WILLIAM

A Coyne Family History

by

Steve Coyne

RB
Rossendale Books

Published by Lulu Enterprises Inc.
3101 Hillsborough Street
Suite 210
Raleigh, NC 27607-5436
United States of America

Published in paperback 2017
Category: Family History
Copyright Steve Coyne © 2017
ISBN: 978-0-244-05397-0

All rights reserved, Copyright under Berne Copyright Convention and Pan American Convention. No part of this book may be reproduced, stored in a retrieval system, or transmitted in any form or by any means, electronic, mechanical, photocopying, recording or otherwise, without prior permission of the author. The author's moral rights have been asserted.

ACKNOWLEDGEMENTS

A book of this kind must first and foremost acknowledge the services of the libraries and record offices of Great Britain and Ireland, most of which remain thankfully free of charge despite many service and staff cuts in recent years. Many visits have been made to the following – the National Archives at Kew, London; British Library Newspaper Library, London; Lancashire Record Office, Preston; Manchester Central Library Archives and Local Studies, Manchester; Blackburn Library; Coventry History Centre; and Birmingham Central Library. In later years many records have also appeared online in digital form. Among these the vast databases of *Ancestry* and *findmypast* have been used sparingly due to their cost, but a special mention is due to the Mormon's giant *familysearch.org* where many records also remain free.

The following facilities have also been used for one or two visits for which thanks are given to the staff of Cheshire Record Office, Chester; Hyde Park Family History Centre, London; Modern Records Centre, University of Warwick, Coventry; Oldham Local Studies Library; Stockport Library and Local Heritage Centre; Tameside Local Studies, Ashton under Lyne; and Teesside Archives in Middlesbrough. In Ireland the excellent National Library of Ireland in Kildare Street, Dublin, deserves the highest praise along with the staff of the Valuation Office in Lower Abbey Street.

In addition the following were unfailingly helpful with written enquiries. Father David Lannon, Diocesan Archivist for the Salford Diocese; St. Mary's Church,

Dukinfield; the Art Keeper (Curator), Blackburn Museum and Art Gallery; Pottsville Free Public Library, Pennsylvania, USA. Information on the personnel of the Shanghai Municipal Police was provided by Professor Robert Bickers.

Special thanks are also due to the Manchester and Lancashire Family History Society of whom I was a distant member for over 20 years. Through their quarterly magazine the *Manchester Genealogist* I kept in touch with local records especially concerning Irish ancestry. The Manchester pages of this book owe much to this Society whose staff, all volunteers, have considerable expertise in family history. Thanks go to the University of Salford Centre for Applied Archaeology, whose open day at the New Bailey Prison dig in 2015 enabled me to visit their site and see the location *in situ*.

Thank you to all those family members who have assisted in many ways, not in the least with sharing their memories and photographs, beginning with Debbie Mellenger in Canada whose interest brought about our family reunion, and has kept alive the connection with our family in Britain since. In the early days I was also thankful that I wrote to two of our oldest relations, both sadly no longer with us. Francis Xavier Coyne in Dorset, and his cousin Winnie Fielding in Lancashire, both sent me a number of letters back in the 1990s informing me of family members I didn't know of, along with many treasured memories which have added to our story. Margaret Mearns also allowed me to copy a number of her family photos from the 1930s to 1950s, while another second cousin, Peter Fielding, helped to clarify the complexities of the 'Fielding migrations'. Chapter Sixteen results from the contributions of the Coynes of White Rock, British Columbia, Canada, which are duly acknowledged. I should not forget to thank my daughter Shona Coyne who from an early age accompanied me on numerous family history trips and more recently improved the quality of a number of images.

Lastly, thanks to Vince at Rossendale Books for help and advice during the publication of my book.

Images

Thank you to Blackburn Library (Blackburn with Darwen Library and Information Services) for their kind permission to reproduce the image of Peter Coyne's premises. This image appeared due to the work of the *Cottontown* digitisation project whose efforts are also acknowledged. The library also gave permission to reproduce the copy of George Howarth's obituary from the *Blackburn Times*. The following also gave permission to use their images – the National Archives for the photo of Terry Coyne and the image of the Fenian Ambush on page 28; the Painter's Society image appears courtesy of the People's History Museum, Manchester. The nineteenth century map of Elphin appears courtesy of the National Library of Ireland, Kildare Street, Dublin. All are thanked for their help. Attempts have been made to gain permission to use all images other than those which belong to the Coyne family. If there are any omissions please contact and it will be corrected at the earliest opportunity.

*Richmond Terrace, Blackburn, in the early 1900s.
The writing on the gates reads
'Peter Coyne. Painter and Decorator'.*

CONTENTS

INTRODUCTION 11

CHAPTER ONE
    Connacht: a Pre-History 15

CHAPTER TWO
    Res Non Verba..26

CHAPTER THREE
    Cheshire & the Great Northern Trek 34

CHAPTER FOUR
    Mancunia 44

CHAPTER FIVE
    Fenians, Sectarians & the Lancashire Irish 54

CHAPTER SIX
    Hard Times in the 1870's 62

CHAPTER SEVEN
    Thomas Coyne, A Sad Decline 1868-1870 67

CHAPTER EIGHT
    Hulme - the Next Generation 84

CHAPTER NINE
    Blackburn..99

CHAPTER TEN
    Years of Struggle in Hyde & Manchester 114

CHAPTER ELEVEN
    Arte et Labore 123

CHAPTER TWELVE
   The Great War 1914-1918 147

CHAPTER THIRTEEN
   The Inter-War Years 166

CHAPTER FOURTEEN
   The Second World War 1939-1945 204

CHAPTER FIFTEEN
   From Austerity to Prosperity 256

CHAPTER SIXTEEN
   The Canadians 282

CHAPTER SEVENTEEN
   Towards the Modern Day 296

POSTSCRIPT 313

APPENDICES 314
   Appendix 1 - Table of Rent: Coyne houses of Hulme and
   Chorlton on Medlock, 1864-1899 314
   Appendix 2 - Coyne Family Addresses in Hulme and
   Chorlton on Medlock 315
   Appendix 3 - Wages in the Building Trades in the U.K. in
   the 19th Century: pre-1859 316
   Appendix 4 - Plasterer's Wages in the 19th Century 318

BIBLIOGRAPHY 321

INTRODUCTION

It is often referred to as the Irish Diaspora. Between 1846 and 1855 two and a half million Irish men and women emigrated. The figure up to 1914 is believed to be between four and a half and five million. Many of these emigrants are known to us, for example among the 805,000 Irish-born found on the 1851 Census of England and Wales. One of these was my great great grandfather, Patrick Coyne. Another, Thomas Coyne – his brother – joined him soon after. Who were these emigrants and what do we know of them?

- They were the young of both sexes, mostly under thirty years of age.

- During the Famine decade from 1845 most emigrated in family groups.

- Few had capital or a skilled trade.

- Seventy-five per cent were labourers or domestic servants. The other twenty-five percent were farmers or in higher occupational groups.

- In Britain, as happened in America, the rural Irish became an urban people.

- After 1840 emigrants were predominantly Roman Catholic.

- Significantly, emigrants to Britain were usually poorer and hoped to return to Ireland.

Patrick Coyne was in England by 1838. Thomas, however, was of the generation of the Great Famine – what the Irish called *An Gorta Mor* or the Great Hunger. The potato beds of Ireland in the 1840s provided the subsistence food for several millions when in 1845 they were visited by a terrible pestilence called *Phytophtora Infestans* by the scientists, but better known as the *pratai dubha* (black potatoes) by the dying victims of the Famine. The fungus which attacked the potato crop reduced it to a stinking, slimy and inedible waste. For Ireland the economic and social consequences were catastrophic. Even for those lucky enough to have work, the average wage in 1845 was a mere ninepence per day

The province of Connacht suffered the highest population loss through death and emigration, a twenty-eight per cent fall. In the counties of Galway, Mayo and Sligo one in every nine people died – a third of them were under ten years old or over sixty. Thomas Coyne, from County Roscommon, joined those emigrants who moved to Great Britain, the country held by many Irish to be responsible for the nation's plight, its land plundered by colonists on behalf of the Crown, over the centuries as we shall see in Chapter One. This was a very different experience to that of the Irish-American, for example, who over the years developed a strong, independent cultural identity such that today a staggering 33 million Americans claim Irish ancestry. If we take America's most famous Irish family, the Kennedys, JFK was the great grandson of famine emigrant Patrick Kennedy who left County Wexford in 1848. In the USA after four generations the family remains indisputably Irish.

But what of the Irish in Britain? In telling the story of our branch of the Coyne family – a story in some ways unremarkable, in others it is a barometer of an Irish family's experience after they moved to Britain, a story of where they lived and of how they prospered. How they joined the vast industrial working class of the nineteenth century, how they endured or overcame poverty, who they married – within their community or outside –which institutions they joined or came up against. A tale of religion and politics, and of changing times. By the process of assimilation they became more British than Irish. Later in the twentieth century they played their part in the major events of two World Wars and in the post-war era we see emigration again – this time to Canada – as the material improvements of the modern world allowed them to prosper. We will also see the changes in employment over time.

Our ancestors among the urban poor faced suspicion and often hostility from the native British. They settled in clusters in well-known districts of the industrial areas, and within each Irish cluster there were county groups based on their counties of origin in Ireland. I have found from my own research, for example, that the present day Greater Manchester was a favoured destination for emigrants from Roscommon. Here according to Christine Kinealy, Professor of Irish Studies at the University of Liverpool, they lived under the strain of trying to remain invisible. A very different experience to the USA.

One enduring feature of Irish identity are the names themselves. In Ireland of course the family name adorns the front of nearly every pub in the land – in Britain on very few. The Irish profile here is harder to find. Today it manifests itself in less obvious ways. Just as at one time the thunder of the *bodhran* stirred the rebel blood Catholicism has largely endured despite the tide of secularism – for are we not all servants still of Joyce's two masters whether in practise or by heritage?

The Coyne family roots go back a long way. The familial bond with Ireland may have broken. We know little of the institutions of the modern Irish state. Whether the music stirs something in the soul – of an identity lost – perhaps a certain humanity, something more decent, more caring, in tune with the underdog perhaps survives? Whatever has changed over the years of assimilation the Irish blood is part of our DNA. The people of Ireland have a unique history and it is one all of our family indeed all those of Irish ancestry can be proud of.

CHAPTER ONE

Connacht: a Pre-History

Many an Irish genealogy has faltered around the year 1800 or shortly after due to the lack of extant parish records before this date. Ours is no exception. It is necessary therefore to take a leap back in time to the pre-history of the province of Connacht to look at what history tells us about the way our people lived.

Some distinguished academic works have been passed down, most famously the *Annals of the Four Masters* which date from the seventeenth century. Thanks to the work of the great nineteenth century genealogist, John O'Donovan – who published his annotated translation of the Annals – we know something of the tribes and customs of the local Connacht families and how their fortunes and power declined ultimately at the hands of the English Crown. In the five counties which made up the province the tribes included the *Ui Fiachra* who possessed land in Sligo, Mayo and much of Galway, and the *Hy-Many* who controlled parts of Galway and Roscommon to the River Shannon. The O'Connors were kings of Connacht while the O'Dowds and O'Kellys were among the most prominent of local chieftains. The Coynes evolved from a minor sept named *O'Cadhain* (i) believed to originate from land in the Partraigh/ Partry Mountains of Co.Mayo. They probably lived on land controlled by the *O'Dubda* (O'Dowd) family of the northern *Ui Fiachra*. Other prominent families in this part of Mayo include the *O'Maille* (O'Malley), Chiefs of

Umhal, who controlled the baronies of Murrisk and Burrishoole near to the holy mountain of Croagh Patrick. While looking broadly at the history of the province our focus is mainly on both Partry and parts of Co. Roscommon with its nineteenth century connection to our branch of the family in the towns of Castlerea and Elphin.

Five counties make up the Province of Connacht

At the same time as the Romans were empire-building in the rest of Europe, the north and west of Ireland in the first century AD was ruled by a tribe called the *Connachta* led by the legendary Queen Maeve. By the fifth century AD the old pagan celtic customs were being challenged by St Patrick(385- 461 AD), probably Ireland's singlemost important historical figure. During these years the first Christian churches were built while according to legend St.Patrick spent his Lent in the year 441 at the top of the mountain which bears his name and a place of pilgrimage for Catholics for one and a half millennia. Croagh Patrick is but a few miles from Partry from the top of which, on a clear day, you can view the former Coyne territory in the area of Partry and beyond near to Lough Mask.

It was Christianity therefore which first challenged the powers of the old pagan chiefs. Datha, son of the warrior Fiachra, was Ireland's last pagan king in the fifth century. He is buried at Croghan, near to Elphin. Abbeys and monasteries emerged as centres of learning, spiritual life and culture, while beyond the shores of the province monks following the ascetic lives of the 'desert fathers' have left a rich archaeology of chapels and beehive huts on such offshore sites as Inishglora and St. McDara's Island.

It is the standing of the tribal chiefs we need to look at however. Throughout Ireland the same system existed – a family/clan or clans under the rule of a chieftain. Irish surnames became more frequently used around the tenth century invariably having a strong geographical basis such that terms such as Joyce's Country and O'Kelly country are still used today. The prefix *Baile* (Bally) for town is used throughout the country with hundreds of examples, eg Ballydonelan (O'Donnellan's town) and Ballydoogan (O'Duggan's town or townland). The Surnames map of Ireland (*ii*) denotes towns, castles and locations with a local name connection. Liscarney in Co.Mayo means Carney's Fort, Ballyconneely in Connemara denotes the ancestral lands of the O'Connollys.

Among the ancient chiefs of Partry were the O'Dorceys, ancestors of the Darceys of Galway and Clifden. Also the *O'Goirmiallagh* (O'Gormleys) who according to Keating(*iii*)were chiefs of Partry which he describes as an "ancient territory". He adds that the present parish of

Ballyovey, shows the situation of this land in the south-west corner of Lough Mask. A few miles to the east from here lies the ruins of Ballykine Castle – *Baile Ui Chadhain* in Irish –meaning O'Kyne's town. Kyne is one of those names which shares a common ancestry with the surname Coyne.

To the north-west of these lands, where they enjoyed considerable prowess on the seas were the O'Malleys who claim descent from the Ui Bruin tribe. As descendants of Brian, fifth King of Connacht their ancestry is believed to link them to the O'Connors, McDermotts and O'Rourkes – all significant families in the province. Grace O'Malley, the "Pirate Queen" who stood up to Queen Elizabeth 1 is remembered in local folklore and by her connection to a number of family castles, eg those at Rockfleet and Clare Island.

To the south of Partry lies the wild west region of Connemara on the northern shore of Galway Bay. These were the lands of the *O'Flathbertaigh* (O'Flaherty), Lords of Iar Connacht after being driven west by the invading Norman tribe, the Clanrickard Burkes. The O'Flahertys also had prominent castles around Connemara from where they enjoyed a formidable reputation – the Ferocious Flahertys – *"who from the shout of battle would not flee"*. Another significant presence around Lough Corrib were the *de Jorse* (Joyce) family. They arrived later moving from Wales during the reign of Edward 1. O'Donovan records that the Joyces had large possessions in the Barony of Ross, still called "Joyce Country". He added that "many of them were remarkable for immense strength and gigantic stature"! Historically these families comprised the Coyne neighbours.

Ancestral lands of County Roscommon

Pre-eminent among the local tribes were the *O'Conchobar* (O'Connor), Kings of Connacht. In the twelfth century Turlough O'Connor and his son Rory became High Kings of Ireland, crowned with due ceremony on the hill at Tara in County Meath. The O'Connors had a number of royal residences at Croghan, near Elphin; and *Cluan Fraeich* near Tulsk four miles away;at Dunmore in Co.Galway; and at Cong in Co.Mayo. Turlough O'Connor is widely claimed to be the last real King of Ireland when he was killed in 1406. History shows the O'Connors to be a war-like tribe, who survive today in the form of their clan chief, the O'Conor Don, who lives at Clonalis House near to Castlerea.

Second only to the O'Connors were the *McDiarmuid* (McDermott) clan. They had an official title as hereditary marshals to the King of Connacht. Their territory comprised superior agricultural land in the present-day Barony of Boyle and nearby parts of Sligo and Mayo. Their chief fortress was on an island in Lough Key, near Boyle. Related to them were the *McDonchaid* (McDonagh) clan. Also in north Roscommon were the lands of the O'Beirne who had territory along the Shannon in the Barony of Ballintobber and to the west as far as Elphin. The *O'Flannagain* (O'Flannagan), Chiefs of the Clan Cathail, also occupied land in the Barony of Roscommon, just north of Elphin.

Also in Ballintobber were the *O'Floinn* (O'Flynn). There is an area called O'Flynn's Mountain today in the Barony of Frenchpark to the west of Castlerea. In this area the River Suck – which flows through the town – acts as the historic boundary of the *Hy-Many* just as it does today covering much of the county's western border. The northern boundary of the Hy-Many was the *'Glaisi Uair'* (cold stream) which passes just to the south of Elphin. This makes Elphin something of a clan boundary for to the south lay O'Kelly's Country.

Just as the McDermotts were marshals, the *O'Cellaigh* (O'Kelly) were hereditary treasurers to the King of Connacht. They held some 200 square miles of territory covering southern Roscommon and parts of Galway to the River Shannon at Athlone. The O'Kellys had fought the O'Connors in the fifteenth century – there was serious strife in 1489 – but gradually they assumed official positions under the Crown and at times fought the native Irish , e.g. at the Battle of Kinsale. A number of the O'Kellys are buried at Kilconnell Abbey.

Other prominent names in the area were O'Madden, *O'Mainnin* (O'Mannion), O'Donellan, and O'Mullally (or Lally). To the south of O'Kelly Country were the lands of the *de Burgos* (Burke) a formidable force who owned vast tracts of eastern Co. Galway from their castle at Portumna. The Burkes were originally Norman settlers who colonised these lands and were known to have driven the original owners, O'Flaherty and O'Halloran, "into the mountain wilds of Connacht". They held a part of Galway called Clanrickard comprising six baronies near the town of Loughrea.

The *de Burgos* dropped their French sounding name in favour of the Irish Burke and adopted local customs – it was said they became *Ipsis Hiberniore Hibernioris* or *'more Irish than the Irish'*. They became the most powerful clan in Connacht and its chief governors under the English Crown. They may, however, have failed to comply with the popular maxim....

> *By 'Mac' and 'O' you'll always know*
> *True Irishmen they say;*
> *But if they lack both 'Mac' and 'O'*
> *No Irishmen are they!*

Here we have a clan system operative during the times of both the Vikings and the Normans. The fearsome Scandinavian invaders influenced Irish affairs for two centuries but little remains of their occupancy. The presence of many red-haired people in the region (including a number in our family!) is believed to be a sign of Viking ancestry!

By 1691 after the failure of James II's campaign in Ireland the *'Wildgeese'* flew to join the army of Louis XIV in France effectively taking the old clan system with them. In its place came continued anglicization indeed colonisation at the hands of the Crown. From the time of Henry II to the Reformation; the Elizabethan campaigns; the Civil War and Cromwell's plunder; the Plantations of Protestant settlers; and the Penal laws, the Crown gradually imposed English laws, English ways, indeed its language itself and sought to impose its Protestant religion. Gaelic Ireland was driven back first 'Beyond the Pale' (Dublin and its surrounds) to rebellious outposts beyond the Shannon and in the south and south-west. This powerful foe succeeded despite numerous rebellions in 1798, 1803 and 1848, through to the Fenians and their successors the republicans of the twentieth century. Only after the War of Independence in 1921-22, building on the Easter Rising of 1916 was Ireland – in part – finally to be free of British rule.

So what did this all mean to the native clans we have noted? Some clan chiefs were hung – Hugh McNavin in 1602 after military intervention by Elizabeth's army. Others were rewarded, e.g. in the sixteenth century when the O'Kellys were appointed Sheriffs of Roscommon. In addition Colla O'Kelly became captain of foot under the Earl of Clanrickard. It was he who dropped the 'O' from his surname at the request of Queen Elizabeth who thought that the prefix tended *"by keeping the clanships of Ireland...to foster disaffection to England"*. Compared to hanging these were subtle means indeed. Castles were rewards for loyalty, land offered with lucrative markets and fairs. Wardships were another means – one was granted to Donagh O'Kelly "to bring him up in the established religion and in the use of the English tongue". They went on to support the Royal cause in the Civil War. If this was bad worse was to come. Oliver Cromwell. *"Spit upon the name of Oliver Cromwell"* raged Morrissey (*iv*) in 2004. In the east coast town of Drogheda at the end of the siege in 1641 the Lord Protector of the Commonwealth put the population to the sword. Elsewhere the O'Mannions forfeited all of their land during the Civil War. The O'Mullalys were earlier driven from their land at Moenmagh. This was repeated right across Ireland.

Elsewhere the O'Flahertys led some resistance to English rule from their Connemara stronghold. .Again the Crown showed its wide range of patronage, granting them their "formerly owned land in the county of Flaherty" called *Iher Connacht*. O'Madden, Chief of the *Siol Anmchadha*, was pardoned for earlier resistance during the reign of James I and it was recorded he *"settled his property and his son's according to the laws of England."*

During the period of the Protestant Ascendancy the screw was further turned. The plantations had brought significant Protestant settlers into Ireland, especially in Ulster, and while the Church of Ireland set up its parallel dioceses, the penal laws sought to rid Ireland of its priests while Catholic landowners and tenants alike were encouraged to convert in order to keep their land and livelihoods. The Saxon was settled in old Hibernia and four centuries of strife were born.

By the time our family story begins the nation had been through an epic pre-history. Our story is rooted in Connacht above all else. Incidentally I was intrigued when writing this up how frequently the Connacht names re-appear among those who we meet later in our family history. Here are a few examples:

McHugh.   Husband of Mary Emma Coyne, 1921
Flannagan   'The sad decline of Thomas Coyne' 1868
Madden   Bridget Madden, Manchester godparent, 1865

If we take the period up to the exile of the *'Wildgeese'* the tribal and clan system served Ireland for over a thousand years. Formed by the pagan Celts power was based on agricultural wealth. In later years the feudal order brought in by the Normans was imposed confronting the clan-based system. The Normans' huge castles took over from the stone *cashels* and *cahir*s of the Gaelic chiefs as a vital defence of their families and cattle. Within the community up to feudal times the structure would have followed the Celtic pattern. The chieftain *(ceann)* and his head-men (sons, brothers and allied kinsmen) led the clan. Below a division of labour between male and female tasks covered the everyday work. Alongside them were a small number of knowledge-based men including craftsmen such as potters and smiths, millers and priests.

In Ireland it was thought that a family was made up of four generations who were all descended from the same great-grandfather and where the land belonged to the whole group. The family head was not necessarily the eldest son. Instead other male relatives could be head, in some cases in Celtic times a woman could lead a family. This system endured for centuries. The old Celtic festivals included *Beltane* (1 May) when open grazing began, and *Samhain* (1 November), when the cattle were killed for food – these were times of great festivals with feasting, drinking, fires and music. In terms of currency, although the Celts did use coins the great currency of trade in kind were cattle. Right up to medieval times "t*hirty fat cows*", for example were traded to settle a fine or a dispute. Other disputes were settled by force. This was a culture rooted in the family and in farming; one whose religion gradually developed from paganism to Christianity; at times war-like with their own language but with little written culture until the arrival of the monasteries. These were the Irish roots conquered by colonists on behalf of the Crown, and once sown were the seeds of conflict in the centuries that followed.

The ruined castles of Connacht today survive as a reminder of the old order. A castle was a symbol of wealth and power. They were frequently built by water or lakes. The O'Malleys even has castles offshore. They varied in size, the most impressive having a tower house. The first Irish castles were built of wood and have not survived but the later stone fortifications have survived well due to their often remote settings. In many cases the medieval fortress was built on the site of an existing *caher*, or stone fort, built by the native Irish for dwelling, protection and storage. This is mirrored by the story of Ballykine, the historic site built on the *'cahir* of the *O'Cadhains'*, where the remains of the *caher* formed a *bawn* for the medieval castle *(v)*

In 1589 the Lord Deputy of Ireland divided Connacht in to the five counties we know today (Galway, Mayo, Roscommon, Sligo and Leitrim). Through the years of war, struggle and famine - from the tribes of the *Connachta* in the first and second centuries AD to the present day province, one of the four provinces with a truly epic history.

i. *According to 'Slainnte Gaedeal is Gall: Irish names and surnames', 1923, the name O'Cadain or O'Coyne was the name of an old family of Partry, still numerous in Connacht. Spellings vary from different sources.*
ii. *Coutts, Co.Cork, 1986*
iii. *Keating,' History of Ireland'*
iv. *'English blood, Irish heart', 2004*
v. *HJ Knox, Galway Archaeological and Historical Society, 1903-04*

CHAPTER TWO

Res Non Verba

Res Non Verba: motto of the Coyne family – meaning 'Facts Not Words'

Hibernian, Mancunian, Blackburnian, Canadian. These are some of the stages of our family's history over a period of some 215 years. The journey began about 1798 , the year of the Great Rebellion in Ireland, in County Roscommon, in the province of Connacht. Soon after came the Great Famine which lasted from 1845 to 1851. As we have seen the failure of the staple food, the potato, brought starvation and disease to the whole country. Death and disease stalked the province of Connacht in the west hardest of all leading to emigration on an epic scale. The population of Ireland is believed to have fallen by half, from 8 million to 4 million during the middle decades of the nineteenth century. The Catholic population was hit especially hard. Under the Protestant Ascendancy the landlords of the great estates – some absentee landlords – began to evict those who could no longer pay their rent bringing a further fall in Catholic land holdings. Evictions were to add impetus to the lure of emigration.

Figures show that most emigrants were young, perhaps under twenty-five years of age. It is known that our ancestors Patrick and Thomas Coyne were among these emigrants. Patrick ' the elder brother left first marrying his wife, Mary Carroll, in Stockport Parish Church, Cheshire in 1838. The Greater Manchester area was second only to Liverpool, both had a great pull for Irish migrants. In Manchester in 1851 the Irish-born accounted for thirteen per cent of the population (i). Thousands of them settled in the cotton towns of Lancashire and Cheshire. Others continued their journeys to the north-east while thousands more – often those with more money- sailed on from Liverpool to the 'New World' of Canada and the U.S.A. The Irish Diaspora of the nineteenth century was one of the great population movements in history.

The Coyne family name is strongly associated with Connacht – particularly in counties Mayo and Galway. In the last chapter we saw how the Partry area is thought to be the place of origin of the Coyne sept. The Irish name *O'Cadhain* is shared with other variants such as Kilcoyne, Kyne and Coen. Translated from the Irish *cadhain* means 'wildgoose'.

I began searching for the Coyne family history back in 1989. I suppose the original idea came about when my father, John Coyne, died in 1986. I got a strong urge to visit Ireland and visited for the first time later that year. I realised how little I knew about the origins of the family and was keen to put this right .Like many others I had caught the family history bug. I have always been proud to have an Irish name – the fact it is now four generations since my great great grandfathers moved to England shows this has endured. In Britain this usually results in being dubbed a "plastic Paddy".

Since 1989 I have slowly trawled through the record offices of England, particularly of Lancashire, purchasing numerous birth, marriage and death certificates of family I never knew existed and acquired some treasured documents along the way which enhance our story. I have maps of the areas they lived in and since the arrival of the internet have discovered more and more as further records came online.

A special mention should be made of the Manchester family. From starting off without a single name and the awareness that just one of my relatives, great aunt Emma McHugh, was believed to be born in the city, I have discovered a whole branch of names who settled mainly in the South Manchester suburbs of Hulme, Chorlton on Medlock, and Moss Side. In 2009, following the early appearance of the 1911 Census I found a new branch of the Mancunians who emigrated to Pennsylvania, USA, in 1914. It is likely that their descendants still live in Schuylkill County to this day, along with the two hundred plus names on the family tree of Thomas Coyne, plasterer, who lived we believe in Elphin, a small market town in Roscommon.

Ireland, 1798. Our story begins in the year of the Great Rebellion. Inspired by revolution in France where the *Ancien Regime* were overthrown in 1789, the rebellion was led by Wolfe Tone and was supported in many parts of Ireland. Thousands of *spalpeens* (ii) armed only with pikes and pitchforks fought for the green flag with varying degrees of success. In County Mayo French troops under General Humbert landed at the small harbour of Killala and marched across the county, on through Sligo and parts of Roscommon before the British Army, under Lord Cornwallis, met the rebels at Ballinamuck and drove them back. Around this time – one of many turbulent periods in

Irish history - my 3x great grandfather, also called Thomas Coyne, was born. We can only estimate his age due to the lack of available records. His son, Patrick, was born between 1817 and 1821, providing the only pointer to his father's age. We know however that he was a slater and plasterer by trade while his place of birth is unknown.

Thomas and his wife may have had a large family as they were unexceptional at this time. The only other child we know of, however, was my great great grandfather, Thomas, born probably in Castlerea, around 1829-1833. Due to a later family marriage Patrick and Thomas are both my great great grandfathers!

Both brothers worked as plasterers in England throughout their working lives (iii). The next generation saw painting and decorating take over as the family trade, indeed it would be true to say that the male members of the Coyne family plastered and painted their way through the nineteenth century and much of the first half of the twentieth until the death of my grandfather, Joseph, in Blackburn, Lancashire in 1947. Much of the family foundations were built on having a skilled trade and although not immune from economic uncertainties and seasonal swings enabled the family to survive alongside others who struggled.

Like many of their compatriots the Coynes were a Catholic family and remain so in parts to this day. Christianity came to Ireland with St. Patrick in the fifth century. Numerous churches and sites are associated with the national saint while the Celtic church's missions spread far beyond Ireland. Economic power in the community still lay with the Protestant landlords such that the ravages of the Famine years left the populace in a desperate state.

It is believed that our branch of the family originated from County Roscommon (iv). In keeping with most U.K. censuses Thomas and Patrick's birthplace was entered only as 'Ireland' giving no hint as to where they were from. It was only in 2009 that I made the discovery that they are believed to hail from Elphin, some ten miles south of Boyle and just to the north-west of Strokestown. The source was the marriage entry for Thomas when he married Emma Cowper at St. Wilfrid's church in Hulme. The Latin text stated that Thomas was the *'filium'* (son) of *'Thomas Coyne Elphin'*. This format followed those of other entries where place of residence followed the father's name. Elphin was an important ecclesiastical centre- a Bishop's Palace remains in the town today. It is also the name of the diocese, the Diocese of Elphin. The name Elphin is an anglicized form of *Ail Finn* or' Finn's stone'. It is claimed the original church was founded by St. Patrick himself, while one of the former bishops of the Diocese was coincidentally, a Bernard Coyne (1854-1926).

The lack of success in tracing Catholic parish records is well known. Few records of baptisms and marriages prior to 1830 have survived. Those that have are incomplete, sometimes damaged and with often illegible handwriting. Their absence means our Irish years are unfortunately incomplete. In Ireland the loss of vital Census records compounds the problem since the nineteenth century Irish censuses were destroyed by fire at the Four Courts in Dublin during the civil war in 1922. For this reason other records have to be used, in particular the records of

Griffiths' Valuation, a national land survey (v) which have become of great importance to genealogists.

In Roscommon county Griffiths recorded five Thomas Coynes on the survey which took place over the years 1856 and 1857. One of them is a Thomas Coyne living at Chapel Street in Elphin. All property details were recorded including a map reference (16.71). The Elphin Thomas Coyne is listed as having a house, garden, offices (outbuildings) and a yard. Its size was one rood and ten perches and was valued at £2.15shillings. It was leased from a lessor, a Robert Lynch. I checked this entry at the Valuation Office in Lower Abbey St in Dublin in what are known as the Cancelled Land Books. They showed that Thomas ceased to lease the land around 1864 when a Margaret Coyne took over the plot. Was Margaret his wife, daughter or other family member?

This entry of course has to be considered with a number of caveats. How do we know the Thomas Coyne born around the turn of the century was still alive in 1856? Civil registration did not begin in Ireland until 1864 and the church, under canon law, did not insist on death records. Griffiths also only recorded landowners and leaseholders so many names do not appear. Coyne was not a common name around Elphin while the population of the town was no more than 1,500. The size of the property found seems to be in keeping with that of a plasterer so on balance it seems there is a good chance this is our man? If so the above information is that of the oldest known member of the family.

On the nineteenth century map of Elphin on page 32, Chapel Street is the main road running west to east.

Reference 16.71 appears about one third of the distance from the left and can be identified from the small graphic at the top of page 33.

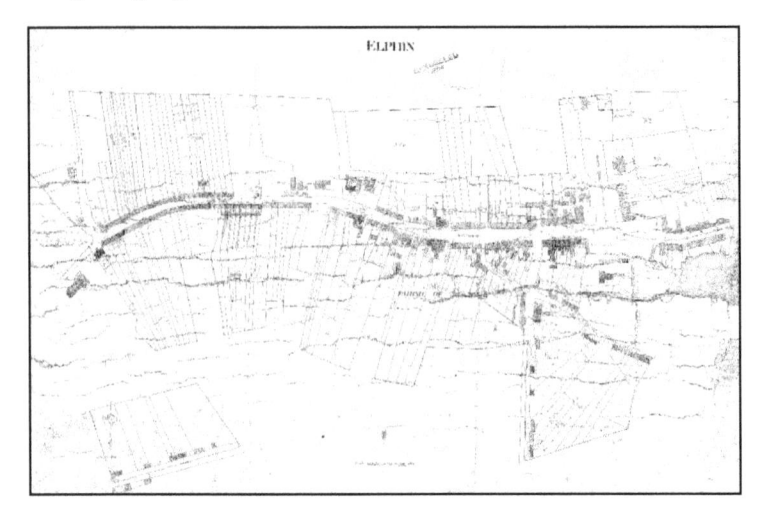

Map of Elphin

Chapel Street, Elphin, today. The house on the immediate left has been rebuilt from the house occupied by Thomas Coyne at the time of Griffith's Valuation in 1856

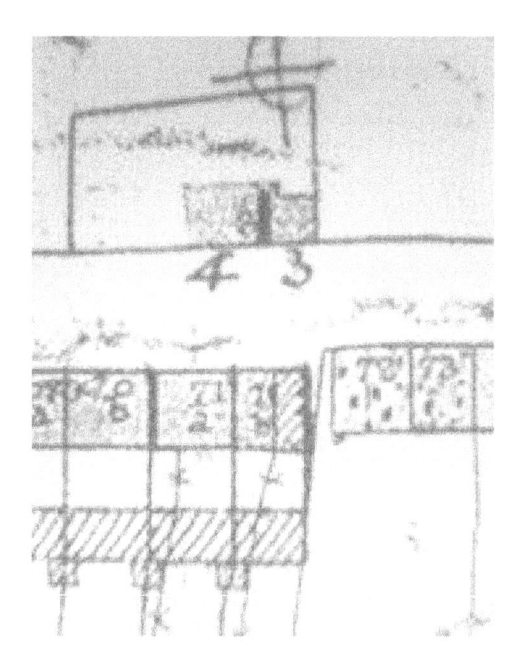

Ref 16.71 is the last house on the south side with outbuildings behind

i. Only Liverpool with 22pc and Glasgow with 18pc had a higher percentage
ii. The rural labouring poor. Spalpeen/spalpin. Itinerant, usually Catholic.
iii. For details of plasterer's earnings in the nineteenth century, see Appendix 1.
iv. Although they may have moved from Mayo or Galway as the name is found more frequently in both counties.
v. Named after Sir Richard Griffith, Commissioner of Valuation for Ireland.

CHAPTER THREE

Cheshire & the Great Northern Trek

Irish emigrants to Britain were known to walk very long distances. From Co. Roscommon Patrick, and later Thomas, very likely walked to Dublin, a distance of some ninety miles before catching an open deck steamer bound for Liverpool. The port of Sligo was nearer but the fare was more expensive involving a journey around the north coast of Ireland. Many emigrant stories have been told of the fate of 'steerage' passengers, denied water and provisions for the journey, forced to share the deck with cattle and animal waste, while sailing the open seas with no protection from the elements (i). They could only pray the crossing was not too rough. A crossing to Liverpool at this time took about thirteen and a half hours after which passengers had to avoid the infamous rogues and scallies who preyed upon the unwary traveller on the teeming Liverpool waterfront when the Irish ships landed at the Clarence Dock. Today this dock has been filled in but the dock gates remain. In 1995 a green plaque was added informing in both Irish and English that...

"Through these dock gates passed most of the 1,300,000 Irish migrants who fled the Great Famine and 'took the ship' to Liverpool in the years 1845-52"

On setting foot in England another forty miles walking was required along the north side of the Mersey estuary via

Warrington and on to Manchester. Our story in England begins on the 1st July 1838 at the parish church of St. Mary's in Stockport market place. Stockport, today a part of Greater Manchester, owes its origins to the Lancashire Bridge, first mentioned in 1282, which was a major crossing-point on the River Mersey – the historic boundary between the County Palatine of Lancaster and the county of Cheshire. It was the presence of the Mersey that may have encouraged Patrick Coyne's arrival for in 1838 Stockport was home to one of the great railway engineering projects of the Victorian era, the Stockport Viaduct. At 2,200 feet in length, 111 feet high and with twenty-seven semi-circular arches the Manchester and Birmingham Railway used some eleven million bricks in the viaduct construction. It was the largest brick structure in the world at the time and with a constant demand for lime mortar over six hundred labourers worked on the site, no doubt including many new arrivals from Ireland.

The parish church was built in the fourteenth century and has a one hundred and twenty-five foot tower rebuilt in 1814, it is claimed, after being damaged by enthusiastic bell-ringing which accompanied Nelson's victory at Trafalgar in 1805. Situated on high ground Patrick may have climbed the steep Rostron Brow between Lower Millgate and the Market Place all of which survives today. In July 1838, however, he had pressing business for it was here he married his young Irish wife, Mary Carroll, from the nearby town of Hyde. She was the daughter of Patrick Carroll, a labourer. Patrick Coyne's address was given as Sandy Brow, Stockport. He signed the register but Mary, unable to write, marked the space with a cross. Patrick and

Mary married in the 'established church' or Church of England. This may have been because Stockport had no Catholic churches at the time. Significantly all of their children were baptised in the Roman Catholic faith.

The town of Hyde, some four miles from Stockport, and its neighbouring towns of Dukinfield and Newton, became the home of Patrick's family up until the 1890s. Although Mary's parents lived in the town which would have encouraged the move, lots of Irish settlers moved to this area in the mid nineteenth century where they found employment in the cotton industry. When I looked at the records of St. Mary's Catholic Church, close to where the family lived, Roscommon featured very prominently among the places of origin of couples marrying at the church.

It was here at St. Mary's that successive Coyne children born to Patrick and Mary were baptised between 1847 and 1853. It seems likely that some of these baptisms took place in the local pub due to the following unusual event. The first St. Mary's in Dukinfield, built in 1847 to accommodate a growing Catholic population was soon abandoned when it was discovered it had been built over a former coal mine and was likely to collapse. For the next ten years, before the present church in Zetland Street was ready, Mass and the sacraments were celebrated in the Old General Inn on the corner of Astley Street and Crescent Road.

The photo above, taken in 2015, shows the Old General still standing but seemingly closed for business.

The first baptism was on the 28th March when Catherine Coyne became the first English-born Coyne. A year later, another watershed year back in Ireland where the' Young Irelander's' rebellion faltered, a son, Thomas, named after his grandfather, was born on Christmas Eve. He was not baptised until 22nd April 1849 when the register records his surname as 'Cone'. This was not the only 'Cone' entry such that at one time I thought it may be a surname variant but the shortage of Cones in Ireland suggests it was probably an idiosyncrasy of the parish priest or clerk. Thomas' godparents were a Charles Ford and Margaret O'Hara.

A second son followed born on 7th January 1851 and he appears on the first Coyne census return in April where he appears as Edward aged three months. Patrick and Mary were then living at 82 St. Thomas Street, Hyde and shows

Patrick, aged 32 years, working as a plasterer. On June 29th Edward was baptised when his surname was again recorded as 'Cone'. Sadly this was the last we hear of Edward. There is no trace of him in later records and we must assume he died as an infant.

The year 1853 saw the first trace in England of Patrick's brother Thomas. By then he was living with my great great grandmother, Emma. Thomas' wife was English, born in Ellesmere in Shropshire. She had been married before to a John Cowper in Salford on 17th November 1846. By the early 1850s Emma, the daughter of Peter Poole Taylor, was living with Thomas Coyne – indeed their first son, Thomas Edward, was born around 1852-3. One later census records him as having been born in Denton, which is just to the west of Hyde. The year began unfortunately in tragedy. Young Catherine, only five years old, died of croup, a childhood disease she had for four days before death involving inflammation of the windpipe and a severe cough. She died at St. Thomas Street on the 16th January and three days later her uncle, Thomas, informed the Register Office of her death. He gave his address as Manchester Road, Denton. On the 18th of the month Catherine was buried in the churchyard of St. Peter's in the neighbouring town of Stalybridge. In February came happier news.

Another son, named John, was born on the 7th of the month. He was baptised at St. Mary's on the 13th March – likely another opportunity to visit the Old General – and this time Thomas had a happier duty to perform when he became a godfather to his nephew.

Where the Wildgeese Roam

These then were the earliest days of the Coyne family in England. At this point the Industrial Revolution in the north-west was providing increased employment as the Victorian towns grew in size. The railways were taking over from the canals as the main form of transport and the cotton industry, despite its intermittent crises, was continuing to expand. While it is true that the wealth created was not shared by all social classes – a fact Marx had pronounced on as early as 1848 – opportunities to make a living were there. For a plasterer the building boom must have provided plenty of work but to survive it was necessary to move to where the work was. Whereas Patrick and Mary stayed in the Hyde area, Thomas and Emma in contrast travelled far across the north over the next few years.

Their journey across Northern England first took them from Denton to Whitehaven, on the coast of what was then called Cumberland, and on to Crook and Stockton-on-Tees in County Durham. It is possible that the Coynes may have moved around quite a bit in Ireland previously if the years 1853 to 1861 are anything to go by. Whereas a rural labourer was tied to the land a plasterer and slater would have had to travel to stay in work. In England these moves involved long journeys. So how did they do it?

These were still the early days of passenger rail travel and like coach travel it was still largely the preserve of the well-to-do. It is possible some parts of the journey may have been taken by train or more likely horse-drawn travel since they had a very young child to take with them. Once again, though, the most likely answer is that they walked over a number of days stopping in towns or on farms along the way.

In 1855 their second son, John, was born on the 7th March when they were living at 75 New Town in Whitehaven, close to both the market place and a street named Irish Street. For this small port on the Cumberland coast was well-known to Irish travellers being an established ferry-crossing route to the North of Ireland. Consequently it had its own Irish community, some of whom were employed in the local coal mining industry. Since Roscommon also had a mining community it is possible that Thomas may have known people in the town.

Back in Cheshire, Mary Coyne gave birth to her youngest daughter sometime around 1856-57. She was called Mary Ann and since there is no trace of a birth record we have to go by a later census entry to establish that her birthplace was at Newton Moor. On the map this is a somewhat isolated and at the time semi-rural area just to the north of Hyde. It was approached by a road called Muslin Street, renamed Talbot Road on the modern map. The significance of this birth is that, given that Mary Ann later married her cousin Peter Coyne, she was also my great grandmother. Mary Ann becomes the first member of the family in "touching distance" since I have a letter from my father's elder cousin, Winnie Fielding ,informing us that she had "ginger hair", a family trait shared by a number of the Coynes.

At some point between March 1855 and 1859 Thomas and Emma moved again, this time going east continuing their trek some seventy to eighty miles into County Durham. This journey with two small boys would have been far from straightforward crossing two physical barriers, the Cumbrian Mountains and the Pennines with several climbs in the region of 2,500 feet. Again walking was the likeliest option – it is known Irish immigrants took this route to reach the Durham coalfield so they were following an established route, possibly taking the old Roman road to Barnard Castle. This route crossed to Penrith, down the Eden Valley to Appleton, across the Pennine hills into Upper Teesdale, reaching Durham along a further stretch of Roman road to Bishop Auckland. A few miles from here is the town of Crook and since Thomas and Emma stated in error on the 1861 census that son John had been born in Crook, it suggests that they also lived there for a while in the 1850s. What is more certain is that between 1859 and 1861 they were living in Stockton-on-Tees.

Many others moved to Stockton following the discovery of ironstone in the Cleveland Hills in 1850, giving rise to the iron-making industry of the Tees-side area. Stockton occupies the Durham bank of the River Tees as it meanders out to the North Sea. In the second half of the nineteenth century when the Coynes lived there its population increased fivefold to reach 51,478 by 1901.

It was here on the 9th May 1859 that my great grandfather Peter Coyne was born and on 26th June he was baptised at St. Mary's Catholic Church in Major Street, just to the north of the town centre. His godparents were a Jonathan Rowe and Mary Ann Irving. Begun in 1842 St. Mary's,- which still stands today- was built with light 'yellow' stone and was only part completed at the time of Peter's baptism. It was designed by the great Victorian architect Augustus Welby Pugin (1812-1852) who drew up the plans for the nave and north aisle. Today the gothic features are apparent with the half tower completed in 1866. Peter was baptised Peter Poole Coyne, his middle name also that of his maternal grandfather, Peter Poole Taylor of Ellesmere, Shropshire.

At the time of the 1861 Census the family now with three sons were living at 14 Tennant Street in the centre of Stockton. This area just to the east of the railway station was built around the time of the Crimean War (1853-56) and its streets bear the names of the battles and officers of the Crimean campaign – Balaclava, Inkerman, Alma, Cardigan and Tennant. At the end of Tennant Street was a Georgian terrace, on Norton Road, which survives today whereas the original Tennant Street has been redeveloped.

Stockton may have provided employment but it did not bring roots. During the 1860s the local newspaper, the *Stockton Herald*, frequently ran anti-Irish stories, maligning the Irish community, their character and their religion. By 1870 following the Fenian activities, clashes took place between the Irish and English communities of the town. It would seem Thomas and Emma left at the right time as around 1861-62 they undertook the third stage of their journey – another eighty miles travelling south-west and across the Pennines again. This time they were to settle moving to the great metropolis of Manchester, to the township of Hulme about a half-mile south of the city centre. They were also now just eight miles from brother Patrick and his family.

I have traced members of the Coyne family living in this locality up to 1948. It is possible some descendants could still be around but generally the Mancunian Coynes suffered greatly from misfortune, lived amongst undoubted poverty, and yet their time in the "world's first industrial city" was shaped by great economic and political events, not least in the city's large Irish community.

i. *'Black '47: Britain and the Famine Irish' by Professor Frank Neal, p.54*

CHAPTER FOUR

Mancunia

Mancunia: the history of Manchester began at Castlefield in AD 79 when the fort of Mamucium was built.

Around 1861-62 our Manchester years began. The city they called *'Cottonopolis'* had by the nineteenth century moved on from its Roman origins to become a real northern powerhouse of industry and commerce. With its cotton mills and stylish 'Venetian gothic' warehouses, it's early canals and railways (i), followed in 1894 by its mighty Ship Canal, this city of landmark Victorian buildings grew rapidly from 400,000 in 1851 to 543,000 by 1901.Successive censuses of the period saw the Irish-born population peak at 52,504 in 1851. They settled close to the city centre, in Ancoats to the north, and where part of the area close to St.Patrick's Church was known as *Irishtown* (ii). In the south of the city Hulme and Chorlton on Medlock were also areas favoured by the Irish.

Friedrich Engels, the German economist, whose factory Ermen and Engels Ltd was over in nearby Weaste, wrote graphically of social conditions in Manchester at the time. He walked the streets of *'Little Ireland'* (iii) with his Irish girlfriend Mary Burns. She was a Manchester mill-hand whose parents were from Tipperary. He reported on the squalor and poverty found in this area just to the south of the present day Oxford Road station in his book *'The*

Condition of the Working Class in England' published in 1849. Another literary giant, Charles Dickens, also visited the city and is believed to have based his fictional *'Coketown'* on his Manchester experience as depicted in his novel' *Hard Times'*.

Manchester was more than a focus for the social observer however. Ever since the Peterloo Massacre took place on the 16th August 1819 when the Manchester Yeomanry charged a vast protest meeting agitating for parliamentary reform in St. Peter's Fields (iv)- their mounted charges with sabres drawn killed eleven protesters and injured some four hundred – the city has been associated with radical activity and protest .Moving on from the Chartists, to Richard Cobden and John Bright, the Anti-Corn Law leaders of the 1840s; to the first Trades Union Congress held at the Mechanic's Institute from the 2nd to the 6th June 1868; to the Pankhursts and the early days of the women's suffrage movement at the end of the century; the city has been involved in all the major movements of the day. For the Irish it was the Fenian movement above all which had the greatest impact. The Irish quarters were an important base for the Fenians and the period from the mid to the late 1860s saw some of the most dramatic events in the history of the Irish in Britain as we shall see in the next chapter.

It was to this backdrop that Thomas and Emma, and their three sons Thomas Edward, John, and Peter moved from Stockton on Tees. For the first time in England Thomas was now putting down roots. He now had family close by, it is possible other members of the Coyne family were also living in Manchester. On the 1861 Census, for example, are the family of James and Bridget Coyne. James, 61, and Bridget, 55, lived at 48 Style Street in Angel Meadow in the heart of *'Irishtown'*. This referred to the area just north of Victoria Station bounded by the Rochdale Road to the east and The River Irk to the west. James, a rope maker, and Bridget had five Irish-born children all in employment. Their eldest, Catherine and Agnes, were both listed as 22 years of age, suggesting that they may have been twins. The youngest child, Patrick, 13, was working in a local cotton mill, while the other two sons, Thomas, 18, and John, 16, - and whose families can be traced through later censuses- were both employed as 'fish curers' (*v*). In 1881 John is recorded as being from Roscommon. It is the possibility of twin girls that arouses interest since we know of several instances in our family. It cannot be proved however whether we are related so we must leave the Irishtown Coynes for now! Another family, co-incidentally a Thomas and Margaret Coyne, lived in Neild Street, Ancoats, in 1861 in the shadow of London Road Station. They came from Castlerea in County Roscommon and could also be related to us. What we can confirm, however, is that the northern trek was over. The next forty years saw the family both increase in size and also branch out within Lancashire, later forming the Blackburn family, while also retaining their Mancunian roots.

Great aunt Emma was the only family member we knew who was from Manchester, and this was about all that was known. The Mancunians were to comprise some thirty-three names who lived in great hardship and for many life was short. The last name I traced I believe died in 1965 with no known surviving relatives. It is possible there may be descendants of one, Lilian Mercer, but I am certain there are none named Coyne.

Back in the early years Thomas and Emma lived in Park Street in Hulme. These were streets of classic, usually two bedroomed, northern terraced houses like so many which defined the townscape of the industrial towns. They were just fifteen minutes' walk from central Manchester. In fact these were the very streets later immortalised by the artist L.S. Lowry who walked these Manchester and Salford streets every day doing his 'day job' collecting rent on behalf of the Pall Mall Property Company (*vi*). Park Street ran just to the east of Great Jackson Street and the house was rented from a landlord, Samuel Evans, who in 1864 charged five shillings per week for the property (*vii*). As can be seen from Appendix 3 this compares favourably with the likely wages of a skilled tradesman at £1. 15shillings per week and gives an idea of the family wellbeing.

Park Street was close to St. Wilfrid's Catholic Church (see picture on next page) which became the Coyne church of the period holding four baptisms and a wedding over the next few years. Nearby at 7 Rial Street at this time lived Mary Burns, mentioned earlier, although she died soon after in 1863, aged just forty.

The most influential event of the times took place thousands of miles away in the U.S.A. The American Civil war (1861-63) had a devastating effect on the Lancashire economy. Dependent on the import of raw cotton from the Southern States, the Union blockade of the Confederate ports brought Lancashire's mills to a grinding halt. Without adequate poor law provision mill workers faced starvation, indeed the period 1861-62 became known as the

Lancashire Cotton Famine. Here is an example how the Coynes' plastering helped them avoid the worst of the crisis felt by many. In 1860 the National Association of Operative Plasterers was formed following lockouts by employers in the building trades the previous year. As one of the earliest trade unions it helped to protect members and to raise wages.

St. Wilfrid's Catholic Church, Bedford Street, Hulme

A second effect of the Civil War also had a direct impact on Manchester. In the United States Irish battalions had fought with distinction on both sides of the conflict. Earlier in 1858 the Irish Republican Brotherhood was formed in New York, with a separate organisation formed by James Stephens in Dublin. By the time the war was over hundreds if not thousands of armed former soldiers were eager to join Ireland's cause. Better known as the Fenians they first tried forays into Canada and in the spring of 1867 there were attempts at both an uprising in Dublin and a failed arms seizure from Chester Castle. Matters came to a head in Manchester in September 1867 when the infamous Fenian Ambush took place on the Hyde Road which will be covered in Chapter Five. A backlash by the authorities led to the execution of three Irishmen, William Allen, Michael Larkin and Michael O'Brien who came to be known as 'the Manchester Martyrs' and whose memorial, a Celtic cross, today stands at St. Joseph's Cemetery in Moston, north Manchester.

Built in 1842 St. Wilfrid's Church became the focus of family life during the 1860s. It was another 'Gothic revival' church, favoured in Victorian times, and designed by the ever-industrious Pugin. Now standing alone as the last survivor of the old Hulme, St. Wilfrid's was deconsecrated in 1990 after its community moved away in the latest of Hulme's redevelopments of the last century. The building is 'Grade II' listed and began a new life as a business enterprise centre. As a reminder of its former glories I leave it to Pevsner, the great authority on architecture who described its Pugin features as of national importance. He called it a *'seminal building in the history of nineteenth century church architecture'*.

The first record of the Coynes at St. Wilfrid's came on the 1st June 1862 when James Patrick was baptised. He had been born at 18 Park Street on the 17th May, the first Lancastrian in the family. The parish register, in Latin, records the baptism of *Jacobus Patricius*, together with the names of two godparents, John and Honor Carroll. The Carrolls were a nephew and aunt who had a provision shop in Hulme and hailed from Westport on the coast of County Mayo. There is nothing to link them with Thomas' sister-in-law Mary Carroll, although again they may have been related. Sadly, aged just six months James Patrick's young life was ended by a deadly disease. On the 25th November he died of *erysipelas*, a highly contagious skin disease from the same bacteria as scarlet fever. Thomas reported the death the next day when he was described as a *'journeyman plasterer.'*

A little under two years Emma gave birth to her fifth son named Robert Joseph. He was born on 1st March 1864 and baptised on the 27th, again at St. Wilfred's. His godparents were a Margaret Lucy and a John Coyne. Despite extensive searches I have been unable to identify 'John the Godfather' who must surely be related. The problem was that there were a number of John Coynes in Hulme around this time and even more within the Manchester conurbation. There was a John Coyne, a labourer living in Howard Street, Hulme, while another John Coyne, an insurance agent born in Co.Roscommon lived at 18 Pomona Square on the 1871 Census. There was also a John Coyne, plasterer, who lived at 13 Bradshaw Street (a mere five minute walk from Park Street) in 1855. Later in 1882, a John Coyne, whose father was called Thomas, married in Hulme but we cannot connect any of them with any certainty nor whether they were around in 1864. We must also consider the family of James and Bridget Coyne who we have already come across. They lived only a couple of miles away and had a son, John, who in 1864 would have been just about old enough to be a godfather. For proximity 'John the Labourer' is perhaps the best match; although 'John the Fish-curer' over in Irishtown has the added confirmation of a Roscommon birthplace; 'John the Plasterer' the family trade; and the 1882 John has a father called Thomas! One of these must surely have been our elusive godfather?

Tragically the curse of infant mortality was to strike again, young Robert died at 18 Park Street on 15th August aged just five. The cause of death was given as *'diarrhoea convulsions'*. As we shall see in Chapter Six with the family of Thomas' nephew, also Thomas Coyne, our family's experience of infant mortality was all too frequent, and by no means unusual in the industrial towns of Victorian Britain. It is not known where the two infants were buried. By 1864 St. Wilfrid's own adjacent burial ground had closed so Thomas and Emma may have had to find a burial plot outside of Hulme.

St. Wilfrid's did hold one family wedding during this period. The marriage register, the *Liber Matrimoniorum*, reveals that Thomas Coyne married Emma Cowper on the 4th October 1864. These are precisely the kind of family secrets which raise all sorts of questions. By 1864 the couple had had five children so why hadn't they married earlier? Successive birth certificates stated that Emma's 'former name' was Taylor when in fact she had married John Cowper in 1846. In 1864 her marital status was a 'widow'. The marriage certificate also presents another conundrum. Thomas' address is given as 24 Great Jackson Street and Emma's as 64 Park Street. And yet it would appear they lived at No.18 for much of the 1860s? They were married by Canon Laurence Toole, one of the longest-serving and best known priests of the diocese (*viii*). Were the two separate addresses required to hide their circumstances from the priest or did he insist on it perhaps? After all the church knew of the earlier baptisms.

The evidence suggests that Emma's marriage to John Cowper had broken down by the early 1850s, by which time she and Thomas Coyne were together. While John Cowper was still alive Emma was not therefore 'free to marry' and in the interim, and during the births of five sons, their marriage would seem to be a 'common law' one. Since they moved town such a lot before settling in Hulme they would easily have passed as Mr and Mrs Coyne. By 1864 it would seem Mr Cowper was deceased and they could then legally marry. It should be remembered that divorce was very rare at this time and the sole preserve of the wealthy. The timing of the marriage so soon after the deaths of two infant sons could also be relevant. These were times when traditional Catholic values were firmly held and perhaps it was felt the blessing of the church may help their situation?

Their next child was born exactly nine months after the wedding when on the 29th June 1865 Emma gave birth to her sixth son. Baptised on the 16th July the choice of name may have surprised. He was named James Patrick, the exact name of his elder brother who had died three years earlier. His godmother was Bridget Madden, the Maddens were to attend a number of family events in Hulme. We can only guess why he was called James Patrick – was it in memory of their earlier son? Some may have considered the name of a deceased child to be perhaps unlucky.

These were to be the good times .A seventh child was born on the 29th March 1867 at 18 Park Street – yes another boy! How my great great grandmother must have wished for a daughter. On the 5th May Francis Joseph Coyne was baptised at St. Wilfrid's. His birth certificate shows Thomas was still working as a plasterer (journeyman). A few months later on the 11th September a major event was to take place just two miles away on the Hyde Road in Ardwick which was to have repercussions for the local Irish community. Alas also for Thomas Coyne parallel events took place which led him on a spiralling decline leading to his tragic death in Prestwich in October 1870.

i. *The Bridgewater Canal opened in 1764. It was followed by others including the Ashton Canal (1797) and the Rochdale Canal (1804). Liverpool Road, the world's first passenger railway station opened in 1830.*

ii. *The Angel Meadow district. Some 8000 lived in the area, many in the infamous and insanitary cellar dwellings. They comprised some one-sixth of Manchester's Irish.*

iii. *'Little Ireland' was Anvil St, Forge St, Frank St and William St.*

iv. *A plaque marks the location, on the wall of the Free Trade Hall, now a hotel.*

v. *Curing was a form of food preservation, often using salt. Manchester Fish Market near to Victoria Station was close by so our fish curers may have worked there. John was still employed as a fish-curer when he died of alcohol poisoning in 1895.*

vi. *Two of Lowry's street scenes are close to where Thomas Edward and Mary Coyne lived in mid-1890s Salford. These are 'North James Henry Street' (1956) and 'Dwellings Ordsall Lane' (1927). Lowry died in 1976 and his paintings now fetch millions on the art market.*

vii. *Manchester Rate Books 1706-1900 (Manchester Central Library)*

viii. *Canon Toole entered the priesthood late at the age of thirty-four. He became Rector of St. Wilfrid's in 1847 holding the position until his death in 1892 (Salford Diocesan Archives)*

CHAPTER FIVE

Fenians, Sectarians & the Lancashire Irish

The decades of the 1850s and 1860s were landmark years in the development of the Irish community in the north-west. During these years, which also included the Crimean War, three major social and political events shaped the period during which the Coyne family settled in Lancashire.

Firstly, in a pastoral address on the 17th October 1850 Pope Pius IX restored the Roman Catholic hierarchy in Britain. There soon followed an expansion of church building to serve the growing Catholic population. They include some of the finest churches built in mid- Victorian times e.g. St. Francis' in Gorton, Manchester, designed by E.W. Pugin and built between 1866 and 1872 and the impressive Jesuit church on Oxford Road, the Holy Name of Jesus, built between 1863 and 1871.

The second impact was felt by the release of anti-Catholic feeling. The Orange Order, which had been banned in 1836, re-emerged in 1846. They had been involved in sectarian disturbances in Liverpool in 1851, while in Stockport riots broke out the following year. Later the 1860s saw the arrival of a Protestant, Tory agitator called William Murphy. Born in Limerick, Murphy appeared in the cotton districts where he whipped up anti- Catholic sentiments. Speeches by Murphy in 1867 and 1868 invariably led to trouble. In the spring of 1868, for example breaches of the peace took place in Stalybridge, Dukinfield, Bury and Rochdale following visits by Murphy. In Manchester the Irish community helped to defend St. Wilfrid's church in Hulme after Murphy targeted it for a 'meeting' in September. The worst of the 'Murphy Riots', however, took place in Ashton-under- Lyne (i) and continued elsewhere until Murphy was killed after an altercation with Irish miners in Cumberland in 1872. What followed was a legacy of sectarian rivalry and mistrust which only slowly declined over the rest of the nineteenth century. In Liverpool it remained never far below the surface.

The third in this series of events was the formation of the Fenian movement, the Irish Republican Brotherhood. The roots of the Fenians can be traced back further through the centuries as Irish nationalism emerged in response to English invaders, settlers and landlords. Anti- English sentiment was strong and as we have seen influenced successive rebellions. In the early 1800s Daniel O'Connell, 'The Liberator', was credited with bringing about catholic emancipation in 1829, but many felt his parliamentary approach had brought few improvements to life at home. The Great Famine, like nothing else gave impetus to those who felt England could have done a whole lot more to relieve the suffering, and now sought more violent ends. By 1865 the Fenians had won support in both the U.S.A. and Ireland. In England, Manchester became a key centre of Fenian activity and it was here on the 18th September 1867 that the Ambush took place beneath the railway bridge on the Hyde Road, triggering events which led to the tragic deaths of the three 'Manchester Martyrs' by public execution on the 23rd November . Our family lived through these times and cannot fail to have been touched by these events. As we shall see later it is possible Thomas Coyne may have been more closely involved.

The Fenians, whose name derived from the Irish '*Fianna*', the warriors of Gaelic folklore, gained experience of armed struggle from the American Civil War. In 1862 it was claimed nearly all the leaders of the Irish Brigades in the Union Army were Fenians. One was Thomas Francis Meagher (ii) of the 69th New York Brigade, later Governor of Montana. Some of these Irish-Americans were among an armed group of some 700-800 in Dublin on the 5th March 1867 when they were rounded up by the Dublin Metropolitan Police. On the 11th February 1867 an attempt to steal arms from a depot at Chester Castle after hundreds of Fenians had assembled in the town. This foolhardy operation had also planned to hold up the *Irish Mail* train bound for Holyhead, but it was the events in September when the "*Manchester Outrage*" took place that most concern us.

The situation began at daybreak on the 11th September when police arrested four men 'loitering' outside a tailor's shop in Oak Street, Manchester city centre. After a scuffle two escaped and the other two – who claimed to be American citizens – gave their names as Wright and Williams, and were detained. The fact that the authorities were on alert can be deemed from the fact that a Mr. Hale, head of the Irish police in Liverpool, became involved. With the help of a Fenian informer, John Joseph Corydon, Hale identified the men as the 'notorious' Colonel Kelly and Captain Deasy. The *Liverpool Mercury* claimed that Kelly stood higher in the Brotherhood even than James

Stephens, its founder. Fenian 'circles' around Manchester were busy in the days that followed as an audacious plot was hatched to free the American prisoners on their route from Belle Vue Gaol to Salford Gaol on the 18TH September. When the *'black mariah'* van reached the Hyde Road railway bridge(iii) a man stepped out from beneath the arch holding a revolver and forced the police to stop. A shot was fired following which some thirty or forty men attacked the van, and called upon the sergeant holding the keys, a Sergeant Charles Brett, to hand them over. Brett refused and an order was given for the lock to be shot off. Most accounts suggest Sergeant Brett was shot accidentally but he nonetheless sustained fatal injuries. Kelly and Deasy escaped using the railway line and nearby fields.

The backlash was immediate and ruthless. Coming soon after James Stephens had been freed from Richmond Gaol, both the Prime Minister, Lord Derby and the Home Secretary demanded action as the number of 'Fenian scares' mounted. The Irish districts and pubs close to the city centre were trawled by the 'peelers'. Over thirty men were arrested and within the next few weeks an incredible twenty-nine men were indicted for murder. Those arrested, mainly from Ancoats, Hulme and other central districts, were described in the *Manchester Guardian* as comprising *'the lower class of Irish'*. This may have been inaccurate since the list of occupations, included seven labourers but also included a schoolmaster, a lecturer, a clerk, three joiners, two tailors, a traveller, two Royal Marines and three residents of the clothes dealers in Smithfield Market from whose premises Kelly and Deasy had alighted. Although there were many witnesses most were unreliable such that the prosecution finally settled on five names – William Allen, Michael Larkin, Michael O'Brien, Edward Condon and Thomas Maguire. The last two were spared from the noose only by American citizenship and an alibi. Michael Larkin, who was to pay the ultimate price, was a close neighbour of the Coynes at this time. A tailor by trade, he was age 32, married with four children, and a resident of Eliza Street in Hulme – just two streets east of Park Street.

An illustration of the Fenian Ambush on the Hyde Road, 18th September 1867.

Amid widespread frenzy the trial was hastily arranged while some two thousand troops were posted across the Manchester area – there were to be no more rescues. Despite the efforts of the distinguished defence team, Ernest Jones and William Prowting Roberts – both supporters of the Chartists and of many liberal causes – to have the case deferred and moved away from Manchester, the authorities were adamant it would go ahead. Initially all five accused were sentenced to death while all protests from radicals, M.P.s and bishops were swiftly rebutted. There was to be a public execution arranged for the New Bailey prison, Salford, early on the morning of Saturday 23rd November.

On the fateful day, watching among a huge crowd, described as "more English than Irish", a reporter from the Manchester Guardian gave an eye-witness account of the proceedings which he reported in the newspaper on the 25th November. He stated that the scaffold was in *"the centre of the east wall of the New Bailey"* and that conditions were foggy. *"Standing upon Albert Bridge the massive dimensions of the prison loomed through the fog"* and visibility was" down to thirty yards". He saw the *"dim outline of the scaffold"* with the priests beside the unhappy men and that *"not one of them flinched"*.

Wall plaque at the site of Ernest Jones' chambers near Albert Square

At 08.03am the solemn voice of the Reverend Canon Cantwell (iv) could be heard leading the procession. Allen, it was noted, walked with a steady step while Larkin appeared on the point of fainting. The public executioner, a man named Calcraft, placed white caps on their heads. O'Brien (referred to as Gould in the report) fervently prayed. As the three priests *"went through the litany of Jesus"* the bolt was drawn. At this point Allen and Gould (O'Brien) cried out *"Jesus have mercy on us"* as the three bodies dropped. Macabrely it was noted that Allen took a minute or so to die – the others much longer. Calcraft had got his calculations wrong. Having hung from the scaffold for one hour, according to custom, their bodies were thrown into quick-lime before burial in the prison yard adjoining Irwell Street. Widespread revulsion around the world ensured that the names of the 'Manchester Martyrs' would live on and the 'men who broke the van' long remembered. Their bodies were later to be exhumed and buried with honour in Glasnevin Cemetery in Dublin.

Much conjecture exists as to how Deasy and Kelly escaped from Manchester. There was talk of them lying low in a church crypt, a recent book about the Burns sisters (Mary and her sister Lizzie) even claimed they hid for a while at Friedrich Engels' house in Ardwick. What is known is that by the end of October Timothy Deasy was triumphantly welcomed in New York and Colonel Kelly followed later both presumably smuggled through Liverpool docks by Fenian supporters.

Nationally the gruesome spectacle of the public execution was to cease soon after. Just six months later another Fenian, Michael Barratt, the Clerkenwell bomber, became the last man to be publicly hung on 26th May 1868. The New Bailey prison was also to close in 1868 but not before another Irishman was to pass through its doors, for our very own Thomas Coyne was to experience the Victorian justice system at first hand as we shall see in Chapter Eight.

i. *Sunday May 10th 1868. Rioting broke out between Orangemen and Irish Catholics. An English mob entered Cavendish Street, drove the Irish out and wrecked their property. St.Ann's RC Church was attacked and the Irish also driven out of Hill Street ('English –Irish conflict in NW England,' by Professor Frank Neal)*

ii. *Meagher incidentally was no stranger to Lancashire where he was educated at Stonyhurst College.*

iii. *Later dubbed 'the Fenian Arch' by the Manchester Irish.*

iv. *The Rev. Cantwell was Parish Priest of St. Patrick's, Livesey Street. Also ministering to the condemned men was the Reverend Charles Gadd, Prison Chaplain of the New Bailey.*

CHAPTER SIX

Hard Times in the 1870's

The Sad Demise of the Coyne family of Newton Moor

We move our attention now to the family of Patrick and Mary Coyne, a few miles to the east over at Newton Moor, part of the town of Dukinfield (i). Firstly a word about the geography of the area to avoid the confusion I experienced when searching for our family. The River Tame (from which the modern Metropolitan Borough of Tameside gets its name) forms the historic county boundary between Lancashire and Cheshire. Ashton under Lyne was in Lancashire while Dukinfield was in Cheshire even though they are joined up. All today are part of Greater Manchester. Newton, sometimes named Newton and Godley, is a district in the town of Hyde which was also in Cheshire and whose vital events (births, deaths and marriages) are registered in Stockport, four miles away! Newton Moor is a placename within Newton and it is this locality which features most in our story.

The 1870s proved to be a troubled decade for our family. Tragedy never seemed far away and by the end of the century my great grandmother, Mary Ann Coyne, was the only survivor of this branch. The decade began happily enough with the marriage of Thomas, eldest son of Patrick and Mary, and the first surviving child born into the family are emigration. On the 16th May 1870 he married Frances Stretton, aged twenty, at St.Paul's Catholic Church in

Newton. Frances was the daughter of John Stretton, a bricklayer of nearby Flowery Field. When the census took place the following year the couple were living at 166 Mount Pleasant, Newton and Thomas, like his father and uncle, was earning his living as a plasterer. Tragically by the end of the year Frances had died, aged just twenty-one years.

Around the middle of 1874 Patrick Coyne became ill at his home in Victoria Street. He died just ten days later on June 13th from "inflammation of the bowels". His son Thomas was with him when he died and it was he who registered the death the following day. Thomas' address at the time was 71 Cotton Street in Ashton, some three miles from Newton. Patrick's funeral took place at St.Paul's. The *Liber Defunctorum*, today held by the Cheshire Record Office in Chester, informs us he departed in communion with the" *sancta matris ecclesia*" (holy mother church), ministered by the Rev. Henry Hopkins and that he was buried on the 17th June at the nearby municipal cemetery at Dukinfield. Two points are interesting. The record at Chester gives his Christian name as *'Joannes'* meaning John. Also the two records of death give his age as forty-five and forty-six respectively. Since he married in 1838, when of full age, both records must be wrong. The name is puzzling – since all other records refer to him as Patrick perhaps John was a second Christian name?

By 1876 Thomas had moved back to Flowery Field. He was living there on the 22nd May when he married Mary Gill, two years his junior and a cotton weaver in one of the town's many cotton mills. Mary lived in Newton Moor and was the daughter of an Irish-born labourer, Thomas Gill.

The marriage again took place a St. Paul's where the witnesses were James Walsh and Catherine Gill, Mary's sister. Sadly this was also to become a marriage of the most terrible tragedy. Between 1877 and 1881 poor Mary gave birth to five children, all daughters, all of whom died as infants. To compound this desperate story Mary herself also met with tragic end when she died in 1894. The cycle of ill-fortune began in 1877 with the birth of her first daughter, named Mary, who survived just one day. She was buried in her grandfather Patrick's grave at Dukinfield Cemetery.

Next, the 1st August 1878. Thomas and Mary were now living at 9 Bagshaw Street, in a stone cottage which still survives today. Bagshaw Street is a small road of terraced housing just east of the Ashton Road opposite the George and Dragon public house. Just a few metres away was the Newton Moor Cotton Mill, established 1861, a reservoir and a foundry. It was here at 9.20am that Mary gave birth to the first of twin girls to be named Ellen, followed later by Mary Helena. Ellen survived for four days, her younger sister for ten days. Firstly Ellen was buried on the 7th August followed five days later by Mary Helena. The twins lay in the Coyne's rapidly filling family grave.

> ### Infant Mortality
>
> It is believed that the main causes of infant mortality fall into four groups:
>
> 1) Development conditions, e.g. prematurity.
>
> 2) Respiratory disease.
>
> 3) Infantile gastro-enteritis/ diarrhoea.
>
> 4) Acute infectious disease.(ii)
>
> Bad housing and malnutrition are also thought to play a part. In the nineteenth century the North West of England had the highest rates of infant mortality. Civil registration figures show that Ashton-under-Lyne, Blackburn, Liverpool, Manchester, Salford and Stockport all had rates of between 25 and 29 per cent of all children dying in their first year.

Our Victorian tragedy goes on with no respite. The year 1878 was to surpass all others with no less than three family deaths. Firstly Patrick's widow, Mary Coyne, died on the 13th March at the age of sixty. Born in Ireland around 1818 she was the last of our three emigrants to die having lived in England for forty years. She died of heart disease worsened by the acute bronchitis from which she suffered for three weeks before her death. Daughter Mary Ann registered the death. She was unable to write and marked the register with a cross. The Rev. Hopkins again officiated at St. Paul's followed by burial at Dukinfield. It may be that the last direct Coyne family connection to Ireland died with her.

Thomas and Mary had two more daughters. In 1880 Annie was born. This time she survived for nine months. Her burial took place on the 20th November 1880. Finally in 1881 Theresa Ann was born. It seemed each child clung to life a little longer each time – this time she survived for ten months. She was buried on the 19th June 1882 which meant that the family grave at Dukinfield Cemetery was almost full. Our Irish ancestors Patrick and Mary Coyne were to share their final resting place with no less than five infant grand-daughters. How their poor tragic parents must have felt? Even by the standards of the high infant mortality figures of the times (see box) these events were indeed shocking. Finally to end a thoroughly tragic chapter on a more cheerful note, Mary Ann Coyne, also had a child around the year 1878. There is no trace of the birth (not all births were registered) but it is believed to have taken place in Manchester. The child's name was Mary Emma Coyne and she was my great aunt, our 'missing link' with the Mancunian family but this story is covered later in Chapter Nine.

i. *Derived from the Danish 'Duc-en-Veldt' meaning 'raven in the field'. It is believed to be a site where the Danes were defeated in battle.*
ii. *Concise Family Medical Handbook, Collins **1991**.*

CHAPTER SEVEN

Thomas Coyne, A Sad Decline 1868-1870

"History... is indeed little more than the crimes, follies and misfortunes of mankind", Edward Gibbon

It was the 8th October 1870. The Reverend Peter Liptrott, Rector of St.Ann's Church, Junction Street, Ancoats, since 1864, made his way to the graveside to officiate at the committal of the body for burial. The authorities until recently had been unsure as to the identity of the deceased. Was he Thomas Coyne? Or was he named Peter Flannagan as we shall see later? Nearby the River Medlock bubbled on its westward journey towards the city, and it is here in the Catholic section of the Corporation cemetery at Phillips Park *(i)* in north Manchester that our story begins.

The Reverend Liptrott was ordained in 1853 and was now at his fourth Manchester parish. Before St. Ann's he had been at St.Wilfrid's in Hulme from 1856 to 1864. He was to stay at St.Ann's until his death in 1893. At the time of this burial his brother, the Reverend Richard Liptrott was also an assistant priest at the same church. By the time the Reverend Peter walked to the muddy graveside, a journey he had done many times before, he was satisfied the man he was burying was Thomas Coyne*(ii)*, plasterer, age perhaps forty-one years, formerly of his old parish of St. Wilfrid's, but more recently resident some three miles away….. at the Lancashire County Lunatic Asylum, Prestwich.

"Requiem aeternum dona eis, Domine et lux perpetua luceat eis. Requiescat in pace."
("Eternal rest grant unto him, O Lord and let perpetual light shine upon him. Rest in peace")

The voice of the priest praying in the Latin could be heard above the Medlock flow. The body, wrapped in cloth, now lowered into the grave – a public grave Thomas was to share with five others. The life of one Famine emigrant was over, just twenty years after his arrival in England. The sparsely attended burial at Phillips Park bore no resemblance to the funeral an Irishman might have expected back home. It is not known whether there were any family present. What exactly had happened to Thomas since we last heard of him, back in 1867, then the father of a young baby, Francis Joseph, still just three years old? The answer is shocking, and assisted by the record-keeping of the Victorian state, it is fulsome in its detail.

Thomas' descent into the abyss began some two years earlier and it is to the nearby town of Oldham that the trail began in the month of May 1868. As we saw in Chapter Five these were troublesome times in south-east Lancashire. From the Fenian activities of the previous year through to the Murphy Riots in Ashton and elsewhere mob rule was apparent on some streets. In Ashton the mob was reported as being some two thousand strong, the Riot Act had been read and on the 10th May gunfire had been heard coming from St. Mary's church attributed to Fenians engaged in its defence (*iii*). During the riots Irishmen from Manchester were known to have gone to assist their countrymen in the cotton towns where it was claimed that Irish homes were gutted with no protection from the police. Was this why Thomas was in Oldham? It is possible since by the end of the month Murphy had moved on to Oldham where St. Marie's Church on Shaw Street was attacked by a mob some one thousand strong who had assembled around Bank Top and Union Street on the 26th May. On the 28th the *Manchester Guardian* reported of 'Disturbances in Oldham' where windows were broken at St. Patrick's chapel. The *Oldham Chronicle* meanwhile had an explanation for the unrest believing that the mobs were "*excited by the rampant attitude of Fenianism*". Later that summer so-called "Orange Riots" brought fighting to the streets of Blackburn, confined to the area around Penny Street, the 'Irish quarter'. This then was the social climate at the time with significant unrest between the Irish and the English, probably the lowest point since the widespread emigration of the Famine years.

Three days on from the Oldham disturbances in the early hours of 31st May sometime between two and three o'clock in the morning a woman named Ellen Travis, aged thirty, who lived at 101 Rochdale Road in Oldham heard the sound of breaking glass at the photographer's shop opposite. She reported the break-in to Thomas Leavis, the owner. Two days later the Oldham Police Court held its Borough Sessions before the Mayor and the committing magistrates Mr. S. Ratcliffe and Alderman W.Knott. The proceedings were reported in the *Oldham Evening Chronicle* on 6th June where in the column 'Police News' a piece appeared headed '*A Lover of the Fine Arts*' and told of "*an individual who gave his name as Peter Flannagan when apprehended, but on being placed in the dock styled* himself *Thomas Coyne"*. Interestingly they reported that Flannagan/Coyne had addressed the court saying that *"the devil was about him when he did it"* for he had *"never stolen a ha'p'orth in his life"*(iv) adding that he was *"quite an honest fellow"*. Here is a man with some remorse, claiming to be of good character – indeed honest up to now – and significantly, in view of later developments, entirely *compos mentis*

The Oldham Express also reported on the same day in a column headed *'BURGLARY'* – *Peter Flannagan alias Thomas Coyne, was charged with having broken into a photographic studio situated in Rochdale Road, the property of Thomas Leavis, on Friday night'*. In court Mrs. Travis said she had no doubt as to the identification of the accused. P.C. Langton also gave evidence stating that *"he was on duty in Rochdale Road about half-past two in the morning. He saw the prisoner coming from the direction of Oldham, and he was carrying the frame. He asked him what he had got there, and he replied a picture he had bought at a place in Oldham, the day before, and that he had given 5s for it."*

He was charged with having broken into the photographic studio and *'he made no reply to it'* The prisoner, who pleaded guilty, had been taken to Werneth Police Station by P.C. Langton who stated he had in his possession of a photographic frame, valued at ten shillings, and specimen portraits valued at fifteen shillings.

The Chief Constable, also present, and who seemingly involved himself in such routine cases, told the court that there was another case against him of breaking into a house and since this was a case of burglary he would have to be sent to Salford for trial. The Bench committed him to the Salford County Prison, better known as the New Bailey, prior to trial at the next Salford Quarter Sessions.

New Bailey Prison, Salford

In May 1868 the New Bailey was in the process of closing after eighty-one years. A new Salford County Prison opened at Strangeways in June, while close by the grand new Assize Courts had appeared on Great Ducie Street in 1864 competing to extol the virtues of 'Victorian Gothic'. Designed by Alfred Waterhouse, who was also responsible for another great gothic building, Manchester Town Hall, no expense was spared in the construction of the courts which became a familiar sight in the centre of the city before they were destroyed by enemy action in World War Two and subsequently demolished. The case of Thomas Coyne thus appeared at the very first Sessions held at the new Assize Court, a building surely designed to intimidate any errant wrongdoer! As we shall see later he did not however appear in person.

The New Bailey prison occupied a site between Salford railway station and Stanley Street which was next to the River Irwell, then as now the boundary between the cities of Salford and Manchester. The main entrance was in the original Georgian building on Stanley Street which also housed the Governor's House and the former Courthouse, venue for the previous Quarter Sessions. The male felons were housed in the semi-circular western side of the prison bastions facing Irwell Street while the female prisoners were held in cells on the New Bailey Street side. The site extended for 685 feet and each wing was forty-five feet long and three storeys high.

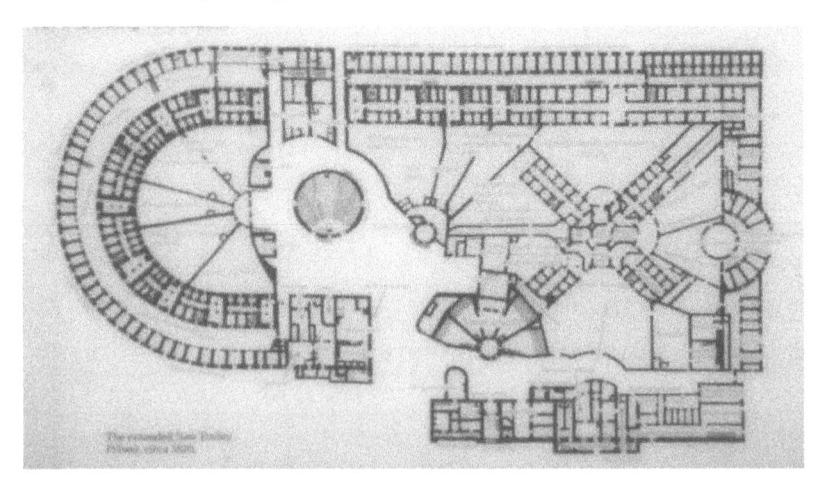

New Bailey Prison plan. Sign. New Bailey Landing Stage, Bridge Street, Salford

The internal buildings included a chapel, a cookhouse and the infamous Treadwheel. Erected in 1824 prisoners would spend up to ten hours per day in unproductive labour turning the wheels. The treadwheel caused many injuries, including miscarriages in women, but were not banned until the late nineteenth century. There were some seven hundred inmates at the New Bailey of whom some two hundred were day prisoners. At the time its regime was considered progressive since they had workshops where prisoners carried out handloom weaving, wool-picking, and rope-making. This was a profitable enterprise for the prison bringing in an income of £3000 per year. At the end of the day the felons returned to their cells, which were single and very small.

In 2015 I attended an open visit to an archaeological dig by the University of Salford and was able to visit the site and took the image below which show the size of these cells which had no fittings and the only ventilation was from an oval opening above the door. Doors were thick and wooden with a second door, one to two feet beyond, made of iron cross-bars.

New Bailey Prison. Excavations in 2015 revealed the size of a typical Felon's Cell.

The photograph above is of a typical cell at the western semi-circular end of the prison. This was at the opposite end to where the notorious execution of the 'Manchester Martyrs' had taken place just seven months earlier giving the New Bailey a hallowed name in Fenian circles. Thomas Coyne was to spend his time here just a few feet from where the Martyrs were buried. Prior to November 1867 executions were infrequent at Salford since the more serious capital offences such as murder were usually tried at Lancaster.

Thomas Sands was an observer for a local literary society who visited the gaol in July 1868. He described the presence of the Irwell alongside as *"black as night"*. It was, he says, dingy and referred to an *"institutional smell"*. He saw prisoners going about their *"melancholic work"* sewing coconut mats. There was gloom and misery everywhere.

Peter Flannagan or Thomas Coyne as he continued to be known spent just twenty-three days at Salford. The Manchester Prison Registers were digitised a few years ago enabling me to view the Felony Register – the entry for 30th May 1868. It contained a great deal of personal detail. The authorities may not have resolved the Flannagan/Coyne conundrum but the details listed below to us show that, beyond doubt, the prisoner was our Thomas Coyne.

Age	35years 7 months (i.e. a birth month of November 1832)
Height	5 feet 8 and a half inches
Complexion	Fair
Hair	Brown
Eyes	Bluish
Occupation	Plasterer
Place of Birth	Castlerea (County Roscommon)
Last residence	18 Park Street, Hulme
Religion	Roman Catholic
Country	Irish
Weight	10 stones 6 pounds
Distinguishing Marks	'Cut on right thumb' 'Sandy whiskers'
Date of discharge	June 22nd. Removed to Prestwich Asylum.

Manchester Prison Registers 1868. Register entry 3064.

Thus ended Thomas' confinement at the New Bailey. It seems strange that they were able to gather so much personal detail, faithfully recorded in beautiful copperplate writing, but failed to resolve the alias situation. We must assume the information all came from Thomas? It is not known at this time if he was still in touch with his wife Emma, or his sons, in view of the uncertainty about his real name we must assume he was not.

Thankfully for us there is the definitive reference to his birthplace in Castlerea and their precise recording of his age. Given the paucity of information in Ireland it is ironic that we have the Victorian prison authorities to thank for finding out where the Coyne family came from! It would seem the 'removal' from Salford was timely since on the very next day, June 23rd, authority was given to remove the remaining prisoners from the New Bailey to the new prison at Strangeways.

Manchester Assize Courts

Before the removal there was business to conduct at the Assize Court. The 'Quarter Sessions for the Hundred of Salford' opened at the new courts (see picture) on Monday 6th July. We can imagine the excitement among the legal fraternity in their new courts, with the stunning *Venetian Gothic* architecture. At 10am the first item on the agenda was the *'Surgeon's Report on New Bailey Prison'*. The Surgeon, Charles Hitchman Braddon, reported on the general good health of the prisoners. He was concerned over the number of prisoners with chest afflictions due to the 'large number of cases of consumption' among the habitual prisoners. The daily average at the hospital was nine men and three women. Mr Braddon concluded, poignantly for us, that "one prisoner, male, has been found insane and removed to Prestwich. He was a trial prisoner of unsound mind when admitted into the prison.

A postcard of the new Manchester Assize Courts on Great Ducie Street

The Quarter Sessions chairman was Alfred Milne, Esq. of Sale in Cheshire who Sands thought had a genial disposition with a word for every prisoner. Sat alongside were the High Sheriff, the Under-Sheriff, and Captain T.H.Mitchell, the Prison Governor for the previous twenty years. Before them was a trial list of some sixty-five names, a Calendar of Prisoners. The first seven cases involved embezzlement, two cases of breaking and entering, and four of stealing. Case Number Two on the list was that of Peter Flannagan, a plasterer aged thirty five years, charged with breaking and entering at Oldham on the 30th

May. Mr. Milne was informed the prisoner was not in attendance and had been 'sent to Prestwich Lunatic Asylum before Sessions'. Of the seven cases at the top of the list only one was discharged, one got seven years penal servitude and four were sentenced to hard labour for periods ranging from three months to twelve months.

Even though the case was not 'heard' it still resulted in a Prosecutor's Bill processed by Redfern and Sons, solicitors of Retiro House' Yorkshire Street, Oldham. A bill for £5. 18s. 8d was submitted being the cost of the prosecution of the Flannagan/Coyne case. This included payment to four witnesses, Charles Hodkinson, Chief Constable of Oldham; Police Constable John Langton; Thomas Leavis, photographer; and Mary Travis, described as a 'married woman'. The latter two were paid one day's expenses of 3s6d each.

The County Lunatic Asylum, Prestwich

Prestwich Asylum occupied a large sixty acre site some three miles from the centre of Manchester in the direction of Bury. It opened in 1851 and the site closed in the 1990s when it was known as Prestwich Hospital. In 1851 the Asylum was built as part of a national response sought by the Victorians to find an institutional remedy to the problems of mental illness along with the treatment of the criminally insane. Prestwich became the Asylum for the whole of Lancashire and by 1868 had expanded in size. By 1863 it had 1,000 beds. In 1868 a Recreation Hall was added and a year later further wards were opened.

In charge of the Asylum was Doctor Joseph Holland, FRCS. Dr Holland was thirty-eight when he was appointed Superintendent and was known as a compassionate man who believed lunacy was a curable disease. Nonetheless many of the Victorian solutions to the challenges of mental health appear inhumane today – straitjackets and restraints, and a liberal use of bromides, for example, all delivered with a hefty dose of Christian zeal. In addition many of the wards were locked in the early days. Over the first five years of its existence 22,000 men and women were admitted to Prestwich, their details initially logged in the Admissions Register.

The Prestwich Register records that on 22nd June 1868 a man named Peter Flannagan alias Thomas Coyne from Chorlton (v) and of unknown occupation was admitted into the Asylum. Prior to the verdict of the Quarter Sessions a decision had been made that he be removed from the New Bailey prison. He would have been taken by a prison van, a black carriage pulled by two horses along the Bury Old Road to Prestwich. He would spend the rest of his days inside the walls of the Asylum.

From the very beginning it is possible to find out how his time was spent at Prestwich since the Asylum had a rigid Daily Routine, as out-lined below.

5.30 am	Day staff on duty
6.00	Patients wakened
7.25 Breakfast	Gruelled water and milk pottage
7.45 Prayers	
8.00 Work	
12 noon Dinner	Mutton or beef broth and flour and rice pudding. 8oz meat every two days.
1.45 – 5.15pm Work	
6.00 Tea	
8.30 Supper	Milk pottage, butter and cheese
9.00	Lights Out

Prestwich County Asylum Daily Routine

Work was considered crucial to the patients' wellbeing with many employed in the kitchens and laundry, in sewing and basket-weaving. Although more people were declared insane during these times, it is apparent the elderly, the physically and mentally handicapped, epileptics and social misfits were readily labelled "pauper lunatics". Alcoholism was another factor affecting both male and female patients in contributing to large numbers of admissions. Clearly anyone deemed difficult in the outside world was at risk of finding themselves confined behind the tree-lined borders of the Asylum. The cost of treatment was chargeable to either the local Poor Law Union or to the state if the patient was either criminally insane or an ex-soldier. The charge per week rose from 7s 3d in the early days to 9s4d by 1913.

Thomas was confined at the Asylum for two years and three months before the night of 4th October 1870. As a very ill Thomas Coyne lay on his Prestwich death bed we can imagine the wind blowing down the airy corridors. In the dark of night time with the sounds of voices, doors slamming and maniacal screams an Irishman far from home in his last hours on earth may hear the wail of the *bean sidhe* (banshee) stalking the dying as many back home still believed. The Medical Case Book reveals little about patient 2267, still unclear who he was, but this time aware that he was a slater by trade (*vi*). They note that he was committed to prison at Salford on a charge of felony. There are only brief details of his medical state but they make disturbing reading. *"He is in a lost demented condition"* it notes charting his decline until death.

The records merely state that he" died this day" at 03.10am on the 4th October. A Notice of Death signed by Joseph Holland stated that" Peter Flannagan or Thomas Coyne died herein in the presence of John Brogden" He had died on his wedding anniversary six years to the day. Later John Watson MD, Medical Officer for the Asylum, certified the cause of death as *"Exhaustion ending General Paralysis"*.

It may be we are no nearer to finding what caused Thomas' sudden decline. Had he succumbed to perhaps lead poisoning since lead was widely used in paint at the time, especially white lead? A plasterer would have worked in many a room dusty with paint debris. Lead poisoning had a number of symptoms, predominantly of the central nervous system and can be responsible for delirium, tremors and convulsions. Alas it is perhaps in the wording of the death certificate where the answer lies.

Lead poisoning may be a possibility but the phrase "*general paralysis*" was widely used by Victorian physicians as a euphemism for advanced syphilis. This is a chronic disease of the brain occurring some ten to fifteen years after contraction that had been left untreated. It would explain a death at such a young age although male life expectancy in mid-nineteenth century Lancashire wasn't much higher, nor was that of the Famine migrants.

It is known that venereal diseases were a problem in Victorian times, especially due to high levels among the military. The 1864 Contagious Diseases Act gave the police powers in some areas to arrest prostitutes for compulsory medical checks. Prostitution in Victorian England is believed to be under-recorded. In Manchester, Angel Meadow was known to be the abode of "hawkers, labourers, vagrants, prostitutes and the Irish poor". Does this explain Thomas' rapid and shocking decline?

Looking back at the events of 1868-1870 it leaves a number of questions unanswered. Just who exactly was Peter Flannagan? Why did Thomas have an alias? Why was he deemed to be an Asylum case when he had spoken so clearly to Oldham Police Court and furnished the authorities with lots of personal detail at the New Bailey Prison? In terms of this last question maybe his condition declined after entering prison.

In 1871 there was a Peter Flannagan living in Hulme. He was Irish-born and lived at 11 Poland Street but it is not known if he was known to Thomas. Perhaps Thomas panicked at Werneth Police Station – an Irishman detained by the English peelers, a not uncommon event in Oldham – and gave a false name. The surname Flannagan however would have been well-known to him. Back to our Connacht history, just north of Elphin, were the ancestral lands of the *O'Flannagain*, in the Barony of Roscommon. An interesting connection perhaps. I saw no others with an alias at the time when going through these records. I will leave the last word with Thomas himself.... maybe it was just a case of *"having the devil about him"*!

Phillips Park Cemetery

In mid-1872, less than two years after Thomas' burial serious flooding took place in the low –lying parts of Manchester. The River Medlock – a section of which meanders around the Roman Catholic part of the Phillips Park Cemetery – was reported as being some twelve feet above its normal height. The *Manchester Guardian* on Monday 12th July also reported it had overflowed its banks and due to the presence of a weir *"the resultant eddies destroyed two hundred and fifty graves"*. Coffins were lifted and broken, corpses in varying stages of decay were swept away by the floodwaters to reappear, horrifically, downstream through Manchester and on to the Mersey.

We do not know whether Thomas was one of them. We can only hope he was able after all to rest in peace.

i.   Phillips Park Cemetery opened in 1866.

ii. Thomas Coyne was buried in Grave 1.879. Grave Receipt No.8692 shows the cost of the burial was ten shillings. Nine shillings for the interment; one shilling for Father Liptrott.

iii. It was the view of Mr Hale (or McHale), Head of the Irish Police based in Liverpool, that groups of Irish four abreast with a horseman at the rear showed an organised response which he attributed to the Fenian Brotherhood.

iv. Short for 'halfpenny worth'. Today worth less than one new pence.

v.   Chorlton refers to the Poor Law Union of south Manchester which includes Hulme.

vi. Thomas was sometimes recorded as a 'slater and plasterer'.

CHAPTER EIGHT

Hulme - the Next Generation

Over the next thirty years up to 1900 the Coyne family of Manchester increased in size as the next generation emerged. They rarely strayed from the township of Hulme, (i) which by 1871 had a population of 74,731. When they did move it was to the neighbouring districts of Salford, Stretford and Chorlton on Medlock. We can track their moves by reference to the Hulme map featured below where each number represents a different Coyne address.

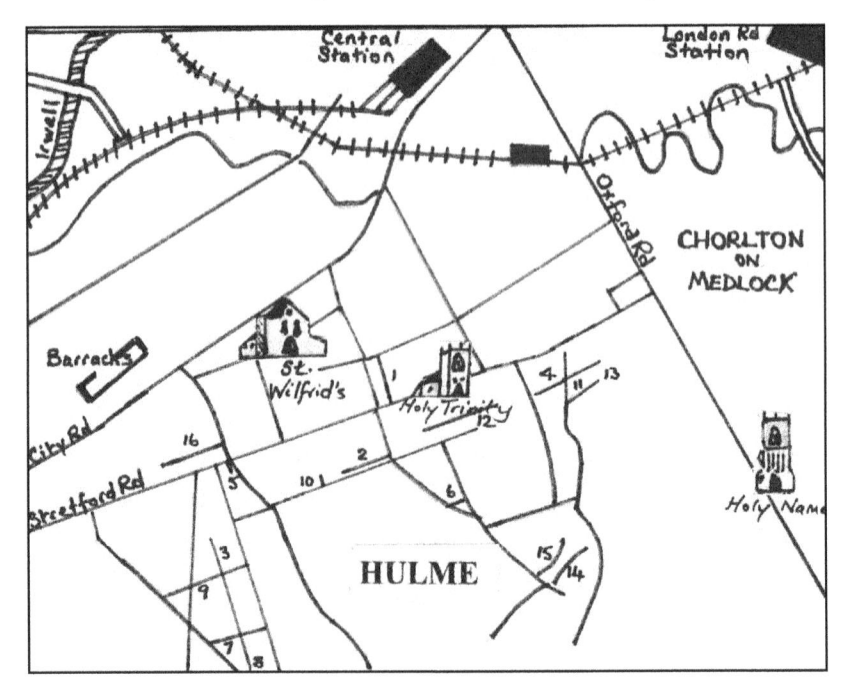

Map of Hulme. See Appendix 2 for the list of Coyne family addresses here numbered 1-16.

Where the Wildgeese Roam | 84

Following Thomas' death it is likely the family, now headed by the English-born Emma Coyne, became less Irish and definitely less Catholic since no family events took place in the Catholic Church in Manchester after 1870. Emma was still at 18 Park Street on 2nd April 1871 when the census enumerator paid her a visit. Now a widow she declared her occupation was *'Manager of her own home'* and with five sons, Thomas Edward, John, Peter, James and Francis, I have no doubt that she was. Significantly three sons were now working. Thomas was an oil merchants' clerk; John an apprentice house painter; Peter at just eleven years of age was an 'errand boy'. Soon after they moved to 27 Union Street in Chorlton on Medlock where Emma had to pay six shillings per week – quite a high rent at the time.

Emma soon remarried. She must have liked Roscommon men since her new husband, Francis McCausland, four years her senior, was also born in the county. The couple married in April 1873 at Manchester Cathedral. Francis was a book-keeper at Manchester Warehouse and their address at the time was 6 Naylor Street, just south of Park Street and close to The Junction (ii), Hulme's major crossroads. The family stayed here a while as Francis was still the tenant in 1879 paying 5s 9d per week rent.

John Coyne would appear to be the first to move out. It was he who began the shift from plastering to house-painting and may still have been an apprentice when on the 23rd September 1876, he and his girlfriend, Hannah Oldham, had a son who they also named John .He was born at 29 Naylor Street but was to die just over a year later in 1877. Despite later assumptions about Victorian morality it shows children born out of wedlock were not as rare as we may think?

The year ended with the first marriage of the new generation. Two days after Christmas Thomas married a young woman named Mary Rideal Cowper at Chorlton Register Office. Mary, 23, was the daughter of William Cowper, a baker, of 32 Tamworth Street, Hulme, who was also listed as a confectioner in the 1871 edition of Slater's Directory of Manchester. Thomas at the time was employed as a 'collector'.

The following May on the 26th of the month John married Hannah Oldham, this time at Holy Trinity church on the Stretford Road. Holy Trinity was at the very centre of Hulme, the Town Hall, the Public Baths, the Register Office and Manchester Free Library were all close by. Significantly it was the local parish church for the Oldham family who lived nearby at 2 Boundary Street. Hannah, aged eighteen was the daughter of James Oldham, a bricklayer. Their address has a famous literary connection since Charlotte Bronte stayed in lodgings at 83 Boundary Street in August 1846 when she accompanied her father Patrick to Manchester for a cataract operation. It was here she started to write her novel *'Jane Eyre'* – it was published the following year- before returning to Haworth in September. This part of Boundary Street was described as *'a quiet terrace of brick houses'* (iii.)

The early part of the 1870s had seen an economic boom. This sense of wellbeing is believed to have led to the highest ever marriage and birth-rates over the years 1876 to 1880. Our family were no exception since four more births took place between 1878 and 1879. Firstly John and

Hannah had another son, named Peter, born in 1878. On the 7th June 1879 a daughter named Amy was born at 2 Boundary Street. The last quarter also saw the birth of

Salutation Inn, Boundary Street West. This is a rare survivor of Victorian Hulme with interior décor dating from the 1840s. It stood here at the corner of Higher Chatham Street when Amy Coyne was born at 2 Boundary Street.

Thomas and Mary's first child, a daughter named Emma Cowper Coyne. The fourth birth however has remained elusive. It was only through the marriages of two James Coynes in Blackburn in the early 1900s that I became aware of James Whittaker Coyne, born around 1876-1878 in Manchester. His marriage certificate declared his father was 'John Coyne, a house painter and decorator'. JWC remains one of the great mysteries of our family history, indeed his footprint is slender outside of the decade from 1901 to 1910*(iv)*. It would seem this James' mother was not

Hannah Coyne (confusingly called Anne or Annie at times). Rather he appears to be an illegitimate son of John. By 1877 things had taken a turn for the worse and in 1878 Manchester was hit by its worst unemployment since the Cotton Famine. This may seemingly have influenced Peter's decision to take the "King's Shilling". On the 3rd November 1876 a young man named Peter Coyne, a painter, from Hulme enlisted into the Army, joining the 1st Dragoon Guards, a cavalry regiment. As can be seen from the Hulme map the Hulme barracks (see box) was close to where the family lived. We will cover Peter's time in the military later.

The year 1881 provides the next census 'snapshot'. The Coynes are now established in Manchester over a period of twenty years. Hulme must have been a lively place at this time. Barely half a mile from the city centre it had major transport routes, lots of industry, shops and a cavalry barracks. By 1869 Hulme it was said there were 500 beerhouses in Hulme (v.)In the 1840s when building began in the area it was acknowledged the area's housing was 'better standard housing for artisans' and compared favourably with those of Ancoats, for example, where serious overcrowding and the infamous cellars had become a byword for squalid living conditions. In 1881 John and Hannah were now living nearby at 5 Russell Square which was just off Warde Street and close to the Junction. Thomas and Mary meanwhile were at 4 Dorrington Street where Thomas was now employed as a coal merchant. Also nearby, a half mile to the west at 33 Clifford Street, Stretford, were the McCauslands.

The census showed that Emma's two remaining sons at home, James and Francis, (here listed by his middle name of Joseph) were both employed as pawnbroker's assistants, aged sixteen and fourteen years respectively. Emma and Francis also had no less than three boarders. They were a James Hesse, born in Washington, USA, a warehouseman at Manchester Warehouse with Francis McCausland ; John Anderson, house-painter; and Thomas Quinn, plasterer – both Irish born. Thus by 1881 Emma now had six wage earners living at Clifford Street. Her husband Francis, however, was to die early in 1882, in Stretford, meaning she was once again a widow. Meanwhile third son Peter Coyne, my great grandfather, was by 1881 living in Oldham. He had effectively left Manchester prior to settling in Blackburn which is covered in the next chapter.

Hulme Cavalry Barracks

The cavalry barracks in the north west of Hulme, close to the Chester Road, was built around 1804. It soon gained notoriety when the 15th King's Hussars left the barracks in 1819 to fatally charge protesters mown down at 'Peterloo.' It housed numerous cavalry battalions until it closed in 1895. Part of the officer's quarters remain in use today. It comprised officers' stables; troop stables; a riding school and a parade ground. In 1839 it had accommodation for 262 horses, 399 men, and 20 officers. In 1868 a local magazine '*The Sphinx*' gave a vivid if misanthropic description of the site....

> "*The main approach to the Barracks is through a street which owing to dirt and dinginess is neither good to the sight or nose. Marine stores, rag and bone shops, public houses of the lowest class give the neighbourhood anything but a pleasant appearance.*
>
> *The male population consists principally of old soldiers, discharged from one cause or another who supplement their pensions (if they have one) by keeping these shops and cleaning old uniforms. The female population is composed of soldier's wives, the wives of old pensioners, and a class of women who are invariably found outside every barracks, and by whose help the British soldier wastes his money, health and character.*
>
> *There is a strong Irish element about the neighbourhood and more children than one would think possible. A general cast-off military air pervades everything and everybody. The public houses show signs patriotic and regimental. Articles of clothing abound on lines, in shop windows, on beggar's backs. Nearly everyone has a moustache and holds himself erect from force of habit, nearly every woman an independent air*".

For now we continue with the Hulme years. There is evidence that the family endured significant poverty during these years. To begin with there is the housing situation. From a local history publication *"From Hulme all Blessings Flow"* (*vii*) there is a description of the houses in Dorrington Street and nearby Booth Street. Although discussing later years, around the time of the First World War, they are the same houses. It was observed that these houses were smaller and the road narrower than most streets in Hulme. The author describes Dorrington Street as *"one of the most unattractive of streets"* and this is borne out by the lower rent Thomas was paying in 1883, just £4.10s *(viii)*.

Like most northern terraces the houses opened onto the street, a local feature here being the raised front doors which had two or three steps and were ever popular for children to sit on! Inside was a front parlour with a black-leaded coal grid. Houses were 'two up and two down' with lobby, parlour, living room, scullery, yard and outside closet. Upstairs were the front and back bedrooms and landing. Below ground level most houses had a cellar and "coal 'ole". The living rooms had stone-flagged floors, usually covered by oilcloths, and another iron fireplace.

The year 1883 began well enough. Early in the year another daughter, Eveline, was born to Thomas and Mary. By the middle of the year events took a turn for the worse when Thomas' brother, James Patrick, was struck down with tuberculosis, one of the most feared of diseases. He died on the 3rd August at 33 Clifford Street where his mother, Emma, was present at the death. A local physician, John Kennedy MD, declared the cause of death as being "tubercular disease of the lungs". James was just eighteen years old. Before the decade was out this deadly disease was to strike again. Before then Thomas and Mary had two more children. Sarah was born in 1884, followed a year later by Lilian. By then the couple were living in Stretford, now with four daughters.

It seems that tragedy was never far away for our family. By the middle of the decade Francis Joseph Coyne had also contracted tuberculosis. He suffered with the condition for four years until his death on the 2nd May 1889 at 29 Upper Tamworth Street, Stretford. This address was just around the corner from Clifford Street. Aged twenty-two years he was still employed in his old job as a pawnbroker's assistant when he died. The cause of death was *'phthisis about four years'* this being an alternative name for tuberculosis. This time his elder brother Thomas reported the death revealing that he and his family had moved again.

Phthisis or Tuberculosis

Phthisis pulmonalis was the name formerly used by the medical profession to describe pulmonary tuberculosis. It is a highly infectious disease of the lungs and accounted for one-fifth of all deaths in the U.K. in late Victorian times. It was especially prevalent in the 18-35 age group.

The disease could incapacitate over a period of years. Its symptoms included coughing up blood, weight loss, tiredness and sweating, especially at night. Overcrowded living conditions were blamed for its prevalence in working class communities. One family member could easily infect others by coughing or sneezing since the germs could survive in the atmosphere for long periods.

It was not until the mid-twentieth century that the disease was largely eradicated in advanced countries

---

On this move, Mary had crossed to the adjoining city of Salford, across the Irwell from Stretford. The family address was now 4 New Park Road, Salford, (ix) overlooking Ordsall Park. This road still features on the modern map but has been redeveloped. It is close to the surviving Dock Offices of the Manchester Ship Canal

Company (see box). Here in early 1890 Mary gave birth to her first son. Almost certainly he was named Francis Joseph after his late uncle whose death had been little more than six months earlier.

Later the same year Emma McCausland married again. She informed the Registrar at Chorlton Register Office that she was fifty-four years old *(x)* when she married William Couttes, aged fifty-two, a Scottish-born widower who was employed as a carter. Both gave their address as 52 Clayton Road, Hulme.

This road was next to the Chorlton Road Brewery whose chimney would have been a prominent local feature. William was one of some 14,000 carters on the streets of Manchester and Salford at the time, this being the last decade of horse drawn transport before the emergence of the electric tramways and of motor travel. They often worked long hours for which they were paid between 17 and 23 shillings a week.

By 1891 Thomas and Mary were at a new address in Salford, at 47 Ellesmere Street, Ordsall, which ran between the busy Regent Road and the north side of Ordsall Park. This area was demolished in the 1980s. On the same census Hannah (Anne) Coyne, and children Peter and Amy were at 24 Anson Street in Hulme, near to the Junction. Anne, as she was now called, was working as a 'charwoman'*(xi)* while Peter, now aged thirteen was in work as a 'telegraph boy'. The rent for the house was, at four shillings per week, the lowest in the street and perhaps shows they were struggling on a low income.

John Coyne was not with them at Anson Street so it is not clear whether they were separated or not? This may be because John, now aged thirty-six, was working away on census night nearly two hundred miles away in the south of England. He was working as a painter while staying in a beerhouse along with five other tradesmen – all from northern counties – in the town of Sunningdale in Berkshire. It is interesting to see how far a painter was prepared to travel for work at this time and probably only possible through advances in rail travel. This was to be the last official record of John whose whereabouts from hereon are less certain. It seems likely that he was already separated from his family.

Manchester Ship Canal

The Ship Canal was one of the great engineering feats of Victorian times. The idea to build a canal large enough for seagoing ships to sail form Eastham Locks on the Mersey into the centre of Salford came from the desire of hard-headed Manchester businessmen to import raw cotton into the city in order to cut out what they saw as the excessive costs of Liverpool merchants and warehouse owners. During the 1880s there were numerous setbacks and three attempts were needed before the Bill passed through Parliament.

Thousands of 'navvies' ,many from Ireland, were involved in the construction – the Irish called it 'the Big Ditch'- before, on 1st January 1894 the first ship moored in Salford Docks. Later that year, on 21st May, Queen Victoria arrived on 'the Enchantress' to officially open the Ship Canal. The docks were full of boats and ships, many decked with flags while hundreds on the dockside celebrated the opening. Overnight Manchester was now an inland port.

> *When Thomas and Mary Coyne lived at New Park Road around 1889-90 the Ordsall area – which became the 'dockers' district' would have been a hive of activity. Over the years seamen from all over the world docked in Salford such that Trafford Road, leading to the Docks became known locally as the "Barbary Coast"!*

The 1890s offered new opportunities for working people, including our family. New public parks, the music halls, the emergence of a tram system (at first horse-drawn) and the new popularity of spectator sports such as Association Football offered exciting new activities available to workers for the first time. This would have offered some respite from the daily grind as long as the family income allowed. It was of course very much a man's world at this time and Hulme's many beerhouses would have offered rival temptations for the drinking man.

It was in January 1894, just as the first ships docked at the newly-opened Ship Canal that tragedy struck again. On the 24th of the month Emma Cowper Coyne, Thomas and Mary's eldest, died of the dreaded phthisis. She had lived just fifteen years. She was buried at Manchester Southern Cemetery on Barlow Moor Road in a new plot which was to become the family grave. Almost exactly a year to the day in 1895 little Francis Joseph, aged five, also died at 46 Clayton Street and was buried with his sister on the 26th January 1895. By this time Thomas was working as a 'commission agent' when he appeared in Slater's Directory for this year.

As we saw earlier identifying the different John Coynes in the Manchester area has not been easy. For this reason the search for a death for our John Coyne was also troublesome! Family documents suggest he was dead before the year 1900. The best match is probably for a death is that of a John Coyne who died on the 16th July 1898 at the North Manchester Workhouse, Crumpsall. His age, forty-three, is exact for a man born in 1855. The occupation given is merely 'labourer on the wards', referring to work after admission to the workhouse. The cause of death was a cerebral tumour and since the informant was the Workhouse Matron there are no family or address details to check. All we can say is this is probably the best match while a cerebral tumour would explain how a man of forty-three could so decline in economic status over the years as to need to enter a workhouse.

Life in Hulme went on in happier circumstances. John's son, Peter, by then aged twenty-one, married Harriet Bott on the 2nd April 1899. Surprisingly the marriage took place at Hednesford Parish Church in the county of Staffordshire. Peter and Harriet were resident at a place called Hazel Grove and Peter was employed as a joiner, possibly with James Bott, Harriet's father, also a joiner. It seems Harriet was already pregnant since their daughter Amy Coyne was born on the 29th October 1899(xii). By then they had moved back to Manchester where Amy was born in Hulme and later baptised at Holy Trinity church. Amy became the first of the third generation descended from her great grandfather, Thomas Coyne, of County Roscommon. With successive family events now in the Church of England had the Mancunians already assimilated?

By the end of the century in the last few years of Queen Victoria's reign, the Coynes were now settled in England. The Hulme years had been hard. Although in employment the work was very low paid and life harsh. The battle against poverty was continuous and life expectancy short. As with Patrick's family over in Newton Moor infant mortality was all too frequent. During these years Peter and Mary Ann Coyne left Manchester and formed our branch of the family. By 1882 they were living in the cotton weaving town of Blackburn, some twenty-five miles to the north, and it is during the years preceding this move that the story continues.

i. *Hulme was originally a Norse settlement. It's name is of Danish origin meaning 'small island by marsh'. It was surrounded by three rivers and became a desirable settlement.*
ii. *Warde Street met Upper Jackson Street by the Grand Junction Hotel. Swales Brewery on Warde Street had a tower clock and was a prominent landmark.*
iii. *'Literary Guide to Great Britain'.*
iv. *A 'cousin James' and 'Auntie Annie' were known in Blackburn in the 1920s (anecdotal, see Chapter Eleven).*
v. *'Old Pubs of Hulme and Chorlton on Medlock' by Bob Potts.*
vi. *1881 Census ref RG11/3887 Folio No. 34-41.*
vii. *'A Collection of Manchester Memories' by H.Watkin.*
viii. *Manchester Rate Books to 1900 (Central Library). For a full resume of Manchester rents see Appendix 1.'Table of Rent Paid. Coyne Houses in Hulme and Chorlton on Medlock 1864-99'*
ix. *No.4 was at the east end of the road farthest from the docks.*
x. *It is likely she was nearer 60 years old. This was her fourth marriage.*

xi. A charwoman was a name in popular use at the time meaning a woman who cleaned a house or other building.

xii. Belle Vue opened in 1825 as a family run concern. It expanded greatly over the years until its numbers peaked on Easter Monday 1919 when 53,300 visited. It closed in September 1977.

xiii. Social Security Death Index (USA).

CHAPTER NINE

Blackburn

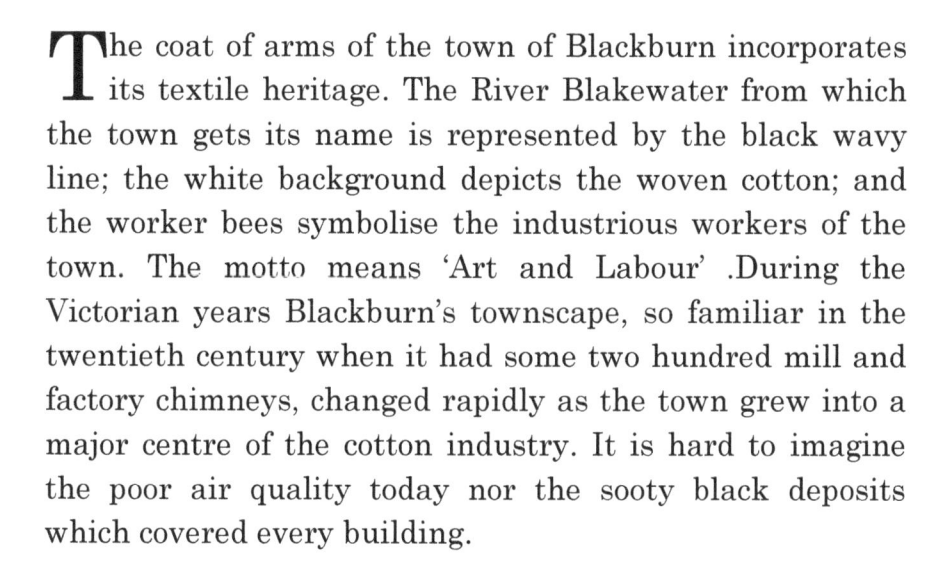

The coat of arms of the town of Blackburn incorporates its textile heritage. The River Blakewater from which the town gets its name is represented by the black wavy line; the white background depicts the woven cotton; and the worker bees symbolise the industrious workers of the town. The motto means 'Art and Labour' .During the Victorian years Blackburn's townscape, so familiar in the twentieth century when it had some two hundred mill and factory chimneys, changed rapidly as the town grew into a major centre of the cotton industry. It is hard to imagine the poor air quality today nor the sooty black deposits which covered every building.

The earliest textiles had been made by handloom weavers but after the technological advances of Arkwright (the spinning frame), Kay (the fly shuttle), and Hargreaves' famous 'Spinning Jenny' the factory system soon took over bringing forth an abundance of cotton mills into nineteenth century Lancashire .The first mill in Blackburn to house power-looms was Jubilee Mill. Erected in 1820 it burnt down in 1842. It was followed by others in Pearson Street and King Street, these early mills were situated near to the Blakewater, as was Brookhouse Mill built by John Hornby in 1828. The river provided water for the mill boilers as well as an outlet for liquid waste. The next mill generation soon followed but this time alongside the Leeds and Liverpool Canal.*(i)*

The town was run by a small number of powerful industrialists, conservative, paternalist men like William Henry Hornby (ii) and Thomas Dugdale who owned Griffin Mill. Both became Mayors of Blackburn. Mill owners like Hornby; Robert Hopwood of Nova Scotia and Crossfield Mills; and Dugdale, were joined by the brewers Daniel Thwaites and Thomas Dutton on the Town Council. Hornby and Hopwood were also magistrates. General Elections were no different, as up to 1906 a member of the Hornby family was elected as Member of Parliament for the town on no less than twelve occasions. Yet another mill owner, William Coddington, won six elections! It was not until the election of a Labour M.P., Philip Snowden, in 1906 that these vested interests were opposed. The mills brought jobs to the town and an influx of migrant labour. In 1821 Blackburn's population was just 17,091. By 1871 this figure had risen to 76,339 a decade before the Coynes first appeared in the town.

On leaving Manchester Peter and Mary Ann Coyne, first cousins, lived for a short time in Oldham, like Blackburn a cotton town experiencing rapid growth and a rise in population. Between 1851 and 1911 Oldham grew from a town of 52,818 to one of 147,483. Thousands moved in to work in the town's 335 cotton mills and whereas Blackburn could claim primacy in the area of cotton weaving Oldham could claim to be the most important cotton-spinning town in the world by the 1860s.

Peter Coyne. Regimental Number 1667

Family history is apt to unearth many surprises and ours is no exception. Until this year it was not known that Peter had spent time in the military but the story of a 'cousin marrying a cousin' did echo down the years within the family. What I have found is that the two issues are connected and explain some of the irregular events and frequent movements between the years 1878 and 1882 when the family first appeared in Blackburn. The Peter Coyne who deserted from the 1st Dragoon Guards on the 19th April 1878 would appear to be 'our Peter' despite some divergence of personal detail. In the absence of a Court Martial it seems he remained at large. Soon after he and his first cousin Mary Ann had a child together and would have appeared to have eloped.

Peter enlisted into the 1st Dragoon Guards in November 1876 and he appears on Pay Lists and Muster Rolls, held at the National Archives, for four quarters in all. At the time of enlistment he was only seventeen years and five months – the Army noted he was aged nineteen. Underage recruitment was rife at the time when new recruits should have been aged eighteen, or nineteen for service overseas. He served for 424 days in total.

On the 19th April 1878 he deserted from his unit in Manchester, an event reported on three occasions in the *Police Gazette* during May. His name appears in a long list published by the War Office headed *'Deserters from H.M. Service'*. A summary of the details are listed overleaf.

Name	*Peter Coyne*
Regimental Number	*1667*
Corps	*1st Dragoon Guards*
Where born	*Hulme*
Trade	*Painter*
Age: *20 yr 6m.* Height: *5ft 7inches* Eyes: *blue* Face: *fresh*	
Coats and trousers	*Regimental*
Date of Desertion	*19 April*
Place of desertion	*Manchester*
Marks or remarks	*Lost tip of right little finger*

Extract from page 4, Police Gazette, 10th May 1878

The two inaccuracies are the age and place of birth. The age can be explained by the fact he enlisted underage. Rather than twenty and a half he was eighteen years and eleven months at the time. We also know he was born in Stockton on Tees in 1859 but did Peter know this since he had no birth certificate? Both Peter and his brother John are listed on different censuses as *'born Manchester'* when neither were.

Desertion from the Army was a serious offence that could even result in the death penalty during times of active service. It can only be tried by a military Court Martial. If caught deserters could be flogged (finally phased out only in 1881) or sent to a military prison, while some were even branded with the initial 'D'. At the time the 1st Dragoon Guards were moving station from the north-west to Aldershot and in the following year they fought in the Anglo-Zulu war in southern Africa. Each quarter payments were made for the apprehension of deserters – a lucrative side-line usually paid to police constables accruing between five shillings and one pound a time. Clearly Peter could not stay in Hulme where the cavalry barracks could not have been nearer. Did he perhaps move eight miles to the east to stay with cousin Mary Ann over in Newton Moor?

Elopement

Mary Ann Coyne was left on her own after the death of her mother in March 1878. There was work in the nearby cotton mill so she could probably afford the rent on her own. In mid-nineteenth century Lancashire this was between 1s 9d and 2s 9d per week. Perhaps Peter helped since this is the time the two cousins began their relationship. By July 1878 Mary Ann was pregnant.

Her first child, Mary Emma Coyne, was born on 19th April 1879 in Manchester. The birth was not registered. Emma – named after Peter's mother? – was baptised at Holy Family Catholic Church at Grosvenor Square, Chorlton-on-Medlock, on 8th August 1880. This was a new parish church, opened in 1876, and suggests they were living just to the east of Hulme at the time. The godparents were interesting. Francis McCausland was now Peter's stepfather, and Bridget Madden had been a godparent when James Patrick was baptised in 1865. I found five occasions when Maddens played a role at Coyne family events suggesting they were related. I found two contemporary Bridget Maddens – it is a Connacht name and one was indeed born in Roscommon. Further Irish searches could prove whether they are related to us. It confirms also that they were still in touch with family members.

There was a Mary Coyne living at Heron Street in St. Luke's Ward, Chorlton-on Medlock, in 1880 in the Manchester Rate Books so this may be where they lived, barely a minute's walk from Holy Family. This was an area close to the Medlock river, frequently prone to flooding and to Oxford Road railway station, indeed not far from what was formerly *'Little Ireland'*. The housing was likely to have been of poor quality.

Mary Ann was pregnant again but before their next child, James Edward, was born in December 1880 they were on the move again – this time to Oldham. For Peter a safer twelve miles from where he was known.

On the Census of the 3rd April 1881 Peter and Mary Ann lived at No. 7 Court, 1 Edge Lane Road in Oldham. The Census was an event where Peter's whereabouts were recorded by the civil authorities and perhaps significantly they were soon to move again. They lived in an area of back-to-back court accommodation where lots of families accessed their homes from a central court, often with a central water standpipe of dubious hygiene.. It was here on the 8th December 1880 that their first son, James Edward Coyne, my great uncle, and grandfather to the Canadian side of the family, was born. He was nearly two before he was baptised and it is from this baptism we are able to date our arrival in Blackburn.

The marriage of Peter and Mary Ann did not take place until 1st October 1882 and also raised a number of curiosities. There was the fact they were first cousins, secondly they married back in Hulme, and thirdly, they married in the Church of England, in the church of St. John the Baptist in Renshaw Street. They gave their address as 28 Hall Street, Hulme, and among the witnesses was Peter's sister-in-law, Hannah Coyne, the wife of John. Their address was in fact the Victoria Hotel at the corner of Renshaw Street and Hall Street. In 1881 the publican was a Joseph Hodgson. The living accommodation housed his wife, two daughters, two servants and a barman.

Peter and Mary Ann were both Roman Catholics, all other family events that followed took place in the Catholic Church, so the Protestant wedding is a curiosity. It may be that the Church of England marriage was a convenience perhaps because a Catholic priest would not marry them? In the nineteenth century marriage between first cousins was not uncommon. Queen Victoria herself on 10th February 1840 married Prince Albert of Saxe-Coburg Gotha, her first cousin, so there could be no higher precedent. In the Roman Catholic Church, however, such relationships came under what was called *consanguinati* (*iv*) which required a Papal Dispensation, an exemption from canon law granted by the Pope, before going ahead. It is known that children born out of wedlock was a great taboo at this time so perhaps the Hulme marriage sought to harmonise a relationship that may have attracted some disapproval.

This may explain also why they moved away to make a new life in Blackburn. I could find no trace of any connection between Peter and Mary Anne and their Manchester relations after their move with the exception of James Whittaker Coyne. Mary Anne's family in Newton Moor may also have died out by this time. The arrival in Blackburn therefore may have been a time of estrangement. They must have been concerned also that James Edward, by now nearly two, had not been baptised since this took place just four days after their wedding in Hulme. On 5th October 1882 he was baptised *'Jacobus Edwardus'*, the start of a long one hundred year connection between the Coyne family and St. Alban's Church. His godparents were a James and Catherine Burton, Their address, the first of many in the town, was at 10 Union Buildings, a street just off the Whalley Old Road.

Before the Blackburn years unfold perhaps it is time to reflect on these events. It must have been a time of considerable anxiety for the young couple. Peter had reason to fear the loss of his freedom, both were initially "living in sin" beyond Catholic conventions, and they had separated from the Manchester family. In addition army desertion, although by no means uncommon, would have been frowned upon. For a family of Irish heritage, however, so soon after the Fenian unrest, desertion from the British Army would have been a lesser concern.

On a brighter note the move to Blackburn was a great success. The family quickly settled into the local community, Peter was initially very successful in the painting and decorating trade and together he and Mary Ann had a total of ten children. By 1900 the Coynes had moved to superior artisan's housing on Whalley Range to the north of the town centre where they were to stay for over half a century (*v*). How they must have enjoyed staying put.

St.Alban's Catholic Church, Larkhill, Blackburn

> **St. Alban's Roman Catholic Church** – *the mother church of Blackburn's Catholic population can trace its origins back to 1773. There was an existing chapel on Larkhill when the parish grew in the nineteenth century. During the ministry of Dean John Newton plans for a new church began. The old St. Alban's was demolished in 1898 and on December 8th 1901 a fine new church built from Yorkshire stone opened. One of the finest in the Salford Diocese there was once a view it would become a cathedral. Newton died in 1896 at a time of considerable rebuilding and it was left to his successor Canon Lonsdale, parish priest to 1915, to open the new church with its imposing tower and ornate doorway. The Coyne family connection to St. Alban's extended over 110 years.*

Their first decade in Blackburn was a momentous one. The local newspapers, led by the respected Liberal weekly, the *Blackburn Times,* espoused civic pride as the building boom brought new public buildings ,a library, churches, public parks such as Corporation Park which had opened on the 22nd October 1857, alongside the houses and the mills. Fine new statues later emerged of *'th'owd Gam Cock'* (Hornby), the Prime Minister (Gladstone) and of Queen Victoria.

But in Blackburn the 1880s meant only one thing – football! No other town in England enjoyed the success of the town's two pioneering clubs, Blackburn Olympic (see box), the first team of working men to win the F.A. Challenge Cup in 1883, and Blackburn Rovers, a club of wealthier backers and considered to be the town's premier club became the only team to win the Cup three years in succession, and by 1891 they had won it no less than five times. If the Coyne family today includes a disproportionate number of football fanatics its origin can surely be traced back to Blackburn in the 1880s!

Blackburn Olympic

The story of Blackburn Olympic is unique in football history. More so than their famous rivals, the Rovers, Olympic FC was rooted in the working people of the town especially in the Brookhouse area where a number of their junior sides played. Formed in 1878 they played at their legendary ground called 'Hole i'th' Wall', now part of the site of St. Mary's College. The pitch occupied a long sloping terrain while the players changed in the adjacent pub of the same name. Hole i' th' Wall often had crowds of 5,000 and during the club's brief existence hosted many epic matches.

Their finest hour came on the 31st March 1883 when Olympic defeated the Old Etonians 2-1 to win the F.A. Cup. Their side included three weavers, a spinner, a cotton machine operative, a dentist's assistant, a master plumber, an iron moulder's dresser, a picture framer and two 'professionals', Jack Hunter and George Wilson. The match was played before a crowd of 8,000 at the Kennington Oval in London. Olympic, who wore light blue shirts, enjoyed great success during the 1880s – in March 1885 full-back Jimmy Ward played for England – but by 1889 the club, facing mounting debts, was forced to sell the ground (briefly to the Rovers) while many of the leading players had already made the same move. Just as Olympic FC reached the end, Blackburn Rovers in 1888 became founder members of the newly formed Football League.

The Olympic players certainly lived close to our family! Cup Final hero Jimmy Costley, who scored the winning goal, worked as a spinner at Hornby's Mill. In 1881 he lived in the next street to us, Pollard Street. In nearby Birley Street club owner Sidney Yates had his Canal Engineering Works, while former England international Hunter, was the landlord of the Cotton Tree Inn. On returning to Blackburn after the cup win the victory procession ended at his pub. Club stalwart Tommy Gibson worked at Yates' foundry and in 1884 he lived at Troy Street, off Whalley Range.

> *For one month after their epic win the famous trophy was displayed in the window of Boyle's Great Clothing Store on Penny Street.*

The first area of Blackburn inhabited by our family was just to the south of the Whalley Old Road, an area with place-names such as Cob Wall and Daisyfield. In 1884 when their third child, Ellen, was born on the 26th March, Peter and Mary Ann lived at 76 Peter Street. The fabric of this road remains today albeit without the old houses. She was baptised at St. Alban's on 27th April when her godparents were James Jack and Mary Holden. In 1886 another son, Frederick, was born on 6th March. He died as an infant on the 8th July the same year (vi). Another daughter named Frances was born next on 14th August 1887.

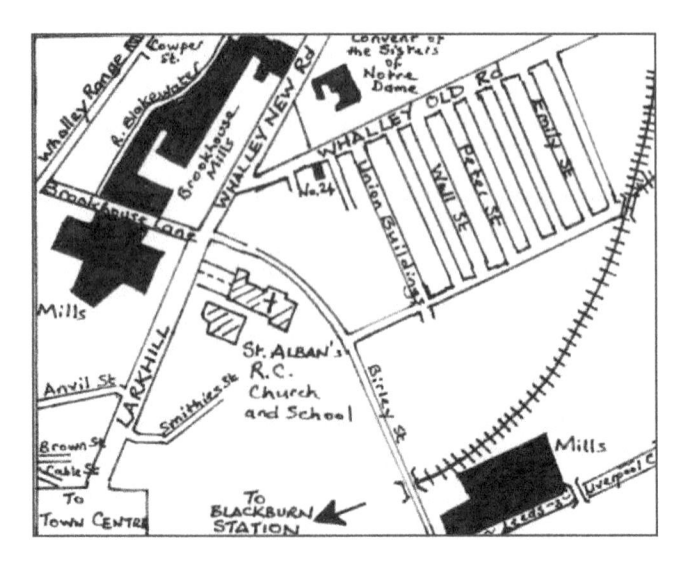

Blackburn street plan showing many of the streets where the family lived from 1880

Where the Wildgeese Roam

They were now living in the next street, at 4 Wall Street, where they stayed for some five years, including the year of the Census of 1891(vii). It was here at Wall Street that my grandfather Joseph Coyne was born on 21 February 1889. He was baptised on 10th March when his godparents were John and Mary Hargreaves.

Into the 1890s the next family address was at 20 Emily Street, again just a few streets away- they possibly moved to a larger property. Here on the 20 September 1892 Mary Ann gave birth to the twins 'Annie' and 'Maggie'. Our family tree reveals a number of occurrences of twin girls born within our branch of the family (viii) but sadly Annie and Maggie were to share the same fate as many other infants at the time. It is thought that Annie died first since only Maggie was baptised (*Margarita*) at St. Alban's on 25th September. She died on the 29th September at her home in Emily Street aged just nine days. The death was reported by her elder sister Emma who was thirteen at the time. The death certificate records the cause of death as 'premature birth – nine days'.

The last two children of this generation were born this decade. Firstly, on May Day 1894, another boy named John, and later to be known as 'Jack' was born at Emily Street. He was baptised on 6th June the same year. Finally, Mary Ann had a tenth child, a girl named Mary Josephine was born on 22nd May 1896 and baptised on the 1st June. 'Jossie,' as she was known, died at the age of four on the 2nd February 1901. The cause of death here was 'febrile catarrh and convulsions'. This meant that of Peter and Mary Ann's ten children only six survived to adulthood, again not unusual for these times.

CHAPTER TEN

Years of Struggle in Hyde & Manchester

We have already seen how the Coyne family settled in South Manchester following their arrival around 1861-62. By the turn of the century it seems likely that John Coyne had deceased. There is also no trace of my great great grandmother, Emma Couttes after the 1890s. With the arrival of Emma's first great grandchild, Amy, the focus now shifts to the younger family members.

The picture over in the Newton area of Hyde was somewhat different. Again it has not been possible to trace the deaths of Mary Ann's two brothers, Thomas, born in 1848; and John, born in 1853. In Chapter Six we saw how the terrible scourge of infant mortality wiped out all of Thomas and his second wife Mary's five children. Of Thomas there is no trace after 1882. His brother John was a coal miner living in a lodging house in the Lancashire town of Leigh in 1881. He was married to his wife Margaret, then aged twenty-four, a 'card room weaver' who adds to our list of millworkers. I have been unable to trace either of them after this date since we do not know if they had any children it is possible their sister, Mary Ann Coyne, was the last of this branch of the family.

There was to be one last unfortunate event which added to the woes of this tragic family whose misfortunes would seem to compare with any horror stories of the times. The tragedy unfolded around midnight on a cold Saturday night between the 27th and 28th January 1894. Thomas' wife Mary – who we remember gave birth to five daughters none of whom survived to their first birthdays – was now aged 44 and had returned from a night out to the house of her mother, at 8 Platt Fold, Newton (i). There she lit a candle with a piece of paper and threw it into the fire with fatal consequences. Her mother, Catherine Gill, had gone to bed but hearing Mary screaming she got up and found her daughter in flames, the fire having engulfed her nightdress. *"She was burning terribly about the arms and lower part of her body"(ii)*. Two doctors, a Doctor Scott followed by a Doctor Kisby attended Mary but found her injuries were so severe they saw no hope of a recovery.

Mary Coyne died at the same address two days later on the 30th January from *"shock to the system resulting from burns"*. At 5pm on the Thursday afternoon Mr Francis Newton, the Coroner for Cheshire, convened a hearing at the Duke of Sussex pub, Newton, where he heard evidence from Catherine Gill and a neighbour. The jury delivered a verdict that Mary had died of burns "received by an accident". Her funeral took place at St. Paul's Catholic Church, Newton, where the *Liber Defunctorum* (iii) recorded that she was buried on the 3rd February at Dukinfield Cemetery. There was no reference to Thomas at this time although the newspaper story described her as a 'married woman' and not a widow. This suggests he was probably alive in 1894.

Back in Manchester things were better. The 1901 Census found Annie Coyne, John's wife, and her daughter Amy living at 20 Stanley Street, Hulme. Annie, now aged 44 years, was a laundress and Amy seemingly worked on a machine attaching collars to shirts. Both jobs would have been very low paid. In 1898 they had lived at 28 Boundary Street having returned to the street where Amy herself had been born in 1879(iv) Annie's son Peter, now married to Harriet, and with their daughter, Amy, born in 1899, was in Yorkshire on Census night. Appropriately for a Lancashire family he was described as a 'visitor' at 1 Portland Street, Altofts, which is near Normanton in west Yorkshire! Employed as a carter it seems they were staying with Harriet's family since the householder was a James Bott.

This leaves the family of Thomas Edward and Mary Coyne. 1901 found them also back in Hulme having lived in Salford for at least the early part of the 1890s. They were to be found at 77 Bonsall Street with their three surviving daughters. Interestingly Thomas, then an insurance agent, was described as an 'employer'. If so he was the only one in Bonsall Street, his neighbours on either side being a 'dock labourer' and a 'corset presser'. By 1906 we also know that Peter and Harriet were again back in Hulme when their son, James, was born on 16th November 1906 at 22 Union Street. Peter was still in work as a carter and it was he who visited the Register Office at Chorlton Town Hall on New Year's Eve to register the birth. James' birth certificate is of some historical significance since Peter met one of the few female registrars in the country at the time. She was none other than Mrs. Emmeline Pankhurst, founder of the Women's Social and Political Union in 1905 and leader of the Suffragettes who by a combination of militant protest and direct action were to bring about 'Votes for Women' in 1918(v). The birth certificate bears the signature of Mrs .Pankhurst.

The Edwardian era was a time of considerable social upheaval. Divisions were apparent not just among the Suffragettes, but within the trade unions the rise of syndicalism brought industrial unrest. The first Labour MPs had been elected bringing representation of working class people for the first time. There was concern also, especially in the new popular press about foreign agitators, while the military build-up took the form of an arms race soon to lead the great imperial powers into a World War. Manchester, meanwhile, had continued to grow shown by its latest prestigious buildings such as the grand Midland Hotel, built by the Midland Railway Company which opened in 1898. Two years later the John Rylands Library opened following a bequest from the department store family. Although the daily grind had eased only slightly there was hope for the elderly with the advent of the Old Age Pension brought in by a Liberal government in 1908.

Hannah (Annie) Coyne was far from pension age when she died in 1907. She had booked herself into the Chorlton Union Workhouse at Nell Lane, Withington, on 26th June and she died soon after on 7th August. She was aged 51 years. There are some records of her admission (*vi*) which state that she was 'Church of England' and from Chorlton on Medlock but no clue as to why she needed to enter the workhouse. The cause of death was given as 'aortic regurgitation' suggesting she had been ill with a heart condition and unable to work. It seems likely that neither Annie nor Amy could afford the medical bills so the workhouse admission may have been the only solution.

> **Withington Workhouse** was built between 1854 and 1855 in Nell Lane, Withington, to cater for the Poor Law needs of the Chorlton Union of South Manchester. It was an imposing structure with a large cruciform shape fronted by a chapel on the south wing. It held 1,500 "in-mates" with female accommodation on the west wing.
>
> Forever linked with 'Dickensian' regimes of the nineteenth century, workhouses housed the destitute poor, the aged and the infirm. Many were just ill or mentally impaired. The regimes were regulated under the strict control of the Workhouse Master with rigid working hours. By the mid-twentieth century many had converted to hospital provision and in 1948 at the onset of the National Health Service Withington Workhouse became a hospital.

Hannah was buried at Southern Cemetery in a private grave *(vii)* later to be shared with the Thursbys – Amy's soon-to-be in-laws. In 1907 Manchester Corporation charged £1.1 shilling for a 'grave space' and 13 shillings for the excavation. Another record of the Withington Workhouse disclosed that the burial, with a private undertaker, was arranged by her son, Peter, whose was then living at 8 Hall Street.

There were happier times to come for Amy. Three years later on 14th May 1910 she married a John Thursby aged thirty –three, who had a good job as a compositor in the printing trade. He was the son of William Thursby, also a compositor of Moss Side, Manchester. The ceremony took place at the Union (Baptist) Chapel on Oxford Road, Chorlton on Medlock. Amy, by then aged thirty-one, was living at Essex Street, Stretford, close to the boundary with Hulme. John had begun his apprenticeship at the age of fourteen so would be well established in the trade by 1910. The couple then lived for a long time in Richmond Street,

Moss Side, close to Alexandra Park, one of the city's finest public parks. It was here at 18 Richmond Street that their only child, John Edgar Thursby, was born on 23rd April 1915.

The year 1911 saw Thomas and Mary still living in Bonsall Street. None of their daughters were yet married so the household income was raised by their respective wages. Both Eveline and Sarah were 'dayservants/charwomen' while Lily, then aged seventeen, was working as a machinist. Thomas was still an insurance agent up until his death the following year on the 31st January 1912 when he died at 162 Tamworth Street, Moss Side, from heart failure brought on by acute pneumonia. So ended the life of Thomas and Emma's eldest son. His working life was different to the rest of the family in that he avoided all the painting and plastering. All his various collecting and agent posts probably didn't amount to much but he was probably well-known around the streets of Hulme.

The 1911 Census also revealed that all was not well between Peter and Harriet, who appeared to have separated. Harriet, Amy and James were living at 78 Phillips Street, Hulme, where they were lodging with another family named Wright. Harriet was working as a machinist producing handkerchiefs while the census also revealed her work was 'at home'. Without support from Peter she would have barely earnt enough to scrape a living and perhaps explains her next move. For Harriet had a surprise in store, emigrating to the USA just three years later. At the time she arrived in the Port of Philadelphia she did not have a cent to her name. Peter Coyne, meanwhile, was to be found living in a 'common lodging house' at 33-34 Richmond Street, Chorlton on Medlock. He was in work as a 'furniture porter', a change from his previous work as a carter.

As the international scene in Europe worsened war had already started when on the 11th November 1914 the *S.S. Haverfield* set sail down the Mersey river and out into Liverpool Bay. On board were Harriet, 38, Amy Coyne, 11, (in error) and young James, aged 7. The port documents record that Harriet was 5 feet 2 inches tall; of medium complexion; with brown hair and eyes. She brought no money with her. Amy was able to read and write, indeed she had left full-time education a year earlier. The records of Vine Street School in Manchester (viii) show that she left school on 7th November 1913 on reaching the age of fourteen, and confirm their address of 78 Phillips Street. There was no mention of Peter.

The *SS Haverfield* arrived in Philadelphia on 25th of the month(x) after a two week voyage. The port documents (ix) give the name of a 'friend ',again James Bott who was already resident in the USA. Harriet's marital status is interesting. She appears to have begun to write 'married' before crossing it out to enter 'widow'. As far as is known Peter was still alive in 1914 so did Harriet try to hide this? It is known that she soon married again in America. Having separated from Peter I can only hope he knew they were leaving the country!

Harriet and family can be traced in the USA during the years following emigration since they appear on both the 1920 and 1930 US Censuses. They settled in a small town in the Appalachian coalfield called Mahanoy City, in

Schuylkill County, Pennsylvania. We will return to them again in Chapter Thirteen.

These then were years of continued struggle in both Hyde and Manchester. To the misery of disease and infant deaths we can add a tragic death in a house fire, and in the workhouse. In between they eked a living from low-paid employment – as carters, laundresses, charwomen, and machinists in the textile trades. After the death of Thomas Coyne in 1870 the Mancunian Coynes appear much less Irish and certainly less Catholic such that we can say that by 1914 they were assimilated into the wider English community. In Hyde they soon died out altogether. This assimilation however would appear to be at odds with the experience of the Blackburn family as we see in the next chapter compounded by the lack of contact between the two branches.

i.	*1891 Census. 8 Platt Fold, Newton. Home of Thomas Gill, 72, and wife Catherine. Both were born in Ireland.*
ii.	*Report, 'North Cheshire Herald', 8 February 1894. Titled 'A Married Woman Fatally Burned at Newton'*
iii.	*Burials 1857-1942. mf 337/13, Cheshire Record Office, Chester*
iv.	*Amy was the tenant rather than Annie at this address in 1898. She was age nineteen and paid 4s 9d to the landlady, Mrs.Mounsey. (Manchester Rate Books 1706-1900)*
v.	*The 1918 Representation of the Peoples Act gave votes to all men over 21, but only to women over the age of 30.*
vi.	*Poor Law records, Manchester Central Library.*
vii.	*Grave ref.J2223. The grave receipts give her address as 8 Hall St. Chorlton on Medlock. This was close to Union St where Peter and Harriet lived.*

viii.   *School Records. The Manchester Collection, findmypast.co.uk.*
ix.   *Philadelphia Passenger Lists 1800-1945, ancestry.co.uk*

CHAPTER ELEVEN

Arte et Labore

Arte et Labore: 'By art and labour' - civic motto of the Borough of Blackburn.

The Coyne family in the nineteenth century, now settled in the North of England, endured all the hardships and survived into the new century. The unforgiving nature of Victorian capitalism had brought misery for many. The Coynes had the advantage of a remarkable consistency of employment. Going right back to the days in Ireland the family were involved in just two trades, painting and decorating, and plastering. To this we can add later, a long period of female employment in the cotton mills, particularly as cotton weavers.

If we take the census records between 1851 and 1911 we can examine family occupations over a sixty year period. If we exclude the Manchester family whose circumstances, as we have seen, were different (they had only one house painter, John Coyne, among them) we have twenty-three instances where an occupation was recorded:

Occupation	Number	Residence
Plasterer	4	Stockton on Tees and Hyde
House Painter	7	Blackburn
Cotton Weaver	10	Hyde, Oldham and Blackburn
Others	2	Blackburn and Leigh

It should be noted that all our cotton weavers were female while the plasterers and painters were all male. Lancashire was perhaps unique in having such high levels of female employment *(i)*

Plasterers

Looking firstly at our plasterers this was a trade brought over from Ireland, an advantage most migrants of the Great Famine did not have. Today a plasterer is viewed as one of the most skilled of the building trades but in the nineteenth century it must have been a tough life albeit with above average wages at the end of the week. Without modern means of transporting materials the plasterer, usually with a 'mate', would have had to transport his sand, lime, and horsehair (used for binding), and tools across town to the place of work. They would also need an old tin bath in which to mix the plaster. Tradesmen of the time usually used handcarts. Limited access to water would have required several buckets. The work was messy and after work the plasterer would have walked home with no protection from the elements in the hope his clothes would be dry by the following day. There is no evidence to show whether Patrick or the two Thomas Coynes *(ii)* worked for a firm of plasterers although these existed within the trade. By 1860 the National Association of Operative Plasterers had formed bringing improvements for the workers (See Appendix 4 *'Plasterer's Wages in the Nineteenth Century'*).

Cotton Weavers

Cotton weaving by the 1880s was long established in Blackburn's mills. Some attribute the town's concentration on weaving to the Blackburn weavers' reluctance to accept the *'Spinning Jenny'*, invented by a local man James Hargreaves in 1765. Weaving was particularly noisy work and the incessant noise of the weaving sheds was responsible for both industrial deafness and the mill hand's skill at lip-reading!

Weavers were paid by piece-rate and later by the number of looms they could work. This trend can be seen by the figures below for Blackburn *(iii)*:

>1886   8,007 weavers worked 27,931 looms.
>Average 3.49 each.
>1906   13,719 weavers worked 47,775 looms.
>Average 3.48 each.

Weavers' wages were regulated by means of a list, the Blackburn List. At times of economic downturn the employers would try to cut wages resulting in industrial strife. In Blackburn in 1892 it was known that 'beamers' and 'twisters' *(iv)* were paid 20 shillings per week. In replies to schedules of questions issued by the Labour Commission of 1891 we can see that a Blackburn cotton weaver was paid between 16 shillings and 24 shillings per week.

Child labour was still used at the time. The 1901 Census shows our own Frances Coyne, daughter of Peter and Mary Ann, working in the mill aged thirteen years. It was not abolished until 1921 when the school-leaving age was raised to fourteen. In 1906 weavers' holidays were raised to 12 days per year, or 106.5 hours, including three Saturdays. These were the conditions experienced by our cotton weavers. Draped in shawls they joined the early morning tide of workers heading towards the smoke of the mill chimney as the hooter abruptly announced the start of another long shift. First was my great grandmother Mary Ann Coyne who may have entered the mill on leaving school. The major employer of the district was the Newton Moor Spinning Company (*vi*) who had two mills, patriotically named Victoria Mill (1862) and Albert Mill (1873-74). Victoria Mill was five storeys high and located off Victoria Road, Newton, where the family were living when Patrick died in 1874. It had 57,400 spindles in 1878.

Mary Ann was also working as a cotton weaver in Oldham in 1881 and in Blackburn in 1891. Her sister-in-law, Frances Coyne, was also a weaver in Hyde in 1871 as was her brother Thomas' second wife, Mary Gill, at the time of their marriage in May 1876. Of the next generation three of Mary Ann's daughters, Mary Emma, Ellen and Frances were also cotton weavers on successive censuses from 1901 to 1911. In 1911 all three were still at home aged 31, 27, and 23 years respectively, providing a significant boost of some £3 per week to the family income.

It seems only one member of the family managed to diversify when it came to occupation. In 1911, the youngest of the family, Jack, then aged 17, was also working as an apprentice brushmaker with Southworth's Brush Manufacturers. Brushmaking was an old established trade while the fact that Jack was not working for his father shows that the painting trade could no longer keep them all. Jack's nephew, Francis Xavier Coyne, remembered him 'driving a trap' for Southworths *(vii.)*

Our weavers' wages then contributed much to the family wellbeing. In Lancashire individual male wages were not the same as family income. The average cotton industry wage of around £1 per week would have been on the border of poverty at the time and contrasts with the operative's reputation for prosperity. The reason of course was the tradition of more than one family member working. For bigger families like the Coynes it meant they enjoyed the living standard of skilled artisans and explained how, at the turn of the century, Peter Coyne could buy his first house at 143 Whalley Range *(viii)*

Painters and Decorators

Painting and decorating became the Coyne family business. Beginning in Manchester in the 1870s the first reference was that of John Coyne on the 1871 Census when he was in employment as a fifteen year old apprentice house painter. By 1881 he had been joined by younger brother Peter. It is likely John started his apprenticeship in 1870, the year that his father died. Peter would have begun in 1873 on leaving St. Phillip's Free School (ix). An apprentice's parents were responsible for paying the master tradesman at the outset so funds must have been available at the time. In 1873 Emma married again to Francis McCausland so he may have helped. In the case of Peter particularly this investment was to reap its reward such that he too, in time, became a Master house painter, a partner in his own business, and with his own painter's yard in Blackburn town centre. During the Edwardian years he employed two sons, James Edward and Joseph, along with a nephew, James Whittaker Coyne, John's illegitimate son, who had been born in Manchester and later moved to Blackburn.

Little is known of Peter's work in the 1880s and 1890s, firstly in Oldham. In the 1880s a qualified painter earned around 6d to 7.5d per hour (*x*) which would give a weekly wage between £1.6s.3d and £1.12s. 9d if we assume a 52 and a half-hour working week. This sum would be subject to seasonal fluctuations, also in the winter hours fell to 48 per week. Peter appears in trade directories from 1900 onwards, particularly Barrett's Directories of Blackburn.

Firstly a look at the painting and decorating trade at the time. One contemporary source is a famous novel, *The Ragged Trousered Philanthropists,* written over the years 1901-11 by Robert Tressell, the pen-name of Robert Noonan, an Irish housepainter, born in Dublin, who after living in South Africa returned to England where he painted around the town of Hastings on the south coast. He wrote his extraordinary and highly political novel about the lives of a group of house-painters while working as a painter himself. The manuscript was kept by his daughter,

Kathleen Noonan, and only came to life after his death in Liverpool in 1911. The novel contains a lot of detail about the trade.

From Tressell we learn that 'regular hands' got most of the work while 'casual hands' were taken on in the spring and often worked for several firms. A casual hand would rarely work for three months without a break in employment. Painting firms had a foreman who often worked as the 'colourman' mixing paints. He writes how painters pushed heavily-laden handcarts around town with broken boots, battered and stained bowler hats *"or caps stained with paint or whitewash"*. It was often the job of the apprentice to push the handcart to the site. In Blackburn, with its cobbled streets we can only imagine how tough it was pushing a handcart up Shear Brow or any other of the town's steep inclines!.

Once on site work would begin on window frames and sashes, old whitewash would be removed from ceilings, and paper scraped from the walls. The air would soon be laden with dust, powdered mortar, lime, plaster and dirt forming layers of debris. Wallpaper would be removed by scraping, soon causing blisters. The labourer would follow filling in cracks and holes and sweeping away the debris. The paperhangers' trestles and boards would be stacked ready for use.

An apprentice painter was bound for five years. He began work in the yard paint shop surrounded by "poisonous pigments". Here he would begin cleaning paint pots and brushes and learning to mix paint under instruction – along of course with making the tea (xi). From the yard heavy loads of paint and white lead, or pails of whitewash, ladders or a 'pair of steps', would be ferried to the job. From yard duties the apprentice would move on to 'plain painting' or 'paste boy'.

Tressell details the tools of the trade – shavehooks, putty knives, paraffin torch-lamps, glasspaper, pumice stone, bottles of oil and turpentine, and tins of putty. He describes the painter's clothing in the novel where Philpott, one of the older painters wore a patched apron, "ragged trousers, old boots, waistcoat, shirt and 'dickey" Painters naturally had paint encrusted caps and clothing worn open –necked in Summer and with a scarf in Winter.

By these times wages had advanced little from the 1880s. In Hastings in 1902 a qualified painter (journeyman) was paid 7d per hour; an unqualified one 5d; a 'mate' or labourer got 4d per hour. A more skilled craftsman such as a signwriter earnt usually one half penny per hour more. For this painters often attended evening classes to learn decorative painting and design and also graining, gilding and signwriting. My great uncle, James Edward, was one of these. In 1900 he is listed under the award winners in Art at the Blackburn Technical School (xii).

There were of course bad times in the trade. Tressell refers to the practice of 'scamping' or shoddy workmanship and the use of cheaper materials. On completion of the job the workman was 'stood off', if there was no more work to go to. He knew of painters who went 15-20 weeks without work and were without earnings. It was here that the benefits of trade union membership (the 'Painters' Society') came into play and this is covered later.

From the information gathered it is possible to estimate James Edward's income for the year he married, that of 1903. Using Tressell's rates and converting to modern currency he would have earnt between £1.68 for a 56 hour week and £2.70 for a 70 hour week. The annual wage would need to consider periods when they were 'stood down' but all in it compares well with the £1 per week of the cotton weaver. By the 1930s Lewery estimated that wages rose to between 1s 6d and 1s 9d per hour.

At the turn of the century – something of a national watershed with the death of Queen Victoria in 1901- Peter and Mary Ann moved to a house at 143 Whalley Range, the first of four houses on this road where family members were to live over the next sixty years. Also in 1902 Peter Coyne went into a business partnership with a John Thomas Whalley, as can be seen from the table on page 132 he appears in the town trade directories of the time. There is even a record of the elusive James W. Coyne then 24 years of age. He was living at 3 Brown Street when he married Margaret Colby, a cotton weaver, at Blackburn Register Office on 15th October 1901. He is described on the marriage certificate as a house painter (journeyman), the son of John Coyne, deceased, a house painter (master). One of the witnesses was James Edward Coyne. This is the record which connects us to James W. and suggests he was the illegitimate son of John. From the directories it seems James W. moved to 3 Cable Street, a short road adjacent to Brown Street, by 1903.

Blackburn Trade Directories

1903 B	Coyne, James	Painter (j)	3 Cable Street
1903 B	Coyne, Peter	143 Whalley Range	and Richmond Terrace
1905 B	Coyne and Whalley	Paint and Varnish Dealers, Paper Hanging merchants	27 Richmond Terrace
1905 B	Coyne, Jas Coyne, Peter	Painter	53 Lawrence St 143 Whalley Range
1905 K	Coyne, Peter	Painter	27 Richmond Terrace
1909 K	Coyne, Peter	Furniture Dealers	162 Whalley Range
1912 B	Coyne, J.E.	Ptr (journeyman)	160 Addison Street
1915 B	Coyne, Peter		175 Whalley Range

B = Barrett's Directory of Blackburn;   K = Kelly's Directory of Lancashire.

Peter Coyne's Painter's Shop. *In 2016 I discovered a Blackburn Library image of Richmond Terrace with accompanying text which stated that "the gates on the left belong to Peter Coyne". I sent for the image and by zooming in was able to discover a lot more about Peter's premises. This image appears as the frontispiece to this book.*

* *It was set about a metre back from the Georgian fronts of Richmond Terrace. To the right was Bolton's Court, while the imposing tower of St. John's church, established 1788, appears in the background.*

* *The tramline from Sudell Cross passes down the centre of the cobbled street. A cobbled entrance extends into Peter's yard.*

* *On the wooden gates is written 'Peter Coyne' with 'Painter and Decorator' below.*

* *On the adjacent wall are examples of signwriting.*

* *The premises is on two floors. There are downstairs sash windows with one large sash window below the roof apex.*

* *Above the window another sign reads 'Coyne' and 'writer' – The word 'sign' is probably hidden.*

In the late 1980s I took the photograph overleaf of the end terrace sandwich shop called 'Tasty's'. The position, size and age suggests this is the very same building albeit with 'modern' features. It reveals a stone-built ground floor with a later addition of a brick upper floor. At the side a door has been bricked –up and probably opened onto the now demolished Bolton's Court. The original photo at the front must date from Edwardian times.

Barrett's Directory of 1905 provides the first appearance of Peter's shop. The entry for 27 Richmond Terrace reads *'Coyne and Whalley wallpaper merchants'*, also listed again under *'paint and varnish dealers'* and *'paperhangers'*. The 1904 Annual Report of the Blackburn Trades Council lists the premises as 28 Richmond Terrace (*xiii*). This street is a surprising venue for a painters' yard since it is an imposing Georgian terrace housing then, as now, the offices of Blackburn's professions- architects and solicitors among them.

Peter Coyne's shop seen here in the late 1980s. In 2016 it was still trading as a sandwich bar.

The exact whereabouts of the premises remained a mystery for a long time. Old maps of this part of the town feature a place called Bolton's Yard – a more likely place I thought,

Where the Wildgeese Roam | *134*

for a painters' premises? On other occasions it is referred to as Richmond Supply Store. In 1905 the premises had a telephone number of 120Y – certainly the first telephone in the family. From 1906 however the business disappeared from the directories and a recent online discovery has explained what had happened.

The Coyne and Whalley partnership struggled in its early days. The expense of running the yard on Richmond Terrace had meant that the business had to borrow from the start. 1906 was a good year when they traded well. Unfortunately 1907 was the exact opposite and with creditors pressing for payment it was apparent by November it was in deep trouble. Realising how bad things were it was agreed to assign the lease on 'Bolton's Yard' over to a trustee. Peter Coyne and John Thomas Whalley were adjudged to be bankrupt on 17th January 1908 and on the 5th February at 10.30am they found themselves before Blackburn Bankruptcy Court. When the Official Receiver received a petition from creditors under the Bankruptcy Act of 1883 their gross liabilities were £788.14s (xiv). The cause given was "bad trade and bad debts". The court proceedings were reported by the *Lancashire Evening Post*. Mr. Robert Ferguson, acting for Coyne and Whalley, stated that the partnership began without any capital. They borrowed £20 from Mrs Alice Whalley, wife of John, and further sums up to £330. 17s. 6d. The business was principally managed by Peter. J.T.Whalley continued his employment at the mill attending partnership business in his spare time. The court was told how they were unaware how bad business was until the assignment of the lease. Peter was questioned about the business telling how 1906 was the only year it really paid. Before then he did not think they made a profit, rather they were "working up the business" with Mrs. Whalley's capital. .He had hoped 1906 would be a turning point and confirmed he had been in business before "on his own account". He was asked about book-keeping and confirmed he "had little to do with it" and that previously he had left it to 'his clerk'.

Mr. Whalley said that he left practically all the business to Coyne but he superintended when the opportunity arose. At this point the examination was adjourned. It was later on the 19th June when Charles Harvey Plant, Official Receiver, of Preston issued a 'Notice of Intended Dividend' followed on the 18th August by a declaration in the London Gazette of a first and final dividend of two shillings and eight and a half pence in the pound.

Peter, with James Edward and Joseph still working for him, had to quickly get back to painting and decorating, back again to 'his own account'. Surprisingly he soon had another venture. In the 1909 Kelly's Directory of Lancashire he appears as 'Coyne, Peter. Furniture Dealer' of 162 Whalley Range. Number 162 was a commercial property next to William Herbert Street with three adjacent shop fronts and a large space to the rear. My father, John, said that these were once called "Hornby's cottages", another part of the empire of the local millowner. It was in later years the premises of Cliff Crook and sons, heating fuel distributors, whose business survives on Whalley Range. I once visited the premises around 1982 with my uncle, Frank Coyne, since the Crooks were friends of the family, when the photograph on the next page was taken. I recall a connection with Peter Coyne so this may have been it. Peter's time as a furniture dealer appears all too brief since there are no further entries in later trade directories.

The Painters' Society

Tressell refers to the trade union as the Painters' Society. It did however have a much weightier title as can be seen from the box on page 139. Trade unionism was one of the great movements of late nineteenth century Britain formed in response to the excesses of employers eager to increase profits at the expense of their workers. The Painters' were one of the old craft-based unions like the engineers and the boilermakers, for example, who sought to defend their apprenticeship- based training not just from employers but also from other workers who may try to 'dilute' their skills. The protection of the interests of 'time-served' men was one of the most frequent grievances aired in the Annual Reports of the Society (*xv*) at this time. Other general workers unions emerged after the 1880s to protect unskilled workers barred by the membership criteria of the craft unions.

162 Whalley Range

The membership records of the Society – unusual for such a long time ago – have survived and our painters are to be found in the records of the Blackburn Branch. The Annual Report of 1905-06 reveals that the branch had 263 members and an income of £834.10s.6d per year. The balance sheet shows that the Society offered more than just a means of dealing with the employer. The main items of expenditure were 'Unemployed Benefit' paid at 10 shillings per week for eight weeks, and Sick Benefit paid at 10 shillings per week for thirteen weeks, followed by 5 shillings per week for a further thirteen weeks. Other benefits included Accident and Funeral Benefit. In 1905-06 the branch paid out £562.13s.10d in Unemployed Benefit alone. These benefits would have been vital at a time when the state made no provision for those not in work. Members' paid one shilling per week in contributions – under two hours pay.

It seems the Coynes were irregular payers of Society subs. Both James E. and James W. were expelled for arrears in September 1906 and December 1906 respectively! (*xvi*) On 24th October 1910 my grandfather, Joseph Coyne, aged 20 years and 8 months joined the Blackburn Branch. On page 140 is a photograph of him taken on a trip to Blackpool a year or so before this date.

These accounts provide one further point of interest. They show that the branch received from Barrow (1) Branch the sum of £103. These would appear to be contributions forwarded to the Blackburn branch on behalf of members working outside the district. Barrow is especially interesting since James Edward was known to have worked painting ships in the Barrow shipyards during the

Where the Wildgeese Roam | *138*

First World War *(xvii)*. This connection may have played a part in his later decision to leave for Canada in 1923. The records show a big demand for

Painters' Society Emblem

The Manchester Alliance of Operative House Painters** was formed in 1856. Following some changes of name to reflect its changing membership it became, in 1880, the General Alliance of House and Ship Painters. In 1886 an amalgamated union, the National Amalgamated Society of Operative House and Ship Painters and Decorators was formed, merging in 1904 with the Amalgamated Society of House Decorators and Painters and some small societies to form......**the National Amalgamated Society of Operative House and Ship Painters and Decorators.

My grandfather, Joseph Coyne (top left) and friends on a Blackpool outing c.1909.

Blackburn painters in Barrow where a major naval shipbuilding programme was underway, part of what became known as the 'naval race' between Great Britain and Germany leading ultimately to the Great War.

By the turn of the century then the Coynes had settled, and had experienced improvements in the family circumstances with the help of abundant female employment in the cotton mills. The first marriage of the new Blackburn family took place on the 27th July 1903 when James Edward married Catherine McCarthy at St. Anne's RC Church in France Street, Blackburn. It is remarkable that a Coyne event took place away from St. Alban's so this may have been the McCarthy's church. Although St. Anne's survives today, now a small red-brick church, the marriage would have taken place in the original chapel which dates from 1849 since the present day church was not built until the 1920s. Catherine was the daughter of James, a 'coachman', and Mary McCarthy of 52 Joseph Street, both parents were Irish-born (xviii) while Catherine, 22, and elder sister Margaret, an assistant school-mistress, aged 26, were born in Denbighshire which makes them Welsh by birth. Margaret was a witness at the wedding along with a James Donlan *(xix)*.

The newly married couple moved to a house at 31 Anvil Street, just to the north of the town centre where the cobbled streets of Brookhouse begin to climb steeply up the hillside. This lower part was demolished during a comprehensive clearance programme in the 1960s. It was here on 6th July 1904 that their first child, named Terence Coyne, was born. He was joined by a brother, Francis, born on 15th July 1906, on St. Swithin's Day. Both boys attended St. Alban's School on nearby Larkhill and it was here that one of our oldest family photographs was taken of Terence (Terry) with other schoolboys taken at the school when they would have been about seven or eight years old. It seems this was a First Holy Communion photograph as some of the boys are wearing sashes and this would date the picture at around 1911-12.

Frank was baptised *'Franciscus'* in July 1906 at St. Alban's when his godparents were a Joseph Cunningham and his aunt, Ellen Coyne. The baptism record (today kept at Lancashire Record Office) confirms he was not baptised Francis Xavier, the name he was known by, so perhaps 'Xavier' was a later confirmation name. James and Catherine seemed to have a fondness for Jesuit confirmation names – St. Francis Xavier being a sixteenth century Spanish missionary known as '*Los conquistadores del animis*', or the conqueror of souls. In our family we were thankful for the 'X' since it enabled us to distinguish between Frank, born 1906, and his cousin, also Francis Coyne, born later in 1928.

James and Catherine may have been doing well while at Anvil Street but nationally things were far from calm. The years to the end of the Edwardian decade (Edward VII died in 1910) were a time of social unrest. The number of strikes had increased in the mines and on the railways particularly; action by the suffragettes in support of women's suffrage was at its highest; and events such as the Siege of Sidney Street in January 1911 saw foreign revolutionaries shoot and kill three policeman on the streets of London. On top of this the international situation was threatening the peace.

Before events escalated into war in just a few years James and Catherine moved around 1911-12 to improved housing, probably still private rented, on the west side of Blackburn, to 160 Addison Street which was to be the family home until at least 1935. Addison Street has a very steep incline at the north end where it joins the busy Preston New Road, home to some of Blackburn's grander houses and from the 1880s, a tramway. Most of Addison Street survives today where the brick-built terraced houses on the west side of the street have survived but unfortunately No.160 on the other side has been demolished.

Among these St. Alban's schoolboys Terry Coyne is third from left (back row).

The west side of Addison Street, Blackburn. The Coynes lived opposite at No.160.

Art

James had other reasons to be pleased with life. A daughter, Catherine (known as Kathleen) was born in

1913, while it has been known within the family that James was an artist as well as a house painter by day. My parents, aunts and uncles often mentioned one of his oil paintings – described as a tall, dark painting of a woman at a loom, believed to be his sister Emma – hanging from the wall of one of the Whalley Range houses as late as the 1950s. Several efforts had been made over the years to discover what became of this painting, including enquiries to Blackburn Art Gallery, but without success.

A few years ago I found out from James' granddaughter, Margaret Mearns, that James was known to have painted members of Blackburn Town Council so I enquired again. At first this was also unsuccessful but I was later contacted by a member of staff who had found a reference to James in a directory of local artists. Below is a transcription of the information received which best explains James' interests.

> *"James Edward Coyne (active 1910-30)*
>
> *Residence: 160 Addison Street.*
>
> *Landscape painter and Black and white illustrator.*
>
> *"Son of P. Coyne, painter and decorator, Mr. Coyne was a full-time painter and a member of the Arts and Crafts Society, of which he was on the committee. In the early 1900s he did illustrations for the Blackburn Weekly Telegraph, but his main interest was landscape painting with a liking for atmospheric effects and the scenery of the Lake District. He also recorded picturesque scenes near Blackburn and did portraits on commission."(xx)*

Just three art works are known to survive within the family. These are two portraits of his sons Terry and Frank when they were about seven years old, along with a competition entry, a drawing of a 'bust of Caesar'! This makes James a very busy man at the time. It is interesting to note that a proficiency in art has been apparent among members of the Blackburn family since.

Two more marriages took place in Blackburn in 1912. On the 4th May Ellen Coyne, 25, married James Kennedy, 24, of 113 Hancock Street, the son of Stephen and Alice Kennedy. James' grandfather, John Kennedy, had earlier moved to Lancashire from Tipperary. Ellen's youngest brother, John, was a witness. Both Ellen (who was always known as Nellie by the Coynes) and James were cotton weavers so may have met at work. During the same quarter Ellen's sister, Frances Coyne, married George Howarth who was also a weaver at Dugdale's Griffin Mill. On the 23rd November, Mary Josephine Kennedy (later to be known as 'Josie') was born and was baptised at St. Alban's on 1st December. Frances and George also had a daughter, who they named Elizabeth, born around the same time.

By now, with the next generation growing it was not events in Blackburn which were to shape our next chapter. Imperial rivalries among the major European powers were soon to explode. It is usually the assassination of the Archduke Franz Ferdinand in the city of Sarajevo on the 28th June 1914 which is recognised as the starting pistol which began the conflagration that was to become the First World War. Few, however, would have anticipated industrial warfare on an epic scale shattering the peace of millions. By the time of the Armistice in November 1918 barely a family in the land was unaffected by the vast numbers of casualties. For the Coyne family these consequences were to be grave indeed.

i. *Female employment in the cotton industry rose to a peak of 61 per cent in 1913. From 1901 there was a legal limit of 55.5 hours per week.*
ii. *Thomas and Patrick Coyne, and Patrick's son Thomas, born 1848, were all plasterers.*
iii. *www.spinningtheweb.org.*
iv. *A beam is a huge bobbin. A beamer makes warp for weaving. A twister joined the ends of threads onto the warp already on the loom.*
v. *Blackburn Times 15th December 190: 'Extra Day for Blackburn Operatives'*
vi. *'Dukinfield Cotton Mills' by Ian Haynes.*
vii. *FX Coyne letter to author 12.2.1993*
viii. *1901 Census: 143 Whalley Range, Blackburn.*
ix. *There are records of Peter's school attendance. He first attended St. Wilfrid's School and was then admitted to St. Philip's Free School in Hulme on 6th January 1868 (Manchester Collection).*
x. *'Signwritten Art' by A. J Lewery.*
xi. *In Lancashire this vital social function would be known as "havin' a brew"!*
xii. *Blackburn Standard: 'Examination Results', 8th September 1900.*
xiii. *List of Trade Union offices and shops, page.26 'Painters and Decorators' (Blackburn Trades Council)*
xiv. *London Gazette: 17th January 1908.p.458.*
xv. *Deposited files of the NASOHSPD (Modern Records Centre)*
xvi. *Under the rules a member who was in arrears for 20 weeks could be expelled.*
xvii. *Letter from his son, FX Coyne, to author 12th February 1993.*
xviii. *County of birth not known.*
xix. *Liber Matrimoniorum, St. Anne's church p.169 (Lancashire Record Office).*
xx. *Email from Art Keeper (Curator) Blackburn Museum and Art Gallery November 2010.*

CHAPTER TWELVE

The Great War 1914-1918

War was declared in August 1914. By then Peter and Mary Ann had lived in Blackburn for thirty-two years, both were now in their late fifties and while there is no record of him in the trade directories it is likely Peter was still working 'on his own account'. By 1911 the family had moved along Whalley Range to a bigger house at number 175, a section of superior housing raised up from the road and with front gardens, known as 'Beaumont Terrace.' These houses were new having been built in 1903. On the slope below leading down to the Blakewater was Hornby's mill. Just to the west was Brookhouse Lane leading down to St. Alban's church and school. On the corner was the local co-operative shop, the Daisyfield Industrial Bees Co-operative Society who had a number of branches in this part of the town. On the other corner was the Whalley Range Inn.

Also living with the family were James and Ellen Kennedy and two year old daughter Josie. It is likely Frances and George Howarth and their daughter Elizabeth also lived with the family for a while before finding their own accommodation (i). Eldest daughter Emma, then aged 36; Joseph 25; and youngest son John completed the family group. Mary Ann we know was called 'Poll', Ellen was 'Nellie', John was 'Jack', Elizabeth Howarth was known as

'Lizzie' and presumably Joseph was shortened to 'Joe'! By modern standards I think we can say they were overcrowded!

Beaumont Terrace. 175 Whalley Range is the first house with the bay window. Two doors down is No. 179. Peter Coyne bought No.175 around 1900.

James Edward was over at Addison Street with his own family and it seems that as the war progressed he spent less time there. Eldest son Terry from the age of ten did a number of casual jobs in the locality to help boost the family income *(ii)*. This would be important as in December 1915 they had another mouth to feed. On the 17th of the month Catherine Coyne gave birth to her youngest son, named James Anthony.

And so to war. The upheaval to family and working life throughout the country, indeed the Empire, had started. On the 4th August Great Britain, in alliance with France and Russia, declared war on Germany and Austria-

Hungary. The Kaiser's designs on Belgium had triggered the declaration and before long the British Expeditionary Force, comprised of the Regular Army, had set sail for France. Blackburn had two recruitment centres in the town, the 4th East Lancashire Regiment had a base at Canterbury Street barracks and the 1st East Lancashire Royal Field Artillery had a HQ in King Street. Early recruits to the military would have 'joined up' there.

On joining up new recruits were given a medical examination, completed their Attestation documents, and if accepted were placed with a corps that was open for enlistment. By January 1915 one million men had enlisted. Many answered the famous recruitment poster depicting the face of Lord Kitchener, Secretary of State for War, imploring' *Your Country Needs You'*. New recruits were referred to as 'Kitchener's Army' and many were enlisted into 'Pals' Battalions' where men – and often boys as well – signed up along with their pals to face military life together. A few miles from Blackburn the 11th (Service) Battalion, East Lancashire Regiment was so formed, forever to be known as the 'Accrington Pals'. Many of these recruits were from Accrington, along with others from neighbouring East Lancashire towns including Blackburn, and we shall return to their fate later in the chapter. By the end of the year two and a half million men had been recruited, all volunteers. It was still not enough. In January 1916 conscription was introduced where all able-bodied men between the ages of eighteen and forty were called up for military service.

During the course of the war four of our family – John Coyne, James Kennedy, George Howarth and Joseph

Coyne signed up for army service. This account is compiled without the benefit of referring to their army service records, held by the National Archives, since it appears all four were among the forty per cent of records lost during a fire at the War Office during the Second World War! For this reason we don't know if they were volunteers or conscripts. It matters not since three of them were to lose their lives in the conflict and only my grandfather, Joseph, was able to return to Blackburn when he was 'demobbed' in 1919.

In addition to these four James Edward was employed on war work in the Barrow shipyards. He spent less time in Blackburn and began the start of his separation from not just the wider family but ultimately from his own wife and children. His son Frank, in a letter to me sent in 1990 wrote that after his father went away on war work "we never saw my grandparents on Whalley Range again". James' separation ultimately led to his emigration in 1923. The final family member, the ever elusive James Whittaker Coyne, it seems had escaped again. Aged around 40 in 1916 he would have been just too old for conscription!

Gunner John Coyne

It seems likely that John was the first to sign up some time during 1914 or 1915. He enlisted at Aldershot in Hampshire into the Royal Field Artillery with the rank of Gunner and was given the service number L/45819. His army cap badge bore the motto *'Quo Fas et Gloria Ducunt' – where right and glory lead.'* By April 1915 when the ill-fated Gallipoli campaign in the Dardanelles resulted in many casualties John would have begun training with his unit, the CXX11(122nd) Brigade. His pay as a Gunner was one shilling and two and a half pence per day- more than that of an infantryman. In addition he would be entitled to one pound of bread and a three-quarter pound of meat. A two pence per week allowance was also paid for the upkeep of his kit. John's previous employment 'driving a trap' may have aided his recruitment into the Artillery whose field guns were pulled by horses. In August 1915 the 122nd Brigade, who were a howitzer brigade, joined the 38th (Welsh) Division and stayed together for the rest of the war. Many of the new recruits spent much of 1915 training but combat drew near in December when the 38th Division were posted overseas. In the same month the 11th East Lancashire sailed from Devonport for Egypt where a Turkish attack was anticipated. When it failed to materialise they were than diverted to 'France and Flanders' where they became part of the Western Front. As 1916 began the Western Front was soon to surpass all others in the scale of the carnage as the great armies of Europe faced each other across the trenches. If the earlier battles in Flanders, around the town of Ypres were fierce enough 1916 gave up a name forever associated with the horrors of war – a river, also a French *departement* by the name of.....the Somme.

1916

With conscription in force from the 1st January 1916 James Kennedy was the next to join on the 19th of the month. In February war in France intensified as the French Army became involved in an epic battle of attrition at Verdun. By the end of the year 300,000 Frenchmen were dead. As the British Army replaced its casualties the 11th East Lancashire arrived at Colincamps in March, now just one and a half miles from the front. Preparations were being made for the 'Big push'. But first, for a family of Irish origin a significant interlude from our srory.

The Easter Rising

Acting on the premise that Britain's problem was Ireland's opportunity rebel forces struck in Dublin during Easter week 1916. Between Easter Monday April 24th and Saturday April 29th rebels led by Patrick Pearse, James Connolly, and others, held strategic positions around the Irish capital and, after the police withdrew, engaged in armed revolt against the British Army. At the end of six days fighting 125 police and military were dead, along with 180 civilians. During the week Pearse was declared President of the Provisional Government and from outside the General Post Office he issued the *Proclamation of the Irish Republic*. The backlash by the authorities was brutal. After the surrender of rebel forces thirteen leaders were sentenced to death by Field Court Martial. Others, such as the Sinn Feiner, Countess Markievicz were given penal servitude. The executions at Kilmainham Gaol were swift and without mercy. The executed men became martyrs to Irish freedom. The poet W B Yeats in his poem '*Easter 1916*' remarked *"a terrible beauty has been born"*. Independence was now within reach.

It would be interesting to know how our family in Blackburn would have viewed these events. John and

Joseph Coyne, and James Kennedy were all grandsons of Irish immigrants who were now serving with the British Army at war over in France. Other army units had to be diverted to Dublin. The rising was not a popular one at the time and was less so among army families so I would think it would be safe to say they perhaps held mixed emotions.

The Battle of the Somme

By the middle of the year the generals were ready. With the British Expeditionary Force and the French facing the Germans across over three hundred miles of trenches which made up the Western Front, on the 24th June the signal was given for a massive artillery bombardment to commence. They kept it up for a week, each battery firing 3,000 rounds of shells per day in the belief they could bomb the German positions out of sight. As an early recruit John Coyne was probably involved in the bombardment as one of 1,500 gun batteries.

The 1st of July 1916 was a bright, sunny day in N.E. France. It was not the weather we remember however. At 7.30am officers sounded their whistles giving the order for 100,000 men to leave their trenches and advance into 'No Man's Land'. It was soon apparent that the bombardment had not worked, it was later estimated that some 30 per cent of shells had failed to explode. More significantly the shells had failed to remove the ranks of barbed wire in front of the German lines. Casualties immediately fell as men, often caught on the barbed wire were mown down by German machine gun and shell fire.

Five battalions of the East Lancashire Regiment fought at the Somme, including the 11th. It is believed the 'Accrington Pals' were mown down in just twenty minutes. Before the clock struck eight o'clock 585 of the 700 men of the battalion lay dead or wounded near to the village of Serre. Worse was to follow. Not for nothing is the 1st July 1916 known as the "worst day in the history of the British Army". Among a staggering 57,470 casualties, *19,240 were killed in action!* Today these figures are truly shocking and whether or not you believe they were 'lions led by donkeys' General Haig and others of the military top brass had little regard for human life.

Private James Kennedy

As word reached back home of the extent of the carnage, albeit a censored one, the war rolled on. On the 7th July the 38th Division, which included John Coyne, suffered huge losses during an assault on Mametz Wood, today the site of the Welsh Dragon Monument, before the area was secured on the 12th July. On the 18th James Kennedy was enlisted into the East Lancashire Regiment (*iii*) where he was placed in the 12th (Reserve) Battalion with the rank of Private. The battalion was a replacement for the Somme losses, by September the battle raged on and had become a sea of mud. Casualties now included many with 'shell shock', their nerves shattered by the barrage of exploding shells. Most of these were returned to the front while others were placed on a charge of cowardice, a charge which carried the death penalty. Of 346 executions during the First World War, all but 24 of them took place on the Western Front.

By this stage of the war Joseph Coyne may have joined the Royal Garrison Artillery, the heavy gun, Howitzer, section of the Artillery (*iv*). It is not known when he joined up but the War Diary of the 158 Siege Battery – Joe's unit- tells us they left Bristol on the S.S. Huntsman on the 10th September 1916 bound for Boulogne. They continued on to the front by train. After the Somme many battalions ceased to exist, remaining personnel were placed with other units, with new recruits added to Reserve or training battalions. James Kennedy's service showed such a move when on 1st September the 12th (Reserve) Battalion of the East Lancashire Regiment became part of the 75th Training Reserve Battalion. In August they were based in Swanage and later at Prees Heath, a training camp in Shropshire. James may have been there when good news reached him from home. On the 10th October his wife Ellen had a second daughter, named Winifred, who was born at 175 Whalley Range. Soon after James was transferred to the 1st Battalion King's Own (Royal Lancaster) Regiment, who were again replacing the huge losses suffered in heavy fighting around Beaumont Hamel and Serre. They moved immediately overseas to France.

The year 1917 was a fateful year for our combatants. Before the year was out only John Coyne was still in action with the 'C' Battery of the 122nd Brigade. Two of our family, James Kennedy and George Howarth were killed in action, and the third, Joseph Coyne was wounded.

First to fall on the 12th February was James Kennedy, killed in action with the King's Own near to the French village of Fins (*v*), again in the *Departement* of the Somme. He was at first buried in the village, but later moved, according to the Commonwealth War Graves Commission, to the Fins New British Cemetery in nearby Sorel-le-Grand. A father of two, his youngest daughter Winnie was just four months old. In 1991 she was able to visit her father's grave along with James' grandsons, Gerard and Peter Fielding, when the image of his headstone was taken. It is not known how James was killed but seventy five per cent of casualties at the Somme were hit by shellfire. He had been in France less than two months and since action in the Somme area was winding down can consider himself unlucky.For the rest of the war the focus was to move to Arras, Cambrai, and again to Ypres. I learnt this year that another of James' grandsons, Philip Eccles, had visited the grave on the hundredth anniversary of his death.

Private George Howarth

South of the Flanders town of Ypres (' Wipers' to the British tommy) is the town of Messines, and it was here another major battle took place between 7th and 11th June 1917.Again a two week artillery bombardment preceded the battle, this time more successful with the mining of explosives below the German lines. Private George Howarth was with the 7th Battalion, East Lancashire Regiment, (number 29040) when he took part in the battle (*vi*).The *'History of the East Lancashire Regiment in the Great War'* has a graphic description of the battle which began at 3.20am on the 7th June. It was noted hot tea and rum was served beforehand...

"The disposition of the 56th Brigade was as follows: the King's Own and the 7/N Lancs in the front line and the 7/East Lancs and the 7/S Lancs in the second line. The 7/East Lancs was directed to attack in four waves. The first two consisted of two platoons of A and B Companies; D Company in a single line formed the third wave with orders to mop up the captured trenches and dug-outs. C Company also in a single line formed the fourth wave and was the battalion reserve"

The Grave of James Kennedy, Fins New British Cemetery, Sorel-le-Grand, France

The battle was only a partial success. Although they had gained territory the low-lying ground near Wytschaete was overlooked by German positions and despite relatively low casualties during the battle they remained open to shell-fire. George Howarth was killed on the 26th June, eleven days after they had been relieved and gone into camp near Locre. There was an account of his death, along with a photograph in the *Blackburn Times* who reported on 7th July that *"Private George Howarth (30) died of wounds on the 26th June from wounds received in action. He leaves a wife and child, now residing with her parents at 175 Whalley Range"* The report includes an account from the battalion Commanding Officer who had sent a letter to Frances explaining how George had died (see over)

The Regimental History adds that from the 19th to the end of June the 7th Battalion were employed in reconditioning the recently captured area and making it serviceable for troops and transport adding that *"working parties were constantly shelled and few days passed without casualties"* (vii). Together this builds a full picture of how George met his fate. He lies buried at Bailleul Communal Cemetery in France, Nord, close to the Belgian border.

Howarth, George

Private George Howarth (30), of the East Lancashire Regiment, died on June 26th, from wounds received in action. He leaves a wife and child,

Private George Howarth.

now residing with her parents at 175, Whalley Range. Writing to Mrs. Howarth the deceased's captain says: "He was severely wounded some days ago by a piece of shrapnel which damaged the spine. We were out on a working party at the time, but were fortunate enough to get him off to hospital almost at once. He has, however, succumbed to his wounds. I would, therefore, like to express my deepest sympathy with you in the loss of your very gallant husband. He was much respected and liked by all who knew him, and as a soldier the company has lost a very gallant comrade. He has been buried in the military cemetery at ——, and his grave has been marked by one of our regimental crosses." He was formerly a weaver at Dugdale's Griffin Mill.

George Howarth - the Blackburn Times report

Gunner Joseph Coyne

From July to November 1917 the war raged on in the form of the third battle of Ypres, better known as Passchendaele. By then deadly mustard gas was being used. The British fared well until October when the infamous mud turned the battle ground into a quagmire engulfing men, horses and equipment alike. Before then September had been warm and dry and it was during this month our third casualty was hit. Gunner Joseph Coyne of the Royal Garrison Artillery, regimental number 103573, was wounded in action.

The RGA were the heavy gun, Howitzer, section of the Artillery and comprised of many siege batteries. From information in the Army Medal Indexes at the National Archives it would appear that Joseph was attached to the 158 Siege Battery. Unfortunately the battery's War Diary for the period (September 1916- August 1917) ends before the time of the wounding. When it ended on August 31st the battery was in action at Feuchy, near the major town of Arras, on the Somme. They had been active in the Somme area since November 1916.

Due to demands at the time for more information about the colossal number of casualties the War Office had by then had time to improve its communications, They could do little about those missing in action or with no known grave, but those identified as killed or wounded had their names published in the *War Office Weekly Casualty Lists* from quite early in the war. By 1917 this publication was listing hundreds of thousands of names and it is from this source, on the Daily List for September 22nd under the heading *'wounded'* and sub-heading *'Royal Garrison Artillery'*, that there is an entry which briefly notes '*Coyne 103573 Gunner J. (Blackburn)*' A cross reference with the medal index confirms this was our Joseph Coyne.

It was only in 2014 that I was able to confirm what had happened to my grandfather and to find out what regiment he belonged to! My father knew he had been wounded, as did his cousin Frank, while his marriage certificate in 1919 described him as 'ex- Army'. Again without his service record we can learn no more of his time in the army. It is possible he even returned to the front as many others who '*took a Blighty*' (*viii*) were patched up and returned to action. It would seem he suffered no long-term disability as he was able to resume employment as a painter and decorator after the war.

1918

The Great War was now in its fifth year. On the 6th February the 7th Battalion East Lancashire regiment – George Howarth's old unit – was disbanded with the remaining men transferred to other battalions. The main change of direction now was that the Germans had closed their Eastern Front where they had faced the new Bolshevik forces after the Russian Revolution of October 1917. This now meant a new offensive on the Western Front.

It came in March when on the 21st attacks drove the British back, suffering some 38,000 casualties in fierce fighting. If it was despairing to think they were now back on the old 1916 battlefield at Peronne, such thoughts were locked away alongside the horror and the grief endured since 1914. But fightback they did with the valiant support of Australian, Canadian, Indian and other Commonwealth, - and from June 1917 American – forces the Germans had been driven back to the Hindenburg Line by August. This formidable barrier extended for some 65 miles of trenches, including a key section between Cambrai and St. Quentin. John Coyne would have been heavily involved. As the 38th (Welsh) Division attacked towards the Canal du Nord, the 122nd Brigade RFA were praised for their heroic action. We can follow their progress from the War Diary (ix) which shows how they helped to liberate Albert.

By now these battle-hardened troops were ready to face anything and were able to move rapidly and set up the next battery position with minimum delay. On the 29th September they camped at Goozeaucourt, and on the 1st October 1918 they were at Fins, a French village on the Goozeaucourt – Cambrai road. This was very close to the place James Kennedy had been killed the previous year, although John was unlikely to know this. By now news of the advance was also reaching home faster. The *Blackburn Times* was able to report how St. Quentin fell on 1st October and how on the 3rd October 'peace at last' came to the beleaguered town of Ypres. This however was a dangerous time. Such rapid progress found the Germans in full retreat while elsewhere fierce resistance was still apparent. This was the experience of the 122nd Brigade, RFA, who by then were in the village of Troisvilles when on the 10th October the War Diary recorded that " *one team was knocked out*" during a big attack. The very next day, Friday 11th October, Gunner John Coyne 'died of wounds' so it would seem this was the attack which caused his death.

Alas poor Jack! He had spent four years at least shelling the German lines before it seems he fatally succumbed to shellfire himself. He was moved to a casualty clearing station where he did not recover. At 24, John was the youngest of our four soldiers – the first to join up and the last to die. Peace was just four weeks away. One week later, on the 18th October, the city of Lille was liberated ending the last German resistance in the area. The 122nd Brigade were still in Troisvilles where many further casualties were reported. It was not until 11am on the 11th November – Armistice Day – that the guns finally fell silent and the war was over.

John Coyne was buried in a war cemetery at Manancourt in the *Departement* of the Somme (See box for details of our three war graves). All four soldiers were awarded the Victory Medal and the British War Medal. Sadly we have no knowledge of what became of these medals as none are known to have survived within the family. On the 16th November the Blackburn Times was able to report that Bishop Hanlon had addressed a large congregation at St'. Alban's and "thanked God for victory". Later the parish provided a fitting war memorial, a marble Pieta on an onyx base, which is positioned just inside the main door of the church. Here three marble wall tablets commemorate those men of the parish who fell during the First World War including the names of John Coyne and James Kennedy. Elsewhere both men, along with George Howarth feature on the Blackburn Roll of Honour, produced by the Town Council.

And so this most brutal of wars was over. The country had suffered some 1.6 million service personnel either wounded or killed – even today the figures are truly astounding. The economic cost would also be evident for decades. For our family two of Peter and Mary Ann's daughters were now war widows with three young children to support. If John had survived we may have had another branch of the family. Thousands of other families were also mourning but the objective at the time had to be to return to normality as soon as possible and to return the world of work and family life. Before then a brief pause to remember our three soldiers who lie today in the war graves of N.E. France.

Name	Service Number	Regiment	Cemetery	Location
James Kennedy	*32538*	*King's Own (Royal Lancaster)*	*Fins New British Sorel-le-Grand Somme*	V111 A.25
George Howarth	*29040*	*East Lancashire*	*Bailleul Communal Cemetery Extension Bailleul, Nord*	111 D.6
John Coyne	*L/45819*	*122nd Brigade Royal Field Artillery*	*Rocquigny-Equancourt Rd BritishCemetery,Manancourt Somme*	Plot 14 Row C Grave 11

The Green Fields of France: Family War Graves

i. Later in 1917, it is known Frances and daughter Elizabeth were back at 175.
ii. Terry informed his granddaughter Cathy that he had a paper round, worked as a lather boy in a barber's shop, and worked as a helper for a butcher and a grocer.
iii. Service number 27888. Later in the King's Own he had a new number, 32538.
iv. The Royal Garrison Artillery (RGA) fired heavier and more long-distance guns than the RFA and were placed farther from the front. The 6" siege gun fired 100lb shells; 8" siege guns fired 200lb shells; and the 9.2" Siege Howitzer fired 290lb shells Their range could reach 14,000 yards.
v. Fins is a village between Cambrai and Peronne.
vi. 'History of the East Lancashire Regiment in the Great War' by Colonel Nicholson, 1936, p.390.
vii. Nicholson, p.392.
viii. 'Blighty' was a nickname for England, common among soldiers overseas. It came from an Anglo-Indian word 'bilayati.
ix. National Archives ref. WO95/2545

CHAPTER THIRTEEN

The Inter-War Years

The years 1919 to 1939 are usually given the somewhat dull title of 'the inter-war years'. For the purposes of family history though they include some of the most interesting years since for the first time we have first-hand anecdotes from two of my father's cousins – Frank Coyne ,born 1906, and Winnie Fielding, born 1916 – both of whom I wrote to when I first became interested in the 'Coyne family history'. I have some seven or eight letters from them dating from the early 1990s which contain information to be found nowhere else about our lives in Blackburn, in the 1920s particularly. I will also return again to the issue of Irish identity, and look again at how our families fared during these years.

The is no doubt these were again tough times economically and include the years of the Wall Street crash in 1929 and the Great Depression of 1931-33. We also have another shock emigration and the beginning of another break in contact between branches of the family. Others also left Blackburn during these times, a trend which was to continue after the Second World War. But first we take a brief detour to catch up with our Manchester Coynes to see how they got on. .

The Mancunians

The three surviving daughters of Thomas Edward Coyne were all married by 1922. In 1915 Sarah Coyne married an Archibald McIlwraith in Chorlton (South Manchester) and the following year they had a son, also named Archie, who sadly died soon after. In 1918 a second child, named Lily was born and she survived into adulthood. Next to marry was the youngest sister, Lilian Coyne, who married on 17th December 1921. She was a café waitress at the time, aged 27, of 16 Percy Street in Hulme, a street next to the busy Stretford Road. She married George Mercer, a warehouse packer, of 4 Edge Street, also in Hulme. Lastly Eveline Coyne married an Edward J. Scannell in 1922. I have only been able to trace one child of these three marriages when Lilian M. Mercer was born to Lilian and George in 1922. Consequently from this date there is little to report.

In 1930 Thomas' widow, Mary R. Coyne, died of bronchitis and 'senile decay'. Aged 77 years she was still at 16 Percy Street where she had lived for at least eight years. In 1934 Amy Thursby, born 1879, died followed in February 1937 by her only child, John Edgar Thursby aged just 22 years. They were both buried in the Thursby grave at Southern Cemetery. This left just Amy's brother Peter who since 1914 had been separated from Harriet and his two children. The search for Peter's death has been less clear – the only match by age was for a Peter Coyne who died on the 11th February 1937, who was from Chorlton on Medlock and employed with a furniture dealers which matches in some way his circumstances on the 1911 Census. If so, he appeared to be the husband of a Catherine Coyne, although I could find no record of a marriage. It may, of course, have been a common law marriage – legally Peter was perhaps still married to Harriet? This Catherine died on the 18th February 1941 aged 59 years, when according to the *Manchester Evening News* she was living in Moss Side and was the *"dearly beloved wife of the late Peter Coyne."*

Contact with the Coyne family in Blackburn had long since ceased such that the largest section of this branch of the family in terms of numbers today are likely to be the descendants of Harriet's children, Amy and James Coyne, who settled n Mahanoy City, Pennsylvania, USA. There is some further information about them at the end of this chapter.

Blackburn 1919

The last casualty of the Great War was the Lancashire cotton industry. Production peaked in 1913 followed after by difficulties during war-time. Firstly there were labour shortages. As more men were called up there was more employment for women and girls in the mills. Wages failed to keep up with inflation and when the supply of raw cotton became scarcer, due to restricted shipping and foreign competition, exports dropped sharply. After the war the industry recovered a little before terminal decline set in. Both home and overseas markets were lost to foreign competition, firstly to Japan and later to India and China. Blackburn's claim to being the world's largest weaving town would soon be over.

The writer William Woodruff came from Blackburn and remembered these times in his book, *'The Road to Nab End'*. He mentioned how the number of war casualties "stunned the whole of Britain" and how black clothing was everywhere. Winnie Fielding also remembered her grandmother, Mary Anne Coyne, draped in black *"I have a feint recollection of her sat in a chair dressed all in black, with the family doing everything for her"* (i). For those in uniform demobilization from the army took many months after the Armistice given the numbers involved. Joseph Coyne when 'demobbed' would have been allowed to keep a 'cardigan waistcoat, necessaries, drawers, one pair of serviceable boots and a kitbag'. On returning to their home town soldiers were then paid one pound if they returned their army great –coat to the nearest railway station.

It is not known when my grandfather met my grandmother, Mary Ann Power, but soon after he was demobbed they married, on the 13th September 1919, at St. Alban's.

A photo of Mary Ann Power probably taken before the First World War

The witnesses were Mary Emma Coyne, and James Littler. Mary Ann was 28 years old, two years younger than Joe, and was a cotton weaver living at 7 Smithies Street. She was the daughter of Fergus Power, a tailor (journeyman). Fergus was born in County Galway and didn't appear in Blackburn until the 1880s, marrying his wife Mary Brett in 1887. In 1919 Fergus was by then a widower, and Mary Ann, an only child, so after the wedding Joseph and his new wife went to live with Fergus. It was a move of some permanence as Fergus continued to live with them until his death in 1931. As a result my father, John, remembered well his Irish grandfather during his early years. John was born at Smithies Street on 11th June 1920 (ii).

Smithies Street was in something of an Irish quarter in Blackburn, centred around St. Alban's and close to Larkhill leading to the town centre about a quarter of a mile away. Several Irish pubs existed in the area including the *Duke of Connaught* on Moor Street, the street where my grandmother was born, and *'Ireland's Glory'*, a street corner beerhouse. Brewing was very much in the air round here as in addition to the Swan Brewery on Moor Street, which backed on to Smithies Street, both Daniel Thwaites' Eanam Brewery and Dutton and Co's Salford Brewery were not far away.

By the time Emma married – at the grand old age of 42 – early in 1921 to Anthony McHugh, an operative cotton spinner, all Peter and Mary Ann's surviving children were now married. Four names in marriage – McCarthy, Kennedy, Power and McHugh – show how the Coynes mainly married within the Irish Catholic community and

Where the Wildgeese Roam | 170

perhaps something of the old Irish identity was invigorated. This contrasts with the Mancunians whose Irish identity was soon lost. Another factor would be that they were all now second generation Irish and in Blackburn, with the patriotic fervour of the Great War so recent, the process of assimilation was underway. What is intriguing is that the years 1921-22 were pivotal in Irish history being the years of the War of Independence, and the emergence of the Irish Republican Army with a violent nationalist agenda, the partition of the country and the creation of the twenty-six county Irish Free State in 1922. Although the Coynes had long since lost contact with Ireland, Fergus Power, for example still had family in Ireland (iii) and would have been in touch during this period of British Army activity in the south and when the notorious' black-and-tans' damaged Anglo- Irish relations for years ahead. As we shall see in Chapter 15 Terry Coyne, born 1904, told his family that he saw army service in Ireland at this time having joined up at the second attempt and may still have been underage.

This separation from Ireland was a watershed for the Irish community in Britain. No longer one of the four parts of the 'British Isles' but now a sovereign country with its own government, institutions and passport. Did this lead to greater assimilation? I would think it probably did. Lancashire is also a county with a strong local identity – indeed its own accent – and thus by now the Coynes would likely have identified themselves as Lancastrians first. Lancashire Irish? English? Perhaps both.

Family Events of the Early 1920s

1921 to 1923 saw significant changes in the family. Not long after Emma's marriage, the head of the family, Peter Coyne, died on the 28th May 1921 at 175 Whalley Range. On his death certificate it states he died of Apoplexy, probably a form of stroke, aged 65 years. He was in fact only 62, the informant, James Edward 'present at the death' was unaware of his father's exact age.

Less than a year later his widow, Mary Anne, who he called *'Poll'*, died on the 10th February

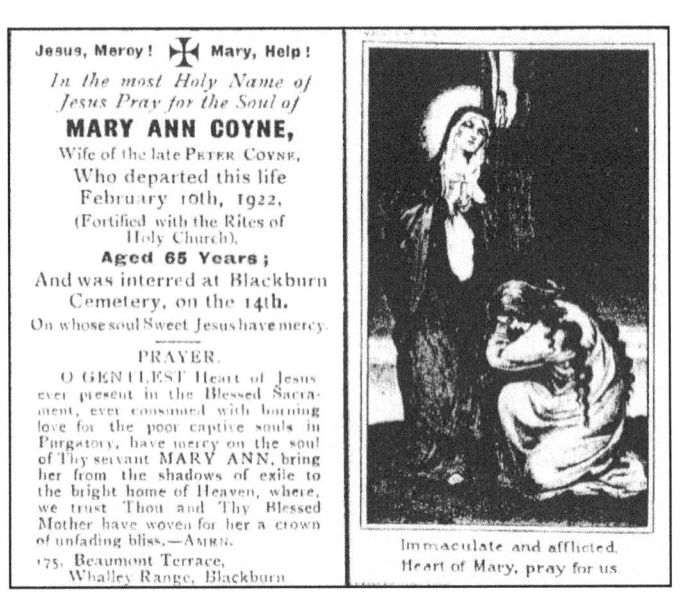

Jesus, Mercy! ✠ Mary, Help!
In the most Holy Name of Jesus Pray for the Soul of
MARY ANN COYNE,
Wife of the late PETER COYNE,
Who departed this life February 10th, 1922,
(Fortified with the Rites of Holy Church).
Aged 65 Years;
And was interred at Blackburn Cemetery, on the 14th.
On whose soul Sweet Jesus have mercy.
PRAYER.
O GENTLEST Heart of Jesus ever present in the Blessed Sacrament, ever consumed with burning love for the poor captive souls in Purgatory, have mercy on the soul of Thy servant MARY ANN, bring her from the shadows of exile to the bright home of Heaven, where, we trust Thou and Thy Blessed Mother have woven for her a crown of unfading bliss.—AMEN.
175, Beaumont Terrace, Whalley Range, Blackburn
Immaculate and afflicted, Heart of Mary, pray for us

Mass card for Mary Ann Coyne

1922 James again reported the death, when it was recorded his mother was 65 years old. The cause of death was 'Mitral Stenosis', a heart condition. The two cousins were buried together at Blackburn Cemetery (iv), the end of lives that had brought them ten children, just five of whom were still alive, and by means of Peter's painting business in the early days had enabled them to buy a good standard family home on Whalley Range. For Mary Anne this had been a tough life, beginning at Newton Moor, pregnant with her first child not long after her parents died, marrying her first cousin, starting a new life in Blackburn, where in between the child- rearing were long shifts in the weaving sheds of the local mill! I have a description of the couple courtesy of their grandson Francis X.Coyne who remembered them. In February 1993 he wrote to me describing Peter as *"a very large imposing man"* and his grandmother as" *quite a well-built lady"*

The focus now moved to my grandparents' generation. Initially it seems that James, the eldest son, took the lead in family matters as in 1922 he was appointed executor of his mother's will shortly before she died. Aware of Mary Anne's failing health and the need to protect the family assets a Last Will and Testament was signed on 16th January 1922,just a few weeks before she died. James as executor was tasked to *'call in, sell or convert'* the estate "for *all my children in equal shares"*. On the 2nd March Probate was granted by the court at Lancaster enabling James to dispose of the effects, the sum of £546.0s.11d. This was a significant sum for the day. Lewery estimated a painter was paid between 1s 6d and 1s9d per hour in the early 1920s which would give a weekly wage of around £3 to £4 per week, so the five beneficiaries were now given the opportunity to secure their futures in the coming years. For James Edward it opened up a particularly surprising opportunity.

For Joseph and Mary Ann at 7 Smithies Street the news of the will would have been welcome as a second child, a daughter named Mary, was born on the 29th September 1922. She was baptised at St. Alban's on the 1st October when one of her godparents was her Aunt Nellie, Ellen Kennedy. The naming is interesting – written as was the practice as the Latin 'Maria' – as my aunt was always called 'Marie' (pronounced 'Marry'). It seems with so many Marys in the family she chose a different form! Around this time our oldest family group photograph was taken of my grandparents and their first two children which dates it around 1923. I have another family document from this time, a Royal Liver Friendly Society (v) policy book taken out by my grandmother insuring the life of John Coyne, issued on 14th February 1921, for the sum of two pence per week. The agent was a J Connaughton – surely a good Connacht name?

Family portrait 1923. Joseph Coyne with John, Marie and Mary Ann.

As ever it seems tragedy was never far away. This was the case for Emma with the death of her husband, Anthony McHugh, towards the end of 1922. She had been married for barely eighteen months. The three Coyne sisters were now all widows, Emma and Nellie continued to live at No.175 whereas Frances and daughter Lizzie had their own place. Although the house was not bequeathed to Emma and Nellie by the will it seems an arrangement was made to secure their housing and they continued to live there until the late 1950s.

I think we can be sure what James Edward did with his inheritance as during the month of February 1923 he emigrated to Canada. He booked his crossing, travelling Third Class, at the firm of J. Robinson, Booking Agents, of Barrow-in-Furness, along with four other men from the Furness district. One was from Barrow and three from the adjoining town of Dalton-in-Furness and it seems likely this group probably all worked together. At the age of 42 James was the oldest of the emigrants.

On the 23rd February the Canadian Pacific liner, the *S.S. Montcalm*, a two funnel liner with a top speed of sixteen knots, set sail from Liverpool carrying 850 passengers bound for the port of St. John in New Brunswick. It arrived seventeen days later when James signed the Canadian immigration form 30A, a *'Declaration of Passenger to Canada'* declaring he was a painter, a Catholic, born in Oldham, and that he had a wife, Catherine Coyne, at 160 Addison Street, Blackburn. The form clearly states he was going to Canada to work and he answered 'yes' to the question – 'Do you intend to remain permanently in Canada?' James also declared he had £40 in his possession on arrival – a sum today worth some £1,983 (*vii*).Later in the year James appears on U.S. Department of Labor immigration documents. On the 1st July at the Port of Detroit, Michigan, he entered the USA with $52 in his possession. This time he was asked if he intended to become a US Citizen and he again replied 'yes'. He gave a forwarding address where he would be staying, with a David Hendrick at 6669 Wales Avenue in Detroit.

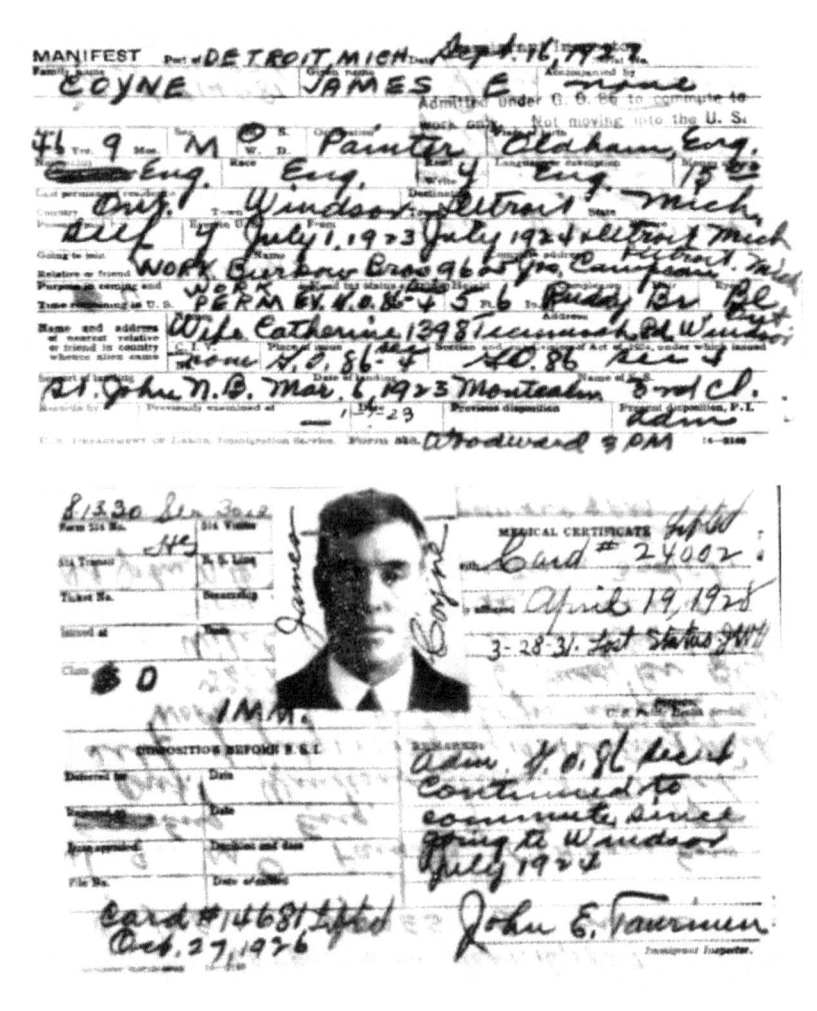

US Immigration documents: the only known image of James Edward Coyne.

Again Catherine was declared and the form also contained some personal details always welcomed by family historians. This told us that James had never been to prison; was not an anarchist; had not visited the USA before; was in good health; his height was 5' 5"; of medium complexion; had brown hair; blue eyes; and had no identifying marks.

Around the same time James' second son, Frank Coyne, also bid farewell to Blackburn. He had shown an aptitude for chemistry and while at school had worked at a chemist's shop on Larkhill, near to the Power home in Smithies Street. It is known he also trained with a prominent Blackburn pharmacist, Charles Critchley whose premises C.A. Critchley & Co., Pharmaceutical Chemists, wholesale druggists, dry-salters, spice, seed and oil merchants, were at 10 King William Street in the centre of the town. Between 1933 and 1935 Critchley was Mayor for two years, and later in 1951 was an Alderman and a member of the Licensing Justices. Around 1923-24 Frank left for Liverpool where he was enrolled at the prestigious Liverpool School of Pharmacy, established in 1849 and whose motto '*Ut Sementem Feceris Ita Maetes* means '*as you sow so shall you reap*'. Frank's daughter, Margaret, told me his fees for the course were paid for by an aunt, either Emma who had no children or perhaps Ellen, his godmother? Frank was to become the first Coyne to achieve a professional qualification which enabled him to have a long career in Pharmacy, including a time when he had his own shop, which will be covered later.

So what had happened to James' family? The exact reasons for the emigration are unknown but James clearly

The mid 1920s

We have a record of a first holy communion from this time. It took place on the 29th March 1924. The certificate below was issued to James Anthony Coyne by Father Cartin at Sacred Heart Church on Preston New Road. This would have taken place at the school chapel at the corner of St. Silas Road and Leamington Road as the present church was not opened until October 1937. A few years later when James was confirmed he took the confirmation name of 'Ignatius' keeping the tradition of Jesuit confirmation names(*x*)

James Anthony Coyne, first Holy Communion certificate, March 1924

By the middle of the decade my grandparents Joseph and Mary Ann had moved to 10 Cowper Street, one of the side streets that descended the slope on the south side of Whalley Range and now much closer to Joe's sisters at 175. Here at their new home in Cowper Street their third child was born on 30th May 1925. She was given a good Irish name, that of Eileen. She was baptised however in the name of *'Maria Helina'* at St. Alban's on the 7th June when her godmother was a Mary McDermott, another family friend with a Roscommon name! It was soon apparent Eileen was not well. She suffered from hydrocephalus, commonly known as "water on the brain". My father, who was five when his sister was born, recalled that she had a "swollen head". The condition was not uncommon at the time but full recovery was unusual. Mary Ann travelled to Edinburgh with her to see a specialist on the condition, but it seemed little could be done. She died on the 14th January 1926 at Cowper Street and her father reported the death of 'Mary Eileen', aged just seven months, the following day.

Cowper Street, Blackburn. Joseph and Mary Ann Coyne moved here in the 1920s. Number 10 was half way down on the right hand side

Both Joe, listed as a house painter, and Fergus Power, a tailor, appear in the 1925 Barrett's Directory at No. 10. My father recalled they also sold paints and decorating materials from the front room at Cowper Street for a while. Fergus had a club foot, a deformity from birth, and wore a raised shoe. John also remembered him at work, always sitting on the floor. It was known that tailoring was a popular trade among those with a disability since it could be carried out from home.

The 1920s despite its later reputation for high society 'flappers', jazz music, and decadence, was a period of further unrelenting toil for most working people. Many of the confrontations between labour and capital that had peaked before the war returned culminating in the General Strike of May 1926, this time caused by attempts to impose wage cuts on members of the Miner's Federation. Woodruff recalls how on May 3rd Blackburn came to a standstill for the eight days duration of the strike. Widely regarded as a defeat it was the first and last General Strike.

The year 1927 brought a major change of career for Terry Coyne who went to live in China after joining the Shanghai Municipal Police. Terry's career in the Far East is covered in Chapter Fourteen along with his war-time service. It seemed that in 1927 he came out of the army after having latterly served in the Sudan Defence Force. The British Empire before World War Two still had spheres of influence all over the world, the Chinese ports among them, and numerous opportunities were there especially for those without ties who were seeking adventure. Terry was to remain in China for ten years.

It was not a pleasant year in Blackburn with two more family deaths. Firstly there was more heartache for Frances when on the 10th August 1927 her daughter, Lizzie, died aged fourteen years. On her death certificate it records that Elizabeth Howarth of 3 Ward Street died of a diabetic coma. She was a shop assistant at a photographic shop and her mother was with her when she died. Like today cases of diabetes often went unrecognised until other medical problems arose and in this case the coma proved fatal. She was buried in her grandparents' grave at Blackburn Cemetery.

Secondly, on the 24th September, Mary Ann Coyne, aged 71 years – better known as 'Auntie Annie' – died at the Royal Infirmary as a result of an accident at her home, 1 Limefield, Preston New Road. These houses, built around 1872, were on the north side of Preston New Road before it reaches Corporation Park. 1 Limefield appears at number 209. These were upmarket houses so it seems likely Annie occupied ground floor rooms in part of a larger house. She died of a fracture to the base of her skull and an intracranial haemorrhage sustained when she fell down the cellar steps the previous day. An Inquest was held at the Infirmary on the 26th of the month presided over by Mr. Thomas R. Thompson, Deputy Coroner for Blackburn. Below is a transcript of the report which appeared in the Blackburn Times on 1st October under the headline "AGED WIDOW'S DEATH. *Fell down Cellar Steps when Cleaning*"

'A son stated that the deceased had been subject to attacks of dizziness, but performed her housework and was active. On returning from work yesterday week he found his mother, who had been alone all day, lying at the bottom of

the cellar steps. She appeared to have fallen and was unconscious, bleeding from a wound at the back of the head. With assistance he carried her into the kitchen, and after medical attention at the house she was removed to the Infirmary where she died, on Saturday noon.'

A Doctor Menzies, house surgeon, confirmed the cause of death and a verdict of "accidental death" was returned. This remains the final mention of James W. who, as ever, has avoided being named. Annie's death certificate stated she was the widow of John Coyne, a Master house painter and decorator. The timing of the death ties in with Winnie Fielding's memories of Sunday visiting which she says stopped around this time. Annie was buried at Blackburn Cemetery in the Church of England section on 29th September.

During the same month we have another little interlude on the new life of James Edward over in Canada, courtesy of some recent online immigration records (xi). This record reveals James crossing from Windsor, Ontario to Detroit, Michigan, an international frontier but also a mere ferry ride across the Detroit River. James was still a painter, Oldham –born, who had entered Canada on the *Montcalm* in 1923, but his complexion was now 'ruddy' and he had seemingly grown one inch – he was now 5' 6" tall. Two other changes were now apparent. He had work, being employed by Burbro Bros, of 9600 Joseph Campsau Street, Detroit and also a wife, still called Catherine. His address was 1398 Tecumseh Road in Windsor. On the reverse of the document, partially covered in shadow, is a signed photograph of James (see page 176), a part of his medical certificate. Looking serious with a full head of hair, smart with collar and tie and a dark jacket, this 1927 picture is the only image of James known to exist.

Piecing together the details given it seems James remained in Detroit for one year after his earlier crossing in 1923. In September 1927 he was crossing the border to work in Detroit and had continued to commute since going to live in Windsor in 1924. In possession he had $15 and was given G.O. immigration status to commute to work only. Detroit at the time was something of an economic powerhouse, James' painting skills would have found him plenty of work in either the city's automobile or shipbuilding industries.

So who is the Catherine referred to as James' wife? The form asked for 'name and address of nearest relative' and he answered 'Wife Catherine 1398 Tecumseh Road'. Does this still refer to our Catherine Coyne or is this another Catherine? From the information given at this juncture James' answers had always been honest so perhaps no bigamous marriage had yet taken place. As we shall see later documents refer to a Margaret Coyne as James' wife so he may have married later. In 1932 we will meet James again where it is apparent that although Catherine didn't know his whereabouts other members of the family did!

1928 F.A. Cup Glory at Wembley

The events of April 1928 were momentous in the history of Blackburn, and were remembered vividly by my father, John, aged seven at the time. On the 21st April Blackburn Rovers beat Huddersfield Town 3-1 at Wembley Stadium to bring the F.A. Cup back to the town for the first time since their great days of the 1880s and early 1890s when they won the Cup on five occasions.

The Rovers, who wore dark blue shirts instead of their usual 'blue and white halves', were not fancied before the game. Huddersfield were a force in the game at the time and hadn't finished below second in any of the previous four seasons in the League. Rovers were mid-table and had conceded 96 goals the previous year. Earlier in 1927-28 they had even sold star player Ted Harper to Sheffield Wednesday and his replacement Jack Roscamp wasn't rated so highly. This was all forgotten on the day, it was after all a 'Roses match' with Yorkshire opponents and it was estimated some 150,000, including many women, travelled south to the match, many knowing they were unlikely to see the game. The first excursion train arrived in the capital at 3am and no doubt some serious drinking took place.

The match began explosively. In the first thirty seconds Roscamp bundled Town goalkeeper, Mercer, and the ball into the net. I heard this story many times from my father who listened to the BBC match commentary on a crystal radio set at a neighbour's house on Whalley Range. McLean put the Rovers two goals up before Town's star winger, Jackson, pulled one back. Four minutes from time Jack Roscamp scored his second, the final score was 3-1 and Harry Healless, the Rovers' skipper, climbed the thirty-nine steps to collect the Cup from King George V.

The winners seemed in no hurry to return. Visiting London was a rare occurrence for most northern folk and it was Monday 23rd before the victory procession took place. The team returned by train to Preston and took the last stage by *charabanc* (open top bus). On entering Blackburn they were led by a band as part of a mile long motorcade. The *Manchester Guardian* reported that the procession reached snail's pace as it dropped down Preston New Road. Eye witnesses estimated crowds of 150,000 as they reached Sudell Cross. Alarmingly serious overcrowding took place in Limbrick and in Randall Street where some of the crowd were crushed. At this point the great procession with Healless at the front holding the F.A. Cup turned into Whalley Range and inched forward until it reached the Bastwell pub. The route took it right past our houses at 175, and at Cowper Street, before returning to the town centre via Penny Street and a civic reception at the Town Hall. This remains the last occasion the Rovers won the trophy. My father could recite the names of the eleven players on duty that day:- Crawford; Hutton, Jones; Healless, Rankin, Campbell; Thornewell, Puddifoot, Roscamp, McLean and Rigby.

This was clearly a good year for the family who celebrated with the birth of another son. My uncle, Francis Coyne, was born to Joseph and Mary Anne at Cowper Street on the 16th November *(xii)*. On the 2nd December he was baptised at St. Alban's where his aunt, Frances Howarth, became his godmother.

The decade ended with the country in economic turmoil after the Wall Street crash which ultimately was to lead to the Great Depression of the 1930s. In 1929 Blackburn was still basking in its football success however when on 2nd March a record attendance of 61,783 crammed into Ewood Park for the FA Cup quarter final with neighbours Bolton Wanderers, a record which will stand for all-time.

Schools

A look now at some of the schools the family attended. In the late 1920s Winnie Kennedy was taking her younger cousins John and Marie (who she called 'May') along to St. Alban's School (*xiii*). Next to the church in St. Alban's Place, this school educated both juniors and seniors from 1870 until its closure in 1947. The route down Brookhouse Lane was extremely well-trodden as the Coyne family carried out their Catholic duties around the religious calendar, as well as to family baptisms, first holy communions and confirmations. My father told me he was an 'altar boy' at St.Alban's and it was probably around 1930 when the photograph on page 189 was taken – originally in sepia brown – of him holding the Bishop's robes following behind the priests, Fathers Tierney and Faulkner.

It was originally thought that the bishop was the Bishop of Salford, head of the Roman Catholic hierarchy for the Diocese of Salford, but on checking Bishop Henshaw, the incumbent bishop, looked nothing like the elderly bearded figure. It appears he was instead bearded Bishop Hanlon of Teos, so named after a former missionary appointment in the Upper Nile and Uganda. Henry Hanlon was born in Manchester in 1862 and ordained in September 1889. In 1915 the "retired missionary bishop" was made parish priest at St. Alban's where he became a prominent figure in Blackburn serving on many committees until he retired through ill-health in 1934.

Altar boy John Coyne behind Bishop Hanlon, circa 1930.

Around 1931 John moved to a new Catholic boy's school, St. Mary's College, at 210-212 Shear Brow. From their earliest days in 1925 in Shear Bank Road, a community of Marist fathers had been invited by Bishop Casartelli to open a school in Blackburn. They later bought the Shear Brow property for £2,650 to build a school for 150 boys. The purchase included grounds, none other than what was formerly *Hole I' th' Wall* – legendary home of Blackburn Olympic FC, who appeared in Chapter Nine –which became the school playing fields. Bishop Henshaw opened the school in November 1930 when the first Headmaster, the Rev. William Fox, S.M. was appointed. Similar to the Jesuits the S.M. in this case stood for Society of Mary. Given the opening date John must have been one of the first pupils. He was a keen learner and since some of his school books have survived from Form III History and

Chemistry we can see he had a high standard of written work. His schooldays however always reminded him of Father Gannon, his form teacher, who he said beat him every day, corporal punishment being common in schools until about the 1960s! He didn't however bear a grudge and years later, on a visit to Blackburn, he bought a St .Mary's College tie from a shop in the town.

For the females of the family another Catholic institution loomed large. The Convent of Notre Dame on Whalley Old Road was built alongside the former Brookhouse Lodge (*xiii*) which dated from 1859 and was originally converted into a ladies' boarding school. Among the ladies of the family, later educated here by the nuns, were Marie Coyne and Winnie Kennedy, who also remembered her cousin Kathleen "two or three years ahead of her at school". She recalled also that, like herself, she had red hair. Apart from Kathleen the education of James' children was different. James, born in 1915, went to Sacred Heart School where there are photographs of him outside in St. Silas Road in 1924. He later attended from 1929 to 1931 one of the town's oldest institutions, Queen Elizabeth's Blackburn Grammar School, whose origins dated back to medieval times, moving to their present site only in 1883.

1930-1935

The fallout from the 1929 crash severely hit the economy of the country. In 1931 the National Government decided to leave the Gold Standard in the belief that it was damaging exports. A period of austerity began bringing huge rises in unemployment. With the cotton industry already in decline

Blackburn, along with many other towns in the north and in Wales, suffered greatly and unemployment rates of 15 per cent were not unusual. As we shall see Joseph's painting and decorating struggled, and although things had begun to recover by 1936 it was not until arms manufacturing took off in 1937 in response to the political situation in Germany that the economy improved.

It was probably around 1930 that Joseph and Mary Ann moved from Cowper Street to 282 Whalley Range which was a bigger terraced house. No.282 was literally just round the corner on the opposite side of the road to his sisters. In 1931 Fergus Power died aged 68 years. Up until this time he was a permanent figure in the life of the family and it was no doubt a time of great sadness. My father always spoke fondly of him and recalled him singing *the Wearing of the Green*'. I don't know if he ever returned to County Galway after moving to Lancashire, although the farm at Annaghbride, near to the town of Loughrea, was still held by the Power family. My grandfather purchased a burial plot at Blackburn Cemetery and Fergus was buried there on 31st May 1931.

The year 1932 brought two family marriages. This was the year that Terry Coyne returned home on leave from China and visited both his family in Blackburn and his brother Frank X. by now living in Birkenhead, just across the Mersey from Liverpool where he had completed his pharmacy studies. By now Frank had his own shop, at 354 Woodchurch Road, a busy route into Birkenhead in the leafy suburbs of Oxton. His daughter, Margaret, recalled it was at the centre of a row of shops and had a painted sign announcing 'F.X. Coyne Chemists'. I visited this area in

2013 where the shop still stands, now trading as an opticians.

Margaret said her parents met at this shop when her mother, then Ann May Hanks, (*xiv*) called in to buy from the chemists. Apparently Frank gave her generous portions and before long the couple were married, on the 7th May 1932 at St. Paul's Church in the nearby Tranmere district of Birkenhead.

Meanwhile back in Blackburn, Frances Howarth, remarried on the 16th July. Then a widow, aged 44, she married Hugh Frost, a widower, aged 53 at St. Alban's. Hugh, known as 'Hughie' was an iron fitter of 30 Ribble Street which was another of the cobbled streets that ran off Whalley Range and was next to Millham Street where James Kennedy used to live. They later lived happily together at nearby London Road for the rest of their days. Frances' brother Joe was a witness at the wedding and probably 'gave her away.'

During the summer Blackburn was also host to the Lancashire County Cricket Club who played for the first time at the Alexandra Meadows ground in a county championship match against Glamorgan. This is the ground of Blackburn's Lancashire League team, East Lancs. Unfortunately two days play were lost through rain, although the county made return visits in 1934 and 1935.

Francis Xavier Coyne behind the counter of his pharmacy on Woodchurch Road, Birkenhead.

During late summer 1932 – before the Chinese winter set in Terry Coyne sailed from Shanghai on 14th August on leave from the Shanghai Municipal Police. He had been promoted to Sergeant in 1930 and it would seem that with a long overseas posting he was entitled to some leave after five years in China. His ship called at Manila in the Philippines, and at Kobe and Yokohama in Japan, reaching Honolulu on the 27th. On the 2nd September he arrived at Victoria, British Columbia on the 'Empress of Russia'. He was surely impressed by the mountains of Canada and the scenery around Vancouver!

For the next stage of his journey back to the UK Terry crossed North America, probably on the Canadian Pacific Railroad to Winnipeg. He broke his journey in the great city of Chicago after crossing into the United States. According to family lore he met with his father, James Edward Coyne, in the 'Windy City' after arriving at Union Station. Given that Terry arrived back in England during the first week in October he must have met his father during the first week of September 1932. We can only speculate how they had managed to keep in touch. Since his mother did not have his address did one of James' sisters give it to Terry? He could then have written to his father giving him his travel details and James probably travelled by rail from Detroit. This was very likely James' last contact with one of his own family.

On the 3rd October Terry completed his circumnavigation across two great oceans when he arrived in Liverpool from New York on the two funnel White Star liner, the *Britannic*. On arrival he stated he was a policeman by profession, that his address in the UK was 160 Addison Street, Blackburn, and that his 'country of permanent residence' was China. We know Terry visited 175 Whalley Range where his cousin Winnie remembered the visit, and he then went to stay with brother Frank in Birkenhead. It was while he was staying on the Wirral that he met his future wife, Bess Muskett, then around 19 years old. Frank X. in one of his letters (xv) described her as *'a young lady from Heswall whose father was a director of Tate and Lyle'*. His niece, Margaret, told me they met at a dance hall in Birkenhead. Terry was keen to drive her home to Heswall in his sports car only to get lost on the journey home!

In January 1933 Terry Coyne married Bess Irene Muskett in the 16th century parish church of St. Peter's in the seaside village of Heswall, next to the estuary of the River Dee. Afterwards Terry returned to Shanghai with his new wife to resume his job with the S.M.P. This was to be a good year with two more births in the family. Firstly, on the 5th April Winifred Sheila Coyne – known as Sheila – was born to Joseph and Mary Ann. She was their fifth and last child and when she was baptised on the 16th April her godparents were George Eccles and her cousin Mary Kennedy (Josie). The godparents were themselves to provide the next family marriage when they married in 1936. On the 8th September 1933 Pauline Margaret Coyne – again to be known by her middle name – was born in Birkenhead to Francis Xavier and Ann. At this time they were living at 12 Allcott Avenue, a terraced road in the Tranmere district.

During the mid-1930s my grandfather Joseph appears in Blackburn trade directories in partnership with another painter, Jimmy Carruthers. They are listed in the Blackburn Town and Country Directory of 1934 as '*Coyne and Carruthers painters and decorators, estimates given*'. Jimmy was a single man, about six years older than Joe, and was born in the U.S.A. according to the 1911 Census. My mother told me the business was struggling at the time, no doubt due to the economic Depression of the time. Not a good time then for my father, John, to enter the world of work. He left St. Mary's College in 1934 aged fourteen years, no doubt glad to see the back of Father Gannon, and went to work for his Dad as an apprentice house painter – the skills learnt here stood him in good stead for later DIY painting jobs. It didn't start so well …on his first day they fell out, John was sent home and only returned after his mother intervened!

Joe had tried to specialise in signwriting, which was more skilled and attracted higher pay- I recall his brushes kept at one of our former homes. Wages had hardly risen over the last two decades such that a painter would earn no more than £4 per week and often a lot less. The business declined and Joe, who had four children to support, left and took up employment with Dutton's Brewery as a painter. Breweries had large tied estates and had plenty of work for in-house painters and although the wage would not be high it offered more security than a trade partnership. In 1935 he was still at 282 Whalley Range, while this is the last time Catherine Coyne appears at Addison Street.

When her son, James Anthony, left the Grammar School in 1931 he moved to Blackburn Technical College *(xvi)*, an imposing Grade II listed brick building built between 1888 and 1894 on Blakey Moor, next to the town centre. He studied at 'the Tech' from 1931-37 leaving with a Technical Certificate in Textile Manufacturing. When he began work it was to be a long way from Blackburn, when he moved to the town of Taunton in Somerset. Meanwhile far away in Shanghai, China, James now had a nephew - Timothy John Coyne was born on the 22nd November 1934, the first child of Terry and Bess. He remains the only Chinaman on our family tree!

1936-39: Years before War

The economic picture showed signs of recovery although in Blackburn the decline of the cotton industry was structural. No-one in 1936 would have foreseen a return to hostilities in just three years, when for the second time in just twenty five years the country was plunged into a world war.

Joseph Coyne certainly must have felt some optimism when he joined the property market. He took out a mortgage with the Leeds Permanent Building Society on the 1st April 1936 when he bought 179 Whalley Range and moved with his family onto Beaumont Terrace, next door but one from his sisters Emma and Nellie. So began the family stronghold on Whalley Range remembered by all of my generation who either lived there as children or visited the houses, and which only ended when Mary Ann Coyne died in 1960. In total the Coynes had now lived at four different addresses on Whalley Range.

During the summer Bess Coyne returned briefly to England from China with her young son Timothy probably to show him to her parents at Heswall. They returned sailing from Liverpool on the 'Menelaus' on the 15th August. The passenger records list Bessie, aged 23, and Tim, aged 18 months, leaving for Shanghai. Back in Blackburn Josie Kennedy married George Eccles and the next year their first child, Mary Patricia Eccles – known as Patricia- was born on the 15th May. She was baptised at St. Alban's on the following day when her aunt, Winnie Kennedy, became her godmother. Josie and George bought a house – a two bedroomed semi-detached – at 76 Plane Street. It was opposite the new Star Cinema and next to a railway line. It was also close to Aunt Emma's baker's shop where Josie worked. The exact location of the shop remains in doubt - its ownership within the family seems to cover a ten year period either side of the war. It may be that there were two shops over the years. It is believed the first one was located near to the Cob Wall railway viaduct.

This year also brought another wedding, and two major family moves. Winnie Kennedy followed her sister when she also married, to Joseph Fielding at St. Alban's. On the wedding photographs of both Winnie, and her sister Josie the year before, their uncle Joseph Coyne is stood to the right –he had very likely 'given them away 'since their father James had so tragically died in 1917. .

James A. Coyne left the town in March 1937 when he took up employment with the textile firm of Harding, Tilton and Hartley in Taunton, Somerset, a distance of over two hundred miles from home. It seems likely his mother, Catherine, gave up the Addison Street house, and along with sister Kathleen, then aged 24, they all moved south. James' job title was that of 'Textile Designer' and they moved to a house at 14 Cranmer Road. This seemed a long way to move for work and is perhaps another sign of the Coyne's 'itchy feet'. Going right back to the earliest days after moving from Ireland moving town either for work or better prospects had been a regular occurrence. This ended the residency of James Edward's family in Blackburn, although two of the three, James and Catherine, were later to return to Lancashire.

In Taunton, Harding's had the worldwide rights to the *Van Heusen* shirt name but whether the job didn't meet James' expectations, or whether it was the beginnings of rearmament in response to events in Europe we don't know what encouraged his next move. What is known is that on the 14th December – barely nine months after moving to

Taunton – James enlisted into the Royal Air Force, signing on to serve for six years with the rank of 'Aircrafthand/ Armourer'. If only he knew what these six years would become! Catherine and Kathleen soon after left for Wolverhampton, where they took up residency at 16 Leyland Avenue, a quiet cul-de-sac of semi-detached houses, just to the south-west of the town centre.

Escape from China

Over ten thousand miles away by sea, Terry Coyne's ten year service in 'the Orient' with the Shanghai Municipal Police came to an abrupt end after increasing Japanese aggression against China led to war, and the rapid departure of western interests from the Chinese ports (see Chapter Fifteen for an account of Terry's Far East years). Terry, Bess and young son Tim departed from Shanghai, under fire, crossing the Pacific Ocean on the *'Empress of Japan'* arriving in Vancouver, Canada, on the 19th October. We can see by now that Terry was no stranger to British Columbia, although on this occasion they resumed their journey from Portland, Oregon, in the USA, finally arriving in Liverpool on 22nd November on the Cunard ship *'Georgic'*. At the port they gave a forwarding address of *'Fairways'*, Chester Road, Gayton, Heswall, the home of the Muskett family. This time Terry had to complete the occupation section by replying 'nil'. During his time in the S.M.P. he had reached the rank of Sub-Inspector latterly working in the force's Special Branch. We will see later that this was to be significant in terms of his next appointment. Meanwhile the family settled back at

Heswall where on the 3rd July 1938, a second son, Vincent Ernest Coyne, was born.

Back in Blackburn Winnie and Joe Fielding had good news when on 18th January 1939 Winnie gave birth to a son, named John. This, of course, was to become the year war broke out again and it was due to the deteriorating international situation that the Government undertook a National Register during the year recording where everyone lived.

Only released in 2015 it gave us a likely match for the whereabouts of the mysterious James W. Coyne. In view of the fact few recalled his time in Blackburn it seems likely he left, perhaps soon after his mother died in 1927. The National Register had a James W. Coyne, born 1 November 1876, living at 17 Brook Drive in the London Borough of Southwark. Apart from the all important 'W' he was a *'Housepainter Decorator'* by occupation and single. It seems a good match for James. If so he probably died in 1953 aged 76 in nearby Lambeth where a James Coyne of 10 Lanfranc Street, died at South Western Hospital, Stockwell. This man was a *'liftman in offices'*- there were government offices just over the road from Lanfranc Street – and there is a good chance this is our James.

The publication of the government's 1939 National Register in 2015 enabled a rare opportunity to trace our family members at the very dawn of World War Two. It was apparent war preparations were already in place since George Eccles' occupation includes that of *'Auxiliary Fireman'* alongside his main job of *'Cotton mill clerk'.* Josie and George were living at 76 Plane Street, off Whalley New Road. Josie's job - a *'Confectioner cake-maker'*- is interesting since it suggests that her Aunt Emma's nearby shop was in the family before the war, while Emma herself appears on Whalley Range as a *'Confectioner maker'*. My father, John Coyne, appears as a painter and decorator, along with his Dad Joe. Also in Blackburn Winnie and Joe Fielding were at 24 Addington Street, Higher Audley. Winnie's occupation was listed as *'Cotton mill unem'*- this was the year her son John was born – and Joe's was entered as *'Corporation electric'*. Katherine Coyne – with her mother in Wolverhampton – was a' *Manageress dairy and provision shop'*. Finally Terry and Bess Coyne had moved to a house on the edge of Heswall, at 74 Downham Road, where Terry was working as *'Transport manager'* for a builder's merchants.

The Coynes of Pennsylvania, USA

Finally, a summary of what became of Harriet's family over in the Appalachian coalfield. Our emigrants can be traced on both the 1920 and 1930 US Census. By 1920 Harriet had married again to a William Davis, when almost certainly she was still married to Peter Coyne of Hulme. They had a son, also called William. Harriet was working in a candy store, described as her own, in the small mining town of Mahanoy City in Schuylkill County. Amy Coyne was also married in 1920, to Elmer*'Duke'* Stride, born around 1892, and a First World War veteran.

A decade later Harriet Davis was the housekeeper of a boarding house. Living with her also was her son, James Coyne (remember him?) now aged 23, and married to his wife Marion since 1928. Elmer and Amy Stride now had three young children born during the 1920s. James E. Stride was born in 1921; Florence Harriet was born in 1926; and another Marion was born in 1928.]

i. Letter 10 June 1991.
ii. My father was baptised on 20th June. His godparents were his grandma, Mary Anne Coyne, and James Littler who may have been an army comrade of Joe Coyne.
iii. Fergus' father Patrick Power had a small farm at Annaghbride, east of Loughrea in County Galway. He died in 1910 when his wife Bridget Power took over the farm. After she died in 1924, Ellen Claffey nee Power, Fergus' sister took it over. It remained in the family until the 1950s.
iv. Grave reference C- 1320 R/C.
v. Head Office: Pierhead, Liverpool. The famous Liver Building.
vi. There is a family story that Anthony McHugh's death resulted from injury or sickness sustained during army service in the First World War. With the assistance of Peter Fielding we have identified an Anthony McHugh who served in the East Lancashire Regt (3443) and latterly in the Labour Corps (253003). This Anthony enlisted on the 6.1.1915 and was medically discharged on 20.2.1919. His medal card reveals he served in the Balkans, at Gallipoli, from 31.7.1915. However, we cannot – in the absence of a service record –prove he is our man.
vii. Historic inflation calculator (online)
viii. Letter 16.1.1996.
ix. Letter 10.6.1991.
x. St. Ignatius Loyola was the founder of the Jesuit order in 1539. As well as Frank having the name 'Xavier' it was thought Terry's confirmation name was 'Aloysius' but this is not certain. Unfortunately we don't know sister Kathleen's.
xi. Detroit Border Crossings: Passenger and Crew Lists 1905-1937. See image on p.62.

xii.   From hereon Francis Coyne, born *1906*, will be referred to as Frank X. to avoid confusion.
xiii. This is the same school Terry Coyne attended when photographed before the First World War.
xiv.   Former home of William Kenworthy, cotton mill owner.
xv.   She was the daughter of William and Margaret Hanks nee Hamilton who also married in Tranmere in *1906*. William died soon after Anne was born.
xvi.   Letter from FX Coyne, *12.2.1993*.
xvii. James' father also attended the Technical College.

CHAPTER FOURTEEN

The Second World War 1939-1945

Airman, Sailor, Soldier, Spy

Just over two decades after the 1918 Armistice the world was again plunged into war when hostilities began on the 3rd September 1939. The cause was the aggressive rise of Nazi Germany under Adolf Hitler throughout the 1930s, assisted by fascist governments in Italy and later in Spain. With its industry on a war footing, policies of racial intolerance and the coveting of neighbouring lands under their policy of *'Leibensraum'*, it was to be the invasion of Poland, however, which brought war with the Allied powers of Britain and France, who were later joined by the Soviet Union and the U.S.A. The war was to last for six years and again our family members played their part. In 1939 James A. Coyne was already serving in the Royal Air Force. The day after war was declared his cousin, John Coyne, entered a recruiting office in Blackburn and joined the Royal Navy. James' brother, Terry, who had considerable army experience prior to joining the Shanghai Municipal Police, had been back in the country less than two years when war broke out. Before long he was to rejoin the Army – possibly for the third time!- this time to join the Intelligence Corps, and in 1941 he became part of a new secret war-time initiative set up under the auspices of the Ministry of Economic Warfare, which became known as the

Special Operations Executive. Finally, our female family members also played their part. Marie Coyne, aged 18 years in 1940, served during the war in the ATS –the Auxiliary Territorial Service, the women's Territorial Army – whose tasks included secretarial, clerical and driving duties in the army. She was based in Yorkshire, a move which was to be significant for her since she met her future husband, Stanley Bentley, who was also in the army. The image below is of Marie in her ATS uniform, aged around eighteen years.

Marie in ATS Uniform

James Anthony Coyne in the Royal Air Force

At the outbreak of war James was serving in the Far East with 34 Squadron, part of 2 Group Bomber Command, which had been formed in 1936. James' service was to include the peak years of Bomber Command between 1943 and 1945 when it was transformed into a vast industrial machine (i) wreaking havoc with a sustained campaign of bombing raids on key targets in Germany, Italy and occupied France. Such was the danger the airmen faced some 55,000 service personnel were killed while serving in Bomber Command during the war.

When James first enlisted in 1937 the Air Force logged his personal details. His service record informs us he was 5 foot 5 and a half inches tall, chest 31 and one half inches, had dark brown hair, and blue eyes. His last address was in Taunton, his religion was Roman Catholic, and his next-of-kin was his mother, Catherine, then living in Wolverhampton. James' first placement was to 1 Depot, Uxbridge, in December 1937 from where he moved on to the Air Armament School with the rank of AC2. This was the beginning of his specialism in the service from where he became a Bomb Aimer, responsible for ensuring bombs were dropped onto their designated targets. Training continued for most of the year until 4th November when he moved to 2 Group, 34(B) Squadron, then based at RAF Upper Heyford, a light bombing squadron at the time flying the relatively new Bristol Blenheim bombers. His role was that of Armourer when on 2nd March 1939 they relocated to RAF Watton. Later on the 12th August James began his first overseas posting, 34 Squadron having joined the Far East Command, stationed at Tengah, Singapore, from the 10th September. By then war had been declared in Europe. The photograph below shows James in tropical kit and was possibly taken in Singapore. What a rarity to have all the names!

RAF group photo

At the end of the year he was promoted to Aircraftsman 1 grade. Over the course of two years in Singapore the Squadron would have been involved in keeping an eye on Japanese military movements in the region. The establishment – of just sixteen Blenheims – was inadequate but such was the confidence in 'Fortress Singapore' the numbers were not increased due to the demands of the war in Europe. When Singapore fell in February 1942 the inadequacy of the air cover was a major reason for the Japanese victory. As we shall see later in this chapter James' elder brother Terry, was from August 1941, also based in Singapore although it is thought they were unable to meet up. James left Tengah on 18th November when he was moved to Southern Rhodesia, where Initial Training Wing (ITW) Bulawayo had just opened as an important training facility for Bomber Command. His departure was timely. Three weeks later the Japanese invaded the Malayan peninsular, by February 1942 'impregnable' Singapore had fallen and the RAF forced to depart for Palembang on Sumatra on the 15th February after suffering many ground losses. Air cover in the region was effectively over.

James was based in Southern Rhodesia (now Zimbabwe) for nine months. It should be emphasised what a vast training operation was required while the war was ongoing to keep squadron manpower at the required level. More airfields, more crew, and more aircraft were needed each year from 1940 to 1945 not just to cover losses but to enable expansion. During these years Bomber Command increased in size from 41 squadrons in 1941 to 73 squadrons in 1944 and began to concentrate on using the new heavy Avro Lancaster bombers which needed a seven-man crew. It took some eighteen months from *'Civvy Street'* to qualify for a frontline squadron. After Air Chief Marshal Sir Arthur "Bomber" Harris took over in February 1942 training was revamped to address pressing operational needs, losses, and poor bombing target results. From hereon there was to be only one pilot per crew and an air bomber added to allow the Navigator to navigate! James time at the ITW would have involved classroom work on technical issues and an Air Observation course. He received his 'Air Obs' badge in August 1942, at the same time as he was promoted to Temporary Sergeant (War Service).

A key operational decision had been made which shaped the future direction of the war. When the Lancaster bomber entered service in March this year it soon proved to be superior to all its predecessors in terms of performance.

The crews were full of praise for the 'Lancs', its controls were easier, while the Perspex cockpit cover gave the pilot commanding views all around. It was to become a landmark aircraft of the war and by mid-1945 over 7,500 Lancasters had gone into service. From this figure some 4,000 were lost on operations.

Once again crews needed further training – the Lancaster Finishing Schools began in 1943, turning out thirty-six crews per fortnight. They were trained in bale-out, dinghy drill, the use of oxygen, use of parachutes and crash drill, all skills regularly required by the bomber crews.

During the course pilots, subject to technical requirements, were able to pick their own crews. At the end of the course they were given one week's leave and then sent to an operational 5 Group at RAF Bottesford, on the border of Lincolnshire and Leicestershire.

He joined 467 Squadron of the Royal Australian Air Force (motto *Adversarius atque ferociter* or 'Your opponents will retreat because of your courage') flying the new Lancaster bombers. For the rest of the war this was to be James' role, as Bomb Aimer of a 7-man Lancaster crew, usually flying at night, on regular bombing raids over the German Ruhr, over Berlin, and other targets in Western Europe

James Coyne (right) with Lancaster crew. Des Sullivan is third from right

From James' own notes it is believed he flew 43 sorties into enemy territory. The pilot on most of these operations was Squadron Leader Des Sullivan, a West Australian, who himself flew over 50 sorties, and with whom James kept in touch after the war.

Bottesford was a typical war-time airfield. Out in the countryside of low-lying eastern England, the staff were accommodated in Nissen huts whose central combustion stoves did little to ward off the winter cold while emitting noxious fumes. The 'early bird' then faced a mile walk to the nearest wash-house! At Bottesford the establishment was sixteen Lancaster bombers plus two in reserve. Overall Bomber Command was still one hundred short of the number needed. It is likely that James' sorties would have begun immediately, as early 1943 was an extremely busy time. The war in Europe only really turned in favour of the

Allies after the success of the Normandy landings on D-Day, 6th June 1944, and in the year before it was the view of Prime Minister Churchill and the military 'top brass' that they could only take the war to the Germans by targeting infrastructure and civilian morale by regular bombing raids. Thus for most of 1943 Bomber Command were involved in almost nightly operations. The industrial heart of Germany was in the Ruhr, especially the town of Essen (iv), home of the Krupps armament factories. The Ruhr was especially well protected by Luftwaffe fighter squadrons, with numerous searchlights and anti-aircraft batteries. Des Sullivan's view was that Essen was the toughest target in Germany for the bomber crews. Twenty-eight raids were sent to Essen; twenty-four to Berlin; twenty-two to Cologne; eighteen to both Stuttgart and Duisburg. 467 Squadron would have been on many of these raids including some of the massive 1,000 bomber raids sent to strategic targets which first took place in 1942.

Des Sullivan had a favourite Lancaster, ED 764 PON, named *'N for Nancy'* and decorated with *Olive Oyl* nose art. Olive Oyl being the hapless girlfriend of strongman cartoon sailor 'Popeye'! There is a photograph online (v) of this particular Lancaster which has been credited to 'J. A. Coyne', seemingly taken by James. Des' crew, like others, were attached to this particular' Lanc' which was unfortunately lost in the following circumstances on 18th August 1943. The story goes that Squadron Leader Sullivan 'lent' N for Nancy to another Australian pilot, Frank Dixon, for an operation over Peenemunde on this night. She was shot down by a night-fighter defending the V-2 rocket station, one of the first victims of the deadly *schragemusik* , a new tactic using stealth to attack from below seeking to hit the bomber's fuel tanks. There was at least one survivor since Sullivan and Dixon met thirty-five years later back in Australia when he was promptly asked *"What have you done with my Lanc?"* Meanwhile James' crew were given a new one but apparently it was not the same.

James' general service ended after five years and two hundred and sixty-two days when on the 1st September 1943 he was appointed to a temporary commission with officer rank. He had crossed one of the great divides of the British class system. Later that year 467 Squadron left Bottesford for RAF Waddington, just south of the city of Lincoln, home to the bomber crew's favourite navigational aid – the towers of the city's massive medieval cathedral. As an officer James' movements were now reported in the *London Gazette,* the official organ of HM Government. One interesting amendment appeared under the heading 'RAF General Duties Branch' (vi) the amendment read *"In notification of 19th October 1943 for James Anthony COYNE (53136) read James Anthony Ignatius COYNE (53136)".*

Did James celebrate his new status by adding his Jesuit confirmation name? Or perhaps there was another airman of the same name? Normally a different service number would be enough. From hereon however every communication from the RAF included the 'I' for Ignatius. Thus in 2014 with the award of the Bomber Command clasp, the award was received by his niece Margaret in the name of J.A.I. Coyne.

From early November James was with the No14 Operational Training Unit leading to a month long course in March 1944 at No.1 Air Armament School at Manby. Here he took a Bomb Leader's course. Back on active duty he received his first bravery award on the 8th June when he was *"Mentioned in Dispatches"*. This occurs in the forces when a Commanding Officer commends a particular act of bravery for recognition by the service.

Such was the turnover of bombing crews airmen were regularly moved. Thus James was transferred to 463 Squadron on the 30th September, still within 5 Group and still with a Lancaster squadron, this time with a strength of nineteen. This was another RAAF squadron. Although by no means all of the crew were Australian they usually had Aussie pilots with crews mustered from around the service. James remembered flying with 463 Squadron for the remainder of the active period of the war until April 1945 when bombing was scaled down.

By then the war was reaching its close, and following the unconditional surrender of the Nazi high command it ended on V.E. Day, the 8th May 1945. Although crews began to be stood-down Bomber Command remained busy dropping food to Dutch civilians and beginning the repatriation of thousands of Prisoners-of-War.

The Distinguished Flying Cross awarded 21 September 1945

In May as squadrons began to disband it was time to reward many acts of heroism. Some like the 'Dambusters' of 617 Squadron, and the crew who bombed the German battleship Tirpitz in September 1944 won popular acclamation. The highest honour in the RAF was the Distinguished Flying Cross. Some 20,000 DFCs were awarded during the Second World War for *'exceptional valour, courage and devotion to duty while flying in active operations against the enemy'*. Although the citation for the award is not known James Coyne was awarded the DFC as announced in the *London Gazette* on the 21st September 1945 (viii). The same month 467 Squadron RAAF – with whom he flew many of his sorties – was disbanded. Over its three year existence they flew 3,997 operational sorties, of whom 105 were missing in action. The total number of casualties was 768, half of whom were Australian.

James was promoted once more to Flight Lieutenant (War Substitute) in August 1945 but his next posting was perhaps a sign of things to come, when on the 1st September he was stationed at Feltwell *'undertaking Administration'*. For the next three years he remained in the Air Force, he had joined before the war and war-time recruits would appear to have been released first, but on 5th October 1948 he resigned his commission. Whether this was because of pressure to reduce manpower or whether James had tired of further administrative appointments, which must have been difficult after intense active service in the bomber crews, is not known. What is known is that after ten years distinguished RAF service – at a time of unparalleled action – James, now aged thirty-three, left the airfields of eastern England and returned to civilian life

James Anthony Ignatius Coyne, DFC

i. Along with air crew, ground crew, admin and logistics, refuelling, rail connections, planning and design, bomb production, supply and loading, aircraft and component manufacture it was estimated over 1,000,000 were involved worldwide.
ii. Prior to leaving James had five days embarkation leave from 27th to the 31st July which he may have taken in Wolverhampton.
iii. From this figure some 4,000 were lost on operations.
iv. Essen had been bombed twice in March 1943 and on 3-4th April, two days before James arrived at Bottesford. 5 Group targeted seventeen Ruhr towns between March and July 1943.
v. www.bottesford.history.org.uk.
vi. The notice was forwarded by the Air Ministry on 7th December 1943 and reported in the Gazette page 5340.
vii. On D-Day Bomber Command despatched 1,333 aircraft, the highest number recorded in the war.
viii. Listed under 'Flying Officers' in the 'Fourth Supplement to the London Gazette' 18th September 1943.

John Coyne in the Royal Navy

On the 6th September 1939 my father, John Coyne, volunteered to join the Royal Navy. His application was dealt with by the Combined Recruitment Centre (Naval) operating from a school in Carlisle Street, Preston. Then aged nineteen years his personal details record he was a painter and decorator; 6 feet tall; chest 34 and a half inches; eyes blue; and complexion 'fresh'. His hair colour was entered, not as ginger, but as an unequivocal 'red'. His Christian names were 'John Bernard'. On his service documents 'Bernard' was entered later and then crossed out – as with his cousin James, Bernard was his confirmation name.

He signed up *'for the period of the present emergency'* and as the war got off to a slow start it was not until late July 1940 when John, by then aged twenty, picked up a railway warrant at Preston and proceeded to Harwich, on the Suffolk coast, to begin inaugural training at *HMS Ganges*, a shore-based RN training ship. His service began on the 30th July with the rank of Ordinary Telegraphist and he remained at Harwich until 13th February 1941. It would seem his future path as a telegraphist was mapped out from the very beginning. On leaving *Ganges* he was posted to another well-known naval port, the vast Devonport naval base, near Plymouth at the mouth of the River Tamar. It was known in the Navy as *HMS Drake*. It was traditional for shore establishments to be given a ship's name and service was treated the same as when sailors were 'on board ship'. New matelots would take the bus from Plymouth and on reaching the base the conductor would shout "Barracks!" and they would disappear into the base where there was an accommodation block for five thousand.

John spent the next three months at Drake during which he also spent time with HMS *St. Christopher*. This was a Coastal Forces training base near to Fort William in Scotland whose purpose was to train crews in the use of inshore patrol craft. They were billeted either in local hotels or in Nissen huts, and training included firing torpedoes and using anti-aircraft guns. Thousands passed through Fort William, students arriving and leaving every Friday evening via the Glasgow train. Once again here is an example of the vast training operation required to support the war effort, not to forget the practise of billeting among the local civilians. John was billeted for a time at *HMS Drake* in the picturesque South Devon fishing port of

Brixham. He stayed with an elderly lady named Ma Tribble. Years later I remember trailing through the back streets above the harbour with my father looking for 115 Mount Pleasant where he had stayed with 'Ma'!

A second placement at *St. Christopher* followed from 21st to the 31st May when he was attached to Motor Launch ML235. He was now ready to start the telegraphist training in earnest. The location was in one of the country's remotest parts, the Outer Hebrides, on the island of Lewis, where the town of Stornoway was home to the base ship, *HMS Mentor*. They would have sailed by motor launch across the Little Minch, a notoriously rough crossing, and John stayed at *Mentor* until 22nd July 1942. He had passed his first O/T Examination at Harwich on the 5th February 1941 involving a paper on procedure, practical procedure, coding and buzzer work (both transmitting and receiving messages). On the latter he scored 100 per cent as shown in the image of his Wireless History Sheet. At *Mentor* he passed the Examination for the Telegraphist qualification on the 1st November and was promoted to the naval rank of Telegraphist.

At this point in the war the Allies had been forced into a mainly defensive position following the retreat from Dunkirk in 1940. Whereas the Battle of Britain was a turning-point defensively, it meant that the Royal Navy were unable to go on the offensive until the North Africa campaign began in mid-1942. In the meantime its ports and bases were regular bombing targets while its lowest ebb was perhaps the 13-14th November 1941(i) when the aircraft carrier HMS Ark Royal was sunk by the German U-Boat U-81 off Gibraltar. This important outpost of the

Empire, at the very tip of Southern Spain was soon to become John's next home base. After leaving *Mentor* he was based at *Drake* again for three months until transferring on the 1st November 1941 to *HMS Cormorant*, shore establishment of the vast Gibraltar naval base.

Gibraltar was home to RN Squadron (Force H) and HQ of the Supreme Allied Commander, General Eisenhower. It had an underground fortress with some twenty-five miles of roads, an airstrip enabling ongoing flights to Egypt, and a fleet of forty ships. The base was of great strategic importance, its position by the 'Pillars of Hercules' enabled monitoring of all shipping entering the Mediterranean Sea. Up to this point in the war ships from Gibraltar had been involved in blockading enemy territory, attacks on enemy shore targets, and escorting Malta- bound convoys where they were handed over mid-sea to the Mediterranean Fleet, based at Grand Harbour, Valletta, on the island.

John's Wireless History Sheet accompanied him throughout his time in the Navy and was filled in every time he was discharged from a ship.

From the onset of 1942, the U.S.A. had entered the war with all the armoury at its disposal. Activity in the Mediterranean increased from this point on. A fleet of 102 US Navy craft sailed direct to Casablanca in North Africa enabling military action in the area to be stepped up. In January 1943 Churchill and U.S. President Roosevelt met in Casablanca and began a strategy of securing North

Africa and invading Europe from its softer southern 'under belly' through France and Italy. In July 1943 the Allied invasion of Sicily began, another significant turning-point in the direction of the war.

John Coyne spent most of the next two years in and around Gibraltar. He was no doubt involved in W/T work at the shore establishment when on 13th November 1943 a change of role saw him serve at sea on *HMS Imperialist*. *Imperialist* was one of four minesweeping trawlers attached to *Cormorant*, one of a number of peace-time fishing trawlers requisitioned and renamed for naval use.

John would have been in the Wireless Room of the ship. Probably with another Telegraphist. From the photograph the full complement would seem to be forty-seven. He would have been very busy dealing with a constant flow of wireless signals to and from every ship in the area, and to the shore base. The *Imperialist* patrolled the Straits of Gibraltar and beyond, trawling for mines and dropping depth charges in search of the deadly U-Boat submarines. He continued on this ship until 8th July 1944, when he stepped up to become a Telegraphist on what became his favourite ship, a 'Danae' class light cruiser, *HMS Delhi*. Built in 1919 on Tyneside, *HMS Delhi*, at 4,927 tons had been in service "in the Med" before the outbreak of war. She had six 6 inch guns and twelve torpedo tubes. After a refit in New York in 1942, when her guns were increased to twenty-five, she served again in the Mediterranean Sea and in early 1944 was in Naples during the Allied landings at Anzio in Italy. After a passage to Gibraltar she resumed convoy duties from April to June. Her captain at the time was Captain G.R.Waymouth.

When John arrived on board the Delhi she had been nominated to take part in a big offensive. Named Task Group 881 she was part of the planned invasion of southern France which was code-named *Operation Dragoon*. After leaving convoy duties on the 2nd August she sailed to join the US Navy-led Task Force where she was deployed alongside HM cruiser *Royalist*, HM escort carriers *Khedive, Emperor, Searcher, Pursuer and Attacker*, and screened by five Royal Navy destroyers and the Greek destroyer *Navarinon* . *Delhi*'s role was to provide anti-aircraft defence during air operations from the carriers. On the 19th she detached from the group to refuel at Maddalena before resuming anti-aircraft duties south of Marseilles on the 21st. She was released from *Dragoon* a week later and spent September deployed in the western Mediterranean. As the enemy was driven from the south of France in 1944 the *Delhi* was present on the 13th September for the formal re-entry of the Free French Navy to their base at Toulon.

With the campaign over *HMS Delhi* moved on to support military operations over in the Adriatic Sea. In October she took a long passage through the Eastern 'Med' and on arrival in the Adriatic provided anti-aircraft defence for convoys and units off the Yugoslav coast. In November she was deployed at the port of Split when on the 10th of the month the formal surrender of German forces took place on board. She remained in Split in support of harbour defences. At Christmas 1944 she was in Split harbour where there was time for shore leave and was still there on 31st January when John's next move came about. This time, surprisingly it involved a long trip back to *HMS Drake* at Devonport, presumably via Gibraltar.

The crew of HMS Imperialist. John is on the back row, centre, bearded with white shirt.

As with James Coyne in Singapore, John was fortunate in the time he left. Less than two weeks after he left, *HMS Delhi* was attacked on February 12th by a German explosive motor craft while at anchor in Split harbour. It is believed that six enemy craft entered the harbour but the main damage was to the *Delhi*'s landing craft, propeller and rudder. It was to be the end of the war for the cruiser, towed back to Malta on the 10th March, and back to HM Dockyard, Chatham, a month later. Here the repair was assessed as uneconomic, the Delhi was "paid off" and within three years, in 1948, she faced the indignity of the breaker's yard at Newport.

The war was not over yet, but moving rapidly in the favour of the Allies. John's next movement was to Copenhagen on the 12th April 1945. He would spend VE Day in the Danish capital where he was part of NP1737 *Royal Philippa*. The number referred to 'Naval Parties' which used royal names, and were involved in land operations after the Germans had left. The Flag Officer 'in charge Denmark' had been based in Kensington, London, but on the relief of Copenhagen was transferred to the *Hotel d'Angleterre* in the city. Naval Party crew were again billeted – in John's case with the family of Herr Madsen. He fondly remembered his time with the Madsens, war was nearly over and the Danes had dairy produce unavailable elsewhere at the time. They had a son, Fredy Madsen, the same age as my father who showed him around the city. He spent his 25th birthday in Copenhagen where the Madsens presented him with a silver cigarette case which they had engraved '*J. Coyne Copenhagen 11-6-45*'. He left Denmark on the 31st August but kept in touch with the Madsen family long after the war *(ii)*.

John Coyne served on HMS Delhi from July 1944 to January 1945

John returned again to Devonport – clearly his 'home' base – and spent the last few months before demobilization at *HMS Drake*, apart from a brief stay in nearby Dartmouth. After six years of war and with VE Day long since gone, war service recruits must have been *'demob happy'*. Finally his papers arrived from the Demobilizing Leave Office, RN Camp, St. Budeaux, on the 22nd November informing him he was released from his service, initially to the navy reserve, due to end on 17th January 1946. In the meantime he was granted 56 days leave effectively leaving the next day. On the 23rd November he sailed for the last time by sea to Liverpool where- safely back in Lancashire- he docked at the mighty Princes Landing Stage. As the story goes he knelt down and kissed the ground in the manner of the Pope himself. As we shall see shortly Terry Coyne's war also ended in Liverpool almost to the day.

So ended John's naval years. It had been undoubtedly character-building and led to his future career in the police force. Despite the dangers, and amid the horrors of war, a love of ships and the sea was born. Leaving Blackburn in 1939, armed with prayer cards and religious medals from his mother (*iii*), he had travelled from the wilds of North West Scotland to the sunny Mediterranean, to North Africa and the Adriatic. On the 8th March 1944 he sent a postcard home describing himself as 'Rock Happy' in Gibraltar. His postcard collection, which survives, ranges from pictures of Barbary apes on the Rock to photographs of naval action in the area.

i. *The Ark Royal was hit on the 13th November and sunk the following day, enabling her crew of 1,487 to be taken to Gibraltar.*

ii.   My parents visited Copenhagen in June 1974. They stayed again with the Madsen family. Fredy was living in an apartment two floors below his parents.

iii.   These included a 'Sacred Heart' and - to protect him from The Devil – 'The Miraculous Prayer of St. Anthony of Padua.'

Terry Coyne in the British Army

Not everyone has a secret agent in the family. With his experience in China between 1927 and 1937 Terry Coyne was recruited into the Special Operations Executive (SOE after he re-joined the Army in 1940. He saw war-time service, probably in the Middle East to begin with, and after July 1941 in the Far East. Much has been written about the activities of the SOE and between these sources and records in the National Archives it has been possible to put together a picture of his activity in the war which was halted when the Japanese invaded the Malayan peninsular, which was to lead to Terry's incarceration in a Bangkok internment camp for three years and eight months in total. Because of the links between the two areas of his secret work we begin by following his years in the Shanghai Municipal Police and finish with a puzzling finale in 1945 with secret service intrigue continuing back in London.

Terry's connection to the Army goes back a long way. Aged ten when the First World War broke out in 1914 he had seen three of his uncles killed in action on the Western Front and a fourth wounded. Relations at home were thought to be strained, his father may have begun to spend time away from the home, and we know Terry undertook a number of casual jobs to help with the family income. Given the climate of war-time pressure many young boys joined the Army underage (it appears very little was done to discourage it) and this is how Terry came to join up for the first time. The official recruitment age at the time was eighteen, an age he did not reach until 1922. It may be he was released when his true age was known but whatever the case he joined again as soon as he was of age. We don't know what regiment he belonged to but it is believed he served in Ireland during the War of Independence which took place over the period 1921-22 and eventually led to the establishment of the Irish Free State along with partition in 1922. Barely seventy years after the Coynes had left Ireland it appears Terry had returned in the uniform of the British Army.

His son, Jim Coyne, told me an interesting tale about his father's time in Ireland. During his thirty-one years as a teacher in British Columbia he used one of his father's stories on his students. Terry had been held at gunpoint, presumably by a member of the Irish Republican Army, and was only released after the intervention of an Irish woman who ran over shouting " *Leave him!*" adding that "*this one was alright*". Jim's conclusion was – be nice to people, you never know – it could one day save your life!

After Ireland Terry continued his army career. Around 1925 he may have served in the S.D.F., the Sudan Defence Force. Sudan was a British colony ruled by the Foreign Office under a Governor- General backed by an elite class of colonial administrator. The SDF was formed in 1925 with their HQ in the capital city, Khartoum. They kept control of the colony when it was surrounded by enemy

Italian territory in Libya, Abyssinia and Eritrea. Sudan was to be Terry's introduction to Africa and the Middle East, a region he would return to in the early days of World War Two.

The Shanghai Municipal Police

On the 15th November 1927 Terry joined the Shanghai Municipal Police and began a ten year association with China. He was promoted to Sergeant in 1930 and Sub-Inspector in 1935. His decade long service was broken only by a return to England between August 1932 and early 1933 during which time, as we have seen, he visited family and married his wife, Bess Muskett, in Heswall. The newly-married couple then returned to Shanghai.

Shanghai in the 1920s and 30s was the sixth largest city in the world. If Terry was looking for adventure he was sure to have found it in Shanghai. By 1930 the city had a population of 2.9million. One million of these lived in the International Settlement along with 36,000 foreigners. The nationalists came to power in China in the 1920s under Chiang Kai Shek and one of his earliest priorities was for the Municipal Council in Shanghai to sweep away the old corrupt police force with its ties to secret and criminal gangs who controlled the city's vast opium traffic. The city was also a centre of entertainment, gambling and vice. Furthermore it was a hotbed of espionage, an area where Terry was to become more involved.

One area of the city, the French Concession was run by the French, while the SMP policed the International Settlement. Within the force the Criminal Investigation

Department had a Special Branch, effectively a political police sensitive to the activities of foreign journalists and visitors. There were numerous White Russians in the Settlement who – just one week before Terry signed up – had been involved in an incident at the Consulate General of the USSR. The White Russians gathered and attacked the building and the SMP did nothing to intervene. The Soviets then opened fire on the crowd and it took riot police one hour to restore order.

Kidnapping was also a problem in the city, while in the early days of motor car traffic the roads were especially dangerous. In 1929 the police recorded 803 street accidents and ten deaths. The burial of corpses was also a responsibility frequently left to the police. After cold winter nights bodies would be found on the streets next morning. During the 1920s it was estimated some 20,000 corpses were found in the streets and alleys of Shanghai. As we can see this was no ordinary police force!

Gambling, vice and narcotics took up a great deal of police time. The Chinese authorities thought that the SMP were not to be trusted in their campaigns against gambling. Luna Park race track, for example, was British owned and frequently had crowds of 70,000 for Saturday meetings. Roulette houses when closed would merely open again in the adjacent French Concession. In 1920 it was estimated there were some 70,000 prostitutes in Shanghai – in the French Concession believed to be comprised of one in every three females. Licensing carried out by the police was largely ineffective after a national ban in China in 1928 brought greater numbers into the International Settlement.

Narcotics dominated the whole economy of the city. Ninety per cent of adult males smoked opium, the supply of which was controlled by the criminal gangs such as the Green Gang. A suspicion of corruption surrounded the question of 'lenient' policing. In the French territory this was more lenient still!

Shanghai 1931. Terry Coyne is third from the left on the front row

The Political Section

Political surveillance was a priority for the Nationalist government due to significant communist activity. The Shanghai Municipal Police was largely a British-run force who were more concerned with unrest among the Indian community in the city due to wider imperial concerns. The Chinese Communist Party were also known to have a cell in the SMP which was not discovered until 1933.

Frederick Wakeman, in his book *'Policing Shanghai'* covers the same years Terry was working for the SMP. It tells us that the Head of the force had frequently seen service in other parts of the Empire while many officers were recruited in England or Scotland to work in the colonial police and later moved on to Shanghai. *"Typically they were men of relatively modest backgrounds, former factory apprentices or soldiers who were especially drawn to Shanghai as it was viewed more favourably by the adventurous and the ambitious"*. They were a recognisable type *"strongly attracted to security work" (i)*

Section 1 and Section 2 of the Special Branch were in close liaison with the CID in Delhi, and with the police bureau in Singapore, especially when Indian nationals were picked up in Shanghai. The Intelligence Group was Top Secret and identified only as Section 4 (S4) who worked closely with the British Consulate, who had offices on the waterfront along the Huangpu River, known as The Bund. Originally a small section interested in "seditious" Sikhs by 1936 S.4 had detailed files on 250 activists, 280 sympathisers and brief notes on 3,500 others. Intelligence reports were shared with other agencies. The *'China Weekly Review'* had no doubt as to the real purpose – *"the CID actually serves as an unofficial branch of the British political intelligence service!"* The Head of the CID, in 1928, W.G. Clarke was thought to be a leading SIS agent in China as was Patrick T. Givens, an Irishman from Tipperary in charge of the Special Branch. There were also numerous foreign agents in Shanghai, which was a key communications hub. Indeed the Far East Bureau of the Comintern was based there.

This then set the scene for Terry's years in Shanghai. A web of espionage and intrigue, with myriad intelligence cliques spying on each other. Like every SMP policeman Terry would have initially worn the uniform of dark serge in winter and khaki drill in summer and he would have carried a Colt .380 semi-automatic pistol. They were known to use them without hesitation when required. Several major events marked his time in the city, the last one in 1937 causing Terry, Bess and young son Tim to return home hurriedly as armed conflict with Japan escalated alarmingly.

Before then in 1929-30 the SMP had begun to involve themselves in anti-communist activity. They clamped down on communist bookshops and meetings and carried out random arrests. On January 17th 1931 The SMP Special Branch arrested thirty-six communists during a raid on the Eastern Hotel. They were all handed over to the Chinese Nationalists and three weeks later twenty three of them were taken away and shot. In 1932 war broke out between Japan and China and the International Settlement was placed under martial law. On this occasion the Japanese invaded parts of Shanghai. This was to prove to be a prelude to the events of August 1937 when Japanese troops invaded mainland China.

By August 11th the Japanese Third Fleet had steamed up the Huangpu River. The warship *Idzumo* anchored directly in front of the International Settlement with twenty six others behind it. Both side put up barbed wire and the Chinese, with 45,000 troops refused to budge. As the situation became extremely tense the residents of the International Settlement could hear gunfire in the distance. Terry was one of 17,000 soldiers and policemen defending the territory. Events however moved rapidly necessitating a hasty departure from Shanghai.

On the 14th August a storm blew up. Gale force winds blew when the Chinese tried to bomb the *Idzumo*. Instead a massive 2,000 pound bomb missed, hitting two hotels and a crowd of refugees on the waterfront. 700 were killed and many maimed. Worse was to come. On "Bloody Saturday" August 23rd 3,000 were killed when wayward bombs dropped by a stricken Chinese plane landed on the French Concession. At this point the Japanese began to land troops. The Coyne family needed to leave hurriedly and it is believed their ship came under fire as they managed to make their way down river from Shanghai. Their journey took them across the Pacific Ocean and back to Britain as we saw in Chapter Thirteen.

Special Operations Executive

In 1940 Terry and Bess were back in Heswall where their third son, James William, was born on the 15th February. They now had their own place at 74 Downham Road, while Terry was working as a Transport Manager for a builder's merchants. The outlook in 1940 was gloomy with Hitler seemingly unstoppable in Europe when, at the age of thirty-six, Terry joined the Army again and by November he had left for Egypt.

Soldiers arriving in Egypt usually docked at Port Suez and continued their journey to the capital, Cairo, by train. Cairo had been for a long time a centre of strategic British interests and despite gaining independence in 1922 the

British Army remained in Egypt until 1956. In 1940 it was another hotbed of intrigue, another centre of espionage where thousands of troops passed through on route to different war zones or back to the U.K. Stories are legion of the heat and the flies, while Cairo's streets were a hive of activity as expensive motor cars competed for space with camels, donkeys, mules and horses. Beggars in filthy robes jostled the newly-arrived while a few miles outside the city off-duty soldiers could enjoy the sights of the Pyramids. Significantly for Terry – who had served in the Middle East before – Cairo was also home to the regional office of the newly formed arm of military intelligence which became known as the SOE, the Special Operations Executive. Their HQ was in the Rustum Buildings on Sharia Kasr and was known as the Middle East Mission along with a range of acronyms. Despite the levels of subterfuge it was apparently well known to the Cairo taxi drivers as "the Secret Building".

The Special Operations Executive was set up by Prime Minister Churchill in July 1940. Its remit was to co-ordinate subversion and sabotage behind enemy lines. It operated mainly in occupied Europe during World War Two but also in the Balkans and in the Far East. It was disbanded in 1946. Its existence was always shrouded in secrecy being an offshoot of the Ministry of Economic Warfare. Its lack of 'official' recognition was at times problematic and the service faced hostility from other military chiefs, diplomats, and especially from the Secret Intelligence Service (SIS) who regarded them as an amateur newcomer to the field. Politically they reported to a minister, Hugh Dalton.

The first Head of the SOE, Sir Frank Nelson, was a former Member of Parliament and a British Consul, who operated from his office in Baker Street, London, which had the typically vague title of 'Inter-Services Research Unit'. Soon the recruitment of officers and training instructors was underway. Recruitment took place by means of interview usually at the SOE's favourite venue, a room in the Victoria Hotel, Northumberland Avenue, which was close to Trafalgar Square.

The hotel was behind the War Office, a labyrinthine neo-Baroque building in Whitehall reputed to occupy seven floors, one thousand rooms and two and a half miles of corridors. By 1940 however the War Office was full! Interviews lasted about forty minutes and, if promising, another was arranged for a few days later during which time a security check was made with M.I.5. Candidates were required to volunteer. Once accepted training then began at a number of locations, usually in country houses. One of the best known was at Arisaig in Inverness-shire in the Scottish Highlands, known as STS 21, and comprised fitness training, weapons training, and unarmed combat. Two officers at Arisaig would have been ver.y well known to Terry Coyne. Among the instructors were Eric Anthony "Bill" Sykes *(ii)* and William Ewart Fairburn, known as "Dangerous Dan". Both were recruits from the Shanghai Municipal Police commissioned as Second Lieutenants on 15th July. Sykes was a Lancastrian, born in Barton on Irwell in 1883, who had lived in Shanghai from 1907. He was a Reserve Officer in the SMP and in July 1940 he was sent to a Special Training Centre at Lochailort. Sykes and Fairburn, both tough streetfighters, were praised for their training methods and were credited with the introduction of a new shooting style

Victoria Hotel, Northumberland Avenue, London

Another name from Shanghai was soon to emerge. Valentine St. John Killery, born in 1900, was an Old Etonian who in pre-war years had been the vice-chairman of Imperial Chemical Industries in Shanghai. In May 1940 he was appointed Head of the Oriental Mission, a further offshoot of the Ministry of Economic Warfare, to be based in Singapore with the objective of running SOE operations in the Far East. Killery soon left for Singapore with another ICI businessman, Basil Goodfellow, where they set up a base in the Cathay Building. Prospective agents followed over the summer of 1941, recruited from all classes. The SOE historian, M.R.D. Foot, described them as the *"strong, silent men of romantic fiction – calm and clear-headed"*. It was during this wave of recruitment that Terry was sent to Singapore. It is not known whether former colleagues from Shanghai recommended him but clearly his experience in the Orient made a good fit for the job. He was already working in Army intelligence *(xiv)* when he was vetted by the SOE 23rd July 1941 and was engaged from 1st August, initially with the rank of Sergeant. He should have felt at home. Ashley Jackson in his book "The British Empire and the Second World War" claimed that the China Sections of SOE and its American counterpart *"were like the Shanghai Club in exile"*. The next section is now part of family folklore. Terry Coyne walked into the famous Raffles Hotel in Singapore and came out with a new identity, new papers, and new clothes. He was now 'Tom Collins', named after the cocktail, a tin miner destined for employment in the tin mines of Southern Siam. Before then he would have attended a Special Training School.

Special Training School STS 101

Whitehall had given Jim Gavin, a captain in the Royal Engineers, a room near the War Office to begin the arrangements for a Singapore Training School. On the 4th April 1941 his establishment was approved and the recruitment of agents began. Gavin arrived in Singapore on the 28th May and premises were found for the new STS 101 at a place called *Tanjong Balai*. The former home of an Armenian millionaire who made a fortune from tin mines, the house occupied a headland connected to Singapore Island by a long narrow causeway at the mouth of the Jurong River. Here in this large bungalow with Chinese-style pavilions Terry began his SOE training among the neighbouring rubber trees and mangrove swamp.

By 26th June staff had moved into *Tanjong Balai* and *Operation Scapula* had begun. By the end of July it was reported the "Scapula parties" had arrived from England joining other arrivals, including Terry, who brought the establishment up to 150 men. SOE Singapore was divided into three sections – a HQ unit; recruitment and liaison under Lt. Colonel Alan Warren – incidentally a former army liaison officer from GHQ Shanghai; and a Country Section. Terry was attached to the latter. In August Freddie Spencer Chapman, a mountaineer who held the army rank of Captain, started as a STS Instructor. He achieved fame after the war with the publication of his memoirs *"The Jungle is Neutral"*, recounting his SOE work and a long period when he was thought to be lost in the Malayan jungle (he was finally rescued by submarine in May 1945). Chapman was to Head the Siam and Indo-China Country Sections and it was to this section that the tin miners were attached. The training itself was not without danger. One mortar practise led to the death of a Sergeant Instructor while a Captain Lowe was badly injured by shrapnel.

A clear plan existed for Siam which awaited the go ahead .The military "top brass" *(xv)*, worried by diplomatic sensitivities, dithered over when to unveil the plan, code-named *Operation Matador*, whereby troops would be sent in to Malaya across the Straits of Johore, as Japanese aggression increased. The SOE were then to be embedded in Southern Siam where they could block Japanese troop movements, capture the important Yala crossroads and seize Phuket Island with its important west coast airstrip. For this operation recruits were found among the European mining population as miners and businessmen alike attended *Tanjong Balai* for training.

Preparations were underway for what were called 'left behind parties'. Supplies were vast (see box) and included two other items. Agents were not to be captured alive and were issued with 'suicide tablets' (cyanide). Finally, each party had a wireless operator, usually from the Royal Signals Regiment, who had been trained in wireless transmission. Unfortunately the wireless sets were to prove unsuitable in humid jungle conditions. Units were required to listen in to Radio Malaya each day at 6am where it had been arranged for a coded message to be broadcast in the event of a Japanese invasion. This was to be the 'green light' for special operations to begin.

In November 1941 another problem emerged at STS 101. Most of the Instructors were struck down by a 'swamp fever' which turned out to be the deadly dengue fever. Chapman was one of those hospitalized. Despite this planning went ahead, and while Killery pressed Sir Arthur Brooke-Popham, Commander-in- Chief Far East until December 1941, to unleash *Matador*, General Percival tried to veto the operation.

1 revolver or automatic	1 fighting knife	1 jack-knife	1 parang (for jungle use)
1 compass	1 steel helmet	1 sub-machine gun and rifle	54 explosives and incendiaries
32 items of food -	cheese, butter, jam	milk, tinned salmon	instant coffee, rice
rice , army biscuits	(all tinned)	25 items of clothing	camping equipment

The Oriental Mission: Supply List for Left- Behind Parties

He may have been influenced by Sir Josiah Crosby, an influential and long-serving British diplomat in Bangkok, ever eager to protect the interests of his 'family and firm' in Siam. Around the 17th November Killery went ahead with the first of his 'left-behind parties' despatched to Siam. By the end of January 1942 forty-five men in eight 'left-behind parties' were in position. *Operation Etonian* had launched, crossing Malaya by road with supplies hidden in car seats and weapons strapped underneath the vehicles. Cruikshank in *"SOE in the Far East"* stated that the operation was commanded by Captain Spencer Chapman and that three of the parties were sent to the state of Pahang – one near Benta led by W.H. Stubbington, a surveyor in peacetime; and one ten miles from Bentong led by J. P. Garden, a tin miner. Terry's cover was that of a tin miner with the Thai Tin Syndicate (*xvi*). Since this company was known to operate in Pahang it seems likely he was sent to one of these two locations, about 80 kilometres north-east of Kuala Lumpur.

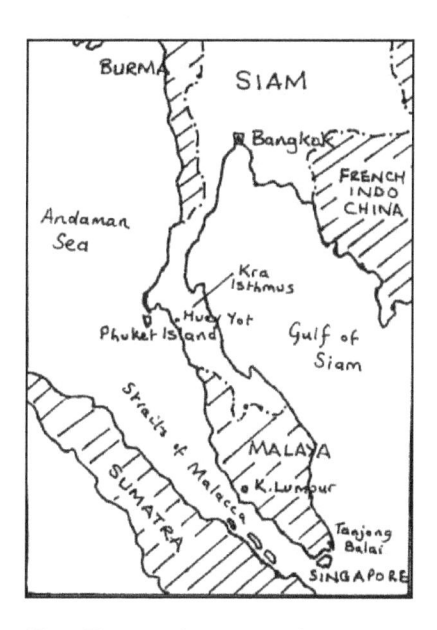

The Far East: The map shows Tanjong Balai,
Phuket Island and Bangkok

Japanese Invasion: the Tin Miners' Destiny

The fate of the 'left-behind parties' was to be determined by the Japanese. While Percival and the GHQ staff continued to believe that Singapore was an impregnable fortress Japanese plans, soon to emerge with deadly intent at Pearl Harbour, brought war to the Far East. In the early hours of Monday December 8th 1941 Japanese forces landed at Kota Bharu, and later at other landings along the Kra Isthmus. Already they were within twenty miles of some of the 'left-behind parties'. Some air resistance was offered in the early days but by the 18th January 1942 the under-resourced RAF units had been damaged beyond use and were withdrawn to Sumatra. The Japanese now rapidly advanced down the Malay peninsula. On the 15th February General Percival, Commander-in-Chief of British forces in Singapore surrendered one of the jewels of the British

Empire to the Japanese and thousands of troops were left to face the brutality of life in many a Far Eastern prison camp.

Before then however the tin miners faced the first wave of Japanese troops. They were notified of the invasion by radio, grouped around their *Philco* wireless sets, listening for the crackling voice of a distant announcer on the 6am news. The coded message when sprung referred to a careless Singapore army officer who had lost his brief case with important papers missing! At first a list of serial numbers were read out with coded instructions for the 'left-behind parties'. The SOE went into action in what proved to be a race against time. The Siamese offered little resistance with the police assisting the invaders in the detention of foreigners. On the west coast the airfield and installations on Phuket Island were seized. Some agents were unsure whether *Matador* had been cancelled and tried to escape back to Malaya. For others escape was not an option.

The Massacre at Pinyok

Pinyok mine was owned by the British-American Tin Corporation and occupied a valley site in Southern Siam where miners' bungalows were built alongside the tin mine. Here arms and explosives had been hidden in a dump in the mountains. Gough in his book on SOE operations in Singapore describes the fate of one of the parties who were arrested, disarmed and escorted back to the mine. They were flung in a store room alongside local civilians and denied food for two days. Japanese soldiers then flung in a grenade leaving behind the dead and those badly maimed. One teenage girl survived to tell the tale. In total nineteen civilians and eight Indian soldiers were massacred.

Elsewhere two of the SOE wireless operators were captured on the 7th December. E.S. Wright, a sergeant in the Royal Signals, was captured. He was later interned and sent to the infamous Burma Railway. The second operator was not so 'lucky' – caught while using his radio he was shot dead. Three mine engineers, D. Reagan and R. Gordon, both employed at Tongkah Harbour tin mine, and H.Wright of Ronpibon Tin were taken prisoner by the Siamese Police. Escaping from house arrest in the mine manager's bungalow they were captured and shot by the Japanese at Sonkhla also during December.

Cruikshank has a chapter on the Oriental Mission recounting the experience of Mr J.W. Omay in the Huey Yat area, twenty miles north east of Trang. Although not mentioned by name 'Tom Collins' may have been there with him since it is known that Omay was employed by the Thai Tin Syndicate (v). We will hear more of J.W.Omay later. His party had heard the warning on Singapore Radio on the Saturday evening, the 6th December, and next morning ordered his colleague R.G. Sarrell (a sergeant in the SOE) To start dismantling the tin dredge. Below he refers to a third person in the 'escape party'.

"Early on Monday 8th December he learned that Singapore had been bombed, and ordered Sarrell to speed up dismantling the tin dredge which proved impossible as workers and a Siamese CID officer were watching. Between 11am and noon the radio news was interrupted and the numerical coded message which Omay had been waiting for

came through at last. However he found that the Nasan bridge was now guarded by armed men; and when he suggested to the District Officer that it might be in their interest to destroy it he received a curt refusal. As he had volunteered for special ops on the assumption Siam would be fighting alongside Britain he felt under no obligation to do anything more. Therefore he and two colleagues made for Phuket Island hoping to find a boat for Penang; but they were arrested by the Siamese police, and taken to Bangkok where they were interned "(vi)

On his release in 1945 Terry Coyne informed M.I.9 (the Escape and Evasion Service)) on a partially completed questionnaire *(vii)* that the place of his capture was 'Pukett, South Thailand'. The above may well be a description of the capture of 'Tom Collins'. Not all of the agents were captured. On the west coast many Australians were evacuated by the Royal Navy. For Terry, however, he would spend the next three years and eight months in captivity. The SOE, undeterred by the ill-fated Oriental Mission, continued their Far East activities away from Siam, with more success in Malaya, Hong Kong and Burma.

Ta Prachan Internment Camp

The Army took the date of 8th December 1941 as the 'date of captivity' for all their tin miners in Siam. Terry joined other captured civilians at the *Ta Prachan* Internment Camp which occupied a riverside location in central Bangkok, capital city of Siam (now Thailand). If the occupiers were aware of his military rank he would either have been shot or detained in one of the many brutal military camps where emaciated and ill-treated captives were put to work by the Japanese. The internment camp was shared with women and children and captives were reasonably well- treated. They were left to organise their own activities and Terry revealed later he had learned languages and tried his hand at basket-weaving.

Back in the UK it took the Government a long time to be aware of these detainees. Not until the 18th November 1942 when the Secretary of State for Foreign Affairs, Anthony Eden, replied to a Parliamentary Question from Mr Hewlett, M.P., was it announced that the *Ta Prachan* camp had opened on the 23rd December the previous year. Mr Hewlett asked whether the Secretary could make a statement as to the treatment of British civilian prisoners "seized at Bangkok by the Japanese". Eden replied he had received reports by which it appeared that the camp was reasonably well-organised, health good, and medical treatment satisfactory. There was a canteen and the general spirit in the camp was 'high' (viii).

Only then were next-of-kin informed since Terry's wife Bess recalled being informed on Christmas Day 1942 having heard nothing for over twelve months. Later, letters written to the camp never arrived due to a lack of co-operation from the captors. One curious fact emerged however. On 1st October 1942 Terry was promoted again to First Lieutenant. The Army List of 1944 under the heading 'Regular Army Emergency Commissions, continued' has the following entry...

'Coyne, T. (WS Lt 1/10/42) spec.emp. 5.7.41'

The 'spec emp' hid the SOE cover. It would appear that Terry was promoted while still undercover in captivity in Bangkok. It is not known why, or how regular this was, but its significance is that Bess would have received a higher ex-gratia payment paid in lieu of Terry's captivity.

The Aftermath: The National Archives Documents

Although Second World War army records remain inaccessible some of the records of the Special Operations Executive have been released in recent years by the National Archives at Kew in London. Among the formerly *'Top Secret'* War Office files are a number of documents about the tin miners and particularly missing personnel. In TNA file HS1/112 are some photographs of some of the men and they include one of Terry wearing a light-coloured jacket, shirt and tie. On the underside is written *'T. Collins alias Terence Coyne.'*

Terry Coyne. The National Archives photo probably taken in 1940.

Significantly, of the eleven photographs, all named, four were marked R.I.P. and included H. Wright and D. Regan referred to earlier as having been shot by the Japanese trying to escape. The photographs were sent to London by BB1 (code for the Far Eastern Bureau in Delhi) on the 12th December 1944. Elsewhere the file contains information about the Siamese tin miners, their rank and remuneration due once the hostilities were over. Telegram No.417 dated 16th September 1945 reported that *'Coyne, T.'* had been recovered, detailed on a list of 'OM Casualties'. He was now back within the Army bureaucracy. Cipher Telegram to Kandy (Ceylon base of SOE Far Eastern office)) dated 28th September 1945 announced that *'Coyne posted back to Army Admin 1st October to facilitate repatriation formalities.'* Tom was now back as Terry, internees from the Bangkok camp were among the first to be released after the atom bombs dropped on Hiroshima and Nagasaki had hastened Japan's unconditional surrender. Air flights from Rangoon in Burma were able to reach Siam with ease.

Already Army finance were working on remuneration. A document dated 23rd October sent to Finance, New Delhi, stated that a 'casualty' with the rank of 2ND Lieutenant was due a rate of £200 per annum. The period of captivity – 43.5 months – meant they were due a payment of £750. While this was going on Terry was on his way home by sea destined for Liverpool and briefly back in his native Lancashire. On the 2nd November 1945 he was promoted again this time to the rank of Temporary Captain (*ix*). All appeared to be a satisfactory conclusion to his period of captivity. Meanwhile however thousands of miles away in Central London, then recovering after six long years of war, an extraordinary episode concerning Captain Terry Coyne was about to unfold.

Room 238, Victoria Hotel, London

The date was 6th November 1945. The blackout screens would by then have been removed from the windows of Room 238 of the Victoria Hotel on Northumberland Avenue, but it is likely the SOE's favourite interview room would have changed little from the early stages of the war when erstwhile recruits to 'the organisation' referred to it as a squalid little room, barely furnished with two folding chairs and a naked light bulb. Seated one side of the table was *"an officer from our Far eastern Section"* who went under the coded initials of B.B.3 (*x*). Seated across from him was an Australian former SOE agent, employee of the Thai Tin Syndicate, and former internee at *Ta Prachan*, none other than Mr J.W. Omay who was at the time staying at the Royal Hotel in Woburn Place. Oddly B.B.3 felt it necessary to use an alias for this interview. Documents in the National Archives state that *"on the 5th November I interviewed J.W. Omay in Room 238 using the alias S.Croft."* During the interview Omay complained about the conduct of Terence Coyne, both before captivity and later during internment. The complaint was that he had been 'indiscreet', particularly that he made no secret of his Army rank or that he was a former Shanghai policeman. The report added that Omay produced statements signed by himself and four other co-detainees which he believed supported his allegations. The meeting also took the view that *"Coyne is not expected to return to the UK, but has remained in the East hoping to go back to*

Shanghai". While this was taking place Terry was actually beginning his journey home by troopship so this was clearly untrue.

The following day, 7th November, B.B.3 sent a report to A/CD (*xi*), with a copy to the security section D/CE. The memo seemed to concur with Omay's view and referred to attached letters (not seen) *"handed to me by Omay from himself, Orton, Turner, and Sarrell"* (*xii*) – all described as *"our bodies"*. On the 9th November A/CD, in a brief confidential memo to B.B.3, suggested *"no action is necessary beyond notification to M.I.5"*. The final word was a letter dated 13th November headed 'Terence Coyne' from an un-signed Major summarising the situation. It pointed out again that Terry was not expected to return and *"that he had not been tackled for his version of events"*. It concluded by placing the comments on record.

So what exactly should we make of all this? Who was J.W. Omay and why did he go to such lengths? Why complain about a fellow officer twice promoted over the period in question? Perhaps it was personal based on years of close confinement in a steamy internment camp. Clearly we shall never know. Using standard genealogical sources I found a little more about Mr. Omay. He was James Watson Omay, born about 1908 in Tasmania who arrived in London on 18th November 1931 from Brisbane in Australia. An engineer by trade he went to the Far East in 1934 when he travelled to Singapore on route for Siam. It would seem he was employed as a Mine Manager on a salary of some £900 per annum. He left Japan in 1938 for San Francisco and may have returned to the UK around the time the Second World War broke out. R.G Sarrell was also an

Australian so perhaps there were national rivalries among the internees. Omay died in Perth, Western Australia, in 1966.

For Terry meanwhile a warm welcome awaited him at Liverpool as more troopships returned after a six week voyage laden with soldiers and liberated prisoners-of-war *(xiii)*. After enduring war, internment and now secret service intrigue a return to family life must have been more than welcome. Amid the murk of the Mersey waterfront in late November 1945, waiting on the quayside were Bess and young sons Tim, Vin and Jim holding a banner with the message *'Welcome Home Daddy'.*

The SOE's Oriental Mission may have lasted just ten months, the 'stay- behind parties' had little time for sabotage before the arrival of the Japanese but if anyone should doubt how dangerous their mission was it can be gauged from the figures below *(xiv)*. Terry received the British War Medal 1939-45.

Malaya Casualties OM: Personnel – Tin Miners

Missing 23

POW 25

Interned 19

<u>Dead 35</u>.

Total 102

Civilian Life

As we saw earlier Marie Coyne was serving in the ATS based in Yorkshire. She had a secretarial qualification so would have been involved in office work. Frank X. Coyne may also have been in the Territorial Army before the war, since we have a photograph of him attending an army camp (*xv*). This was the first war however to impact heavily on civilians who became targets of German bomber raids, known as the Blitz. The Coynes in Birkenhead, particularly, were on the receiving end of regular raids as the Luftwaffe targeted both the Liverpool docks and the Cammell Laird shipyards on the Birkenhead side of the Mersey which was heavily involved in naval work. Between 9th August and 23rd October 1940 Merseyside was subjected to 200 air raids, beginning at Prenton in Birkenhead, very close to where Frank, Ann and Margaret lived. In March 1941 further raids hit nearby Wallasey, leaving 174 people dead. A further Blitz in May killed 1,741. Margaret Coyne (now Mearns) remembered this time and recalled how her father bought a large house at 32 Egerton Park *(xvi)* in Rock Ferry because it had large cellars to protect them from the raids. As a child she remembered the A.R.P (Air Raid Precautions) wardens on duty at the large gate post marking the entrance to the Egerton Park houses. The threat from the air raids became so severe that Margaret, then around eight years old, was evacuated to her grandmother's house in Wolverhampton, where she lived for a time with her grandmother and her Aunt Kathleen.

It is perhaps surprising that the only civilian casualties experienced by our family at the time were accidental rather than war-related. In June 1940 two members of the

Manchester family died tragically on the same day. Sarah McIlwraith, aged 55, a cousin of my grandfather, and her daughter, Lily, aged 22, both died in a house fire at 8 Alexandra Grove, Chorlton on Medlock, about one mile east of Manchester city centre. Lily's death certificate stated that she was employed as a *"waterproofer's doper"*, that she was the daughter of Archibald McIlwraith, deceased, and that she died of "severe burns when the house caught fire while she was in bed at home (*xvii*). The *Manchester Guardian* reported the story the following day in a news report headed *"Two Burned to Death in House Fire"*. The report included an eye witness account from the A.R.P. warden, Mr. T.H. Williams, who had briefly attempted a rescue despite uncertainty whether the McIlwraiths were at home. He was treated at the nearby Royal Infirmary and told the reporter he could not reach the upper floors due to smoke.

An inquest took place on the 17th June. The *Manchester Guardian* headline *"Fire Started by Cats"* on 18th June covered the verdict of Mr G. Jessel Rycroft, Coroner for Manchester. It was an "Accidental Death". The Coroner noted that while, both women smoked, it was usual for three cats to be left overnight in the kitchen at Alexandra Grove, where it was known the fire started. Both women were buried at Southern Cemetery on the 18th June in the grave of Archie McIlwraith.

Finally, there was also our U.S. family, the Davis' and the Strides in Mahanoy City, Pennsylvania. From the brief window afforded by the 1940 U.S. Census it showed that seven members of the family were all living together at 302 East Centre Street, Ward 4, Mahanoy City. Harriet Davis was then 62 years old, her son William, 24, while Elmer and Amy Stride were aged 46 and 40 years respectively. James Stride was now 19 years old, and his sisters Florence and Marion were aged 14 and 11 years. There was no trace of Harriet's son, James Coyne (born Manchester1906) anywhere on the Census. At this point the United States was not yet involved in the war while evidence from the Census shows the family were struggling economically. Their only income appeared to be labouring and included many weeks with no work. They rented a property valued at $3000.

Overall this chapter has provided a snapshot of the enormous effort required to defeat the German war machine, familiar to families throughout the land and beyond. The many military movements and transfers; the thousands of hours of training; the vast amount of capital invested in weaponry and infrastructure. At the same time on the 'home front' the civilian population suffered the privations of food rationing, blackouts, the terrors of the air raids, and for many the loss of their homes. Recent television programmes have emphasised the self-effacing and dutiful contributions of the people involved. They have been described as our "greatest generation". No-one should under-estimate their legacy and we can be proud of the immense contributions of the members of our family whose fate determined their involvement in the Second World War.

Life had to go on around all the upheaval. Two more children were born during the war years. In March 1942 Winifred Pauline Eccles (again to be known by her middle name), the second daughter of Josie and George Eccles, was born in Blackburn, where on the 25th June 1944 her cousin Peter Fielding was born, the second son of Winnie and Joe. As life slowly returned to something like normality a new chapter awaited, one of reconstruction, of optimism and eventually progress.

i. Page 142, Wakeman
ii. Named after character in Dickens' 'Oliver Twist'.
iii. According to the London Gazette, published on 31 July 1942, Terry was promoted to Second Lieutenant on the 5th July .He was named as Sergeant Terence Coyne of the I.C. (Intelligence Corps)
iv. These were led by General Percival, GOC Singapore, and Air Vice Marshal Sir Arthur Brooke-Popham, Commander in Chief, Far East.
v. A British owned company with a Head Office at 65 London Wall in the city.
vi. Cruikshank., 'SOE in the Far East' p73.
vii. National Archives reference WO344/370.
viii. Historic Hansard Vol 385, 18th November 1942.
ix. Army List January- March 1946.
x. BB was 'Delhi Group'
xi. Since CD was known to be the Head of The Special Operations Executive, A/CD may have been an assistant. CD at the time was Major- General Colin Gubbins. Gubbins was a Scot, bald with a clipped moustache, described as having the look of a bank manager. He was a veteran of the Somme in World War One.
xii. R.L. Orton was a Second Lieutenant like Omay. A.E. Redford, R.G. Sarrell and R.K. Turner were Sergeants ('UK Civilian Casualties - tin miners in Thailand 'document dated 23'10.1945)
xiii. The RMS Mauretania, the Cunard liner being used by the Government as a troopship, berthed in Liverpool on the 25th November bringing 6,000 home from the Far East. Press reports mention an earlier arrival in Liverpool. Family recollections think Terry was perhaps on the earlier ship.

xiv.   *TNA reference HS1/112.*
xv.   *Frank was clearly a very busy man. As well as the chemist's shop he also completed an external degree in Engineering during the 1930s.*
xvi.   *The property still stands on the north side of the enclave. On visiting in 2013 the numbers had changed .It had been in use as a nursing home.*
xvii. *Manchester Guardian Friday June 14th 1940, page 10.*

CHAPTER FIFTEEN

From Austerity to Prosperity

Recovery and Family Migrations: 1945 – 1960

With the war over lives began to be rebuilt after years of turmoil. The war-time leader, Churchill, was soon ousted as Prime Minister in the 'Forces Election' of the 5th July 1945 which resulted in a landslide victory for the Labour Party led by its unassuming and somewhat taciturn leader, Clement Attlee (i). Churchill had been good for wartime morale but many already knew of his past political record. Others had enjoyed a relaxation of Britain's class divide during the war and were in no mood for a return to the "know your place" days of pre-war. They remembered all too well the Great Depression during which a Conservative- led National Government had ruled. Attlee's Government faced up to the 'Brave New World" with a radical programme of nationalisation of key sectors of the economy, notably the mines and the railways. Its greatest achievement, however, battled through against powerful vested interests in 1948, was the creation of the National Health Service which had much to do with the rising living standards in the decades that followed. On the down-side those less keen on state control viewed events differently seeing it as the onset of national decline as the sun continued to set on the British Empire.

Economically things remained very serious despite the changes. Most troublesome was the continuation of rationing, a necessity in wartime when supply ships were regularly sunk, but many had hoped it would end soon afterwards. Under the austere Chancellor, Sir Stafford Cripps, the economy only recovered slowly. Work had to be found for the demobbed millions, wartime industries had to return to peacetime markets and there was a major housing shortage. Not in the least, much of the country's infrastructure and many city centres had been bombed to destruction. Rationing of basic foodstuffs like meat, eggs, butter and tea continued, while it was not until 1948 that bread rationing ended. Clothing was also rationed until May 1949(ii). After a very severe winter in 1946-47 potato rationing had to be introduced. Tea was rationed from 1940 to 1952, sweets until 1953. It was as late as 1954 before food rationing finally ended in Britain.

It is little wonder then that many who found it difficult to acclimatize after the war thought of emigration. As we shall see our family was no different with an unprecedented interest in emigration – to Canada in particular – during this period. Not all felt this way though. Others successfully adapted to life in peacetime. New houses sprang up, and full employment became a possibility with many more public sector jobs. Manufacturing industry began to pick up and by the end of the 1950s the modern advertising-led and consumer-driven lifestyles had established with fridges, telephones, televisions, transistor radios, vacuum cleaners and washing machines produced in greater and cheaper quantities improving life for many. In addition luxury items, such as foreign holidays and motor cars began to filter down to the masses during this period. More and more of our family began to own their own homes, although often a period of several years back home with parents or in-laws was still required in order to afford the mortgage.

This was the situation then at this watershed year of 1945. The Coyne family of Joseph and Mary Ann remained in Blackburn along with the Fielding and Eccles families, and Joe's sisters Emma, Nellie and Frances. Over on the Wirral and in Birkenhead were the families of Terry Coyne and his brother Frank X ; in Wolverhampton there was Catherine Coyne and daughter Kathleen, while James remained in the RAF until 1948. Finally there were those with whom we had long since lost touch. James Edward Coyne, who we later found was still alive in Windsor, Ontario, and from the Manchester family Lilian Mercer was living in Old Trafford, with the largest of this group now that of the Davis and Stride families over in the United States.

First off the mark after the war was John Coyne and his sister Marie. John joined the Blackburn Borough Police on the 7th January 1946, starting his long police career with the number PC 103. No doubt after six years in Navy uniform it was a good fit for *"Civvy Street"*. Over in Birkenhead Terry Coyne almost made the same move. He applied to join the Birkenhead Borough Police with whom his brother had a connection as a duty 'police chemist' (iii). Maybe it was a far cry from Shanghai to the dark and windswept frontage of Birkenhead's docks and shipyards but he decided not to join.

Marie Coyne, meanwhile, had her marriage to consider. She was to marry Stanley Bentley, aged 27 years, a Yorkshireman she met while in the ATS. They married at St. Alban's on the 16th February 1946.

Wedding of Marie Coyne March 1946. Sister Sheila and brother Frank are first and second left. To the right of Marie is her father Joseph Coyne –his last photo – and on the far right is elder brother John.

Three days later she sent a postcard from Scarborough (where else would a Yorkshireman go for his honeymoon?) to John which started *"Dear Ging"* and thanked him for his assistance as Groomsman, i.e. looking after Stanley the night before the wedding. From the card Marie is obviously keen to find out what they got up to but must seemingly remain in the dark.

Significantly the address on the postcard was to have a bearing on John's own future. It was addressed to No.4 District Police Training Centre at Ryton-on- Dunsmore, near Coventry. It was while at Ryton, on a visit to a dancehall, that my father met my mother, Winifred Abbott, one year younger and who had lived all her life in

Coventry. They later got engaged at the top of the city's medieval Cathedral spire, the third tallest in England at 295 feet, and a landmark survivor of the Blitz which destroyed the Cathedral in November 1940.

Around the same time Terry and Bess waved good-bye to the Wirral and moved over two hundred miles away – a day's journey by rail - to the seaside port of Weymouth on the south coast. Here they took over a guest house, the Crofton Hotel, at 36 Lennox Street which they ran for a short period. The hotel had a good location being only 150 metres from the seafront and close to the railway station. It still trades today(see below) with eight rooms and in 2011 Terry's son – also Terry – and daughter, Debbie, were able to stay at the Crofton on their visit to the UK from Canada. The visit was a return for Terry since he was born in Weymouth on the 4th May 1947.

The Crofton Hotel

Vincent Ernest, Timothy John and James William Coyne:
Weymouth beach 1946 or 1947

It is not known why things didn't work out in Weymouth, - the rate of taxation in Britain at the time may have been a concern - but not long after, on the 20th October, Terry, Bess and the four boys, emigrated to Canada, travelling on the Cunard ship *RMS Aquitania* (*iv*), sailing from Southampton bound for Halifax, Nova Scotia. It has been said the Coynes had 'itchy feet' meaning a predilection to moving home (certainly this book bears that out) but perhaps they were drawn to the prospect of a better life on the Pacific coast which had clearly impressed both on their journey home from China a decade earlier. As we shall see in the next chapter, after the vast fourteen day odyssey, the family settled in White Rock, to the south of Vancouver in British Columbia, where they happily reside to this day.

Two other family members settled their futures in 1947. On the 31st May my parents John and Win married at

Christ the King RC Church in Coventry. My mother at the time was working as a clerk in the Motor Tax Division of Coventry Corporation. They spent their honeymoon at Broadstairs in Kent, and with John due back on police duty in Blackburn their first home was with the family at 179 Whalley Range. Soon after they were rehoused in what was a pioneering solution to the immediate housing crisis. They moved into what was called a prefab (prefabricated house) at 38 Guide Square a new estate built on higher ground on eastern edge of the town.

PC 103 John Coyne outside 38 Guide Square

Meanwhile Kathleen Coyne's life was about to change also. Before the war she had been the Manageress of a dairy and provision shop. Now aged 33 years she was still with her mother in Leyland Avenue, Wolverhampton, when she met a Canadian serviceman named Michael Wecko. Michael, who was five years older, was born in a place called Rakiw, in Galicia, Ukraine. His family had emigrated to Canada in 1921 settling in the State of Alberta. Why he was still around in Wolverhampton in 1947 is not known (he had served in the Canadian Army during the war) but according to her niece, Margaret, Kathleen had only known Mr. Wecko for six weeks before he had to return to Canada. He had asked her to marry him and it was then she too decided to make a new life in Canada, effectively one of the last of some 48,000 'war brides'. I don't know what her mother Catherine thought – apparently there was a suggestion she may join her later – but this wasn't to be.

Kathleen left England on the 8th October 1947, we think for the last time, aboard the transatlantic liner, *the Empress of Canada*. The quayside of Liverpool's famous waterfront had seen many a family arrival or departure over the years and it was here that she was waved off by Frank and Ann Coyne. She had bravely embarked, on her own, on an epic 4,000 mile journey to a town called Medicine Hat in Alberta where she was to marry Michael Wecko.

Kathleen Coyne photographed before she emigrated to Canada in 1947

Nationally these years after the war were a peak time for both marriages and births and we were no exception. The following family members were born at this time.

1946	*Gerard Fielding*	*Blackburn*
1949	*Hilary Susan Coyne*	*Blackburn*
1949	*Philip Eccles*	*Blackburn*
1950	*Christopher Paul Bentley*	*Spen Valley, Yorkshire West Riding*
1950	*Joseph Paul Fielding*	*Blackburn*

In keeping with family tradition names are either shortened or middle names have precedence. Gerard is Ged; Hilary is Susan. Shortly before the birth of Philip, the Eccles family moved to a new house at 4 Tintern Crescent in Little Harwood in the summer of 1949.

1947 was certainly an eventful year. Sadly it also brought, on the 30th September, the death of my grandfather, Joseph Coyne, aged 57 years. It seems his death was from a form of lung cancer. He had lived through two world wars having fought in the first one, and lived long enough to give away his eldest daughter Marie and saw his eldest son John marry just four months earlier. My mother remembered meeting him for the first time in Blackpool before his illness when he was up a ladder painting a seafront pub! He was interred at Blackburn Cemetery on the 4th October 1947 in the plot he had bought when Fergus Power died in 1931. So ended the life of the last painter and decorator in the Coyne family – he was still listed as such in Barrett's Directory in 1947 – ending the trade which had sustained the family for the best part of a century. He was a painter all his life apart from his wartime years as a

Gunner. Joe was a man of gentle temperament, spoken well of by those who knew him. On his death my grandmother, who still had Frank and Sheila at home, was able to claim a Widow's Pension.

All that remains of the family trade?

The following year, on the 3rd June, Lilian Mercer aged 53 years, a cousin of Joe's but one he had possibly never met, died of a haemorrhage at Park View Hospital, Davyhulme, in Manchester. She was survived by her husband, George, a storekeeper. At the time they were living at 52 Hullard Street, Old Trafford, near to the Lancashire County Cricket Ground. This was the last event I have found for the Mancunian Coynes, although Lilian's sister, Eveline may have lived until the 1960s (*v*).

Other family members started out or returned to the world of work. In Blackburn Frank Coyne followed his brother initially in joining the Royal Navy as an Ordinary Seaman but by 1950 he was also a Police Constable with Blackburn Borough Police. He was still in the Navy in 1947 when he was granted leave (*vi*) to attend John's wedding in Coventry while serving at HMS Raleigh, a shore establishment in the Plymouth area. It is known he was a P.C. in Blackburn in 1950 however since a report in the Burnley Express on the 8th November 1950 referred to an arrest of a burglar carried out by P.C. F.Coyne after a bicycle chase. Two months later when the case came to Blackburn Quarter Sessions he was complimented by the Recorder, a Mr. Scholefield (*vii*). If painting and decorating had been the Coyne trade since the nineteenth century, the uniformed services had seemingly taken over by the midtwentieth.

In 1948 James A. Coyne resigned his commission on the 8th October having served eleven years in the RAF. He fell back on his pre-war textile studies becoming the manager of a cotton mill in the small Lancashire town of Croston, near Preston. Hereon, for the rest of his working days James, who never married, seems to have enjoyed a quieter life after Bomber Command, in his own words *"growing roses and watching cricket"*.

It is perhaps surprising during an era of austerity and slow recovery that a number of the family had businesses at this time. Frank X. Coyne, the first of the family to go onto Further Education, still had his successful pharmacy business in Birkenhead. He appears in a trade directory for 1946 (xviii) as *'Coyne, Fras. Xavier M.P.S. 354 Woodchurch Road'* and also a separate listing as a resident at *'Ellesmere, Egerton Park, Rock Ferry'*. I photographed the shop in 2012 when it was still trading as an optician's. Frank continued to run the shop for most of the 1950s during which time they moved to a large semi-detached house at 23 Carlaw Road, just down the road from the shop.

Terry and Bess, as we saw also ran the Crofton guest house for a while but perhaps the most surprising business was that of great aunt Emma McHugh, started it seems when she was in her fifties. The Eccles' believe the baker's shop was owned by their Grandma Kennedy and Emma although it was the latter who appears as a *'Confectioner maker. shop'* on the 1939 National Register. She is also in a trade directory for 1947 but by 1951 it had changed hands. The shop was fondly remembered by the family. It is now thought that over a ten year period there may have been two shops. The first as previously mentioned was near to Cob Wall where it is recalled Josie Eccles worked. The second – listed in the Directory - was located at 24 Whalley Old Road at the west end of the road and close to Belper Street baths. The shop, no more than a house front in width, and typical of the many residential 'corner shops' of Victorian streets, stood between Edward Street and Pollard Street – three doors from the latter. Opposite was another row of houses adjacent to the Convent of Notre Dame. All of this area including some of the Coyne's first Blackburn houses were demolished during redevelopment of the area in the 1960s. It would have enjoyed a steady trade from the nearby streets. Emma would have known this area well as she had grown up around these streets in the 1880s.

Among the staff at the shop Josie was joined in the late 1940s by her cousin, Sheila Coyne, who in her first job trained as a baker and confectioner. In 1939 Josie was listed as a *'confectioner/cake maker'* so likely opened the shop each day. It is not known exactly how long the shop traded or the extent of the produce beyond cakes. It seems to have been open during the war and amid post-war rationing which may explain why it didn't last long. Living close by Josie would have opened the shop at 6am six days a week which she found hard after the birth of her second daughter in 1942. All who remember the shop mention that Emma took sole charge of the money! Prior to this venture she had only worked as a cotton weaver so perhaps this was an attempt to provide work for the family during meagre times?

The next business emerged in the mid-1950s when Winnie and Joe Fielding, for about three years, ran a fish and chip shop at 114 Scotland Road in the Audley Range district. I was informed by my uncle, Terry Hoyle, that it was a *"good 'un"*. The shop was sold in 1956 in preparation for the last of the 'Fielding migrations'. It was known that Winnie and Joe were unsettled in Blackburn during this period and they made some four attempts to emigrate. The first in 1948 they lived for a year in Canada; then there was an enquiry about going to Australia; in 1953, of great interest to our story, was an attempt to emigrate again to Canada when they were in touch with Winnie's 'Uncle Jim' –none other than our elusive James Edward Coyne. Finally in 1956 there was another attempt leading to a 'long summer holiday' in Canada. This was really the last decade of transatlantic sea travel and it is worth taking a look at these trips.

The Government of Canada at the time were keen to encourage immigration and ran an Assisted Passages loan scheme for immigrants. In 1951 15 percent of the country's population were immigrants of whom 44 percent came from the UK, and a further 8 percent from Ireland. As we have seen the Atlantic crossing was a well-established emigration route. The moves began on 18th June 1948 when Joe Fielding of 13 Lincoln Street, Blackburn, travelled ahead on the *'Britannic'* from Liverpool to New York and on to Toronto. Later that year Winnie and the three boys joined him this time sailing from Southampton to Halifax, Nova Scotia, an eight day voyage continuing by train to Toronto. They stayed for a year returning on the *SS Samaria*, arriving in Liverpool on the 25th July 1949. They then stayed with the boy's Grandma Kennedy on Whalley Range before renting a house in William Hopwood Street.

In 1948 there had been no contact with James Edward Coyne and no trip to Windsor. What took place in 1953 has only recently come to light. Great aunt Emma, ever formidable, and keeper of the family secrets, would appear to have kept in touch with her brother some thirty years after he left. After briefly considering Australia, the Fieldings tried again to move to Canada. Uncle Jim, it seems, had agreed to sponsor them and it was intended they would stay with him in Windsor. Travel arrangements were made and a date fixed. In these days before most people had telephones, letters were sent but unfortunately they were not returned. A deadline had to be set for contact from Uncle Jim in order to allow time to cancel and receive a refund, which they had to do one week before they were due to sail in May 1953. Two days after they cancelled a letter arrived from James to say he was travelling up to

Montreal to meet them. Winnie sent a letter of explanation but this was nor replied to. A few years ago I discovered that James – then 72 years old – died in Ontario on 1st August 1953, which perhaps explains why this attempt failed. But for a delayed letter and the untimely death might this attempt have succeeded?

The final attempt took place in 1956. As before Joe, then aged 44 years, went ahead with the two eldest boys leaving Liverpool on the 20th May 1956 on the *TSS Columbia* bound for Hamilton, Ontario, after completion of the 3,093 mile crossing to Montreal. Winnie stayed behind in Blackburn with the two youngest boys while she sold the fish and chip shop and house on Scotland Road, intending to join the others later. Another attempt was made to contact Uncle Jim in Windsor to arrange a visit. Tellingly, a response was received from his 'son' saying they knew nothing about us or a connection to England! It would seem James' origins had remained the deepest of secrets during his years in Canada?

This final 'migration' was again unsuccessful. It may have been that Joe's trade, a cable joiner, was not compatible with the work in Canada, as by 18th September Joe, John and Peter had returned to Liverpool on the Canadian Pacific liner, the *Empress of France.* They returned first to 158 Audley Range but around this time they moved instead to Fleetwood on the Lancashire coast. Yet another return to Blackburn was too much and finally they settled in the seaside town and fishing port on the Wyre estuary, around which Winnie and Joe were to spend the rest of their days. The first house in Fleetwood was at 72 London Street, conveniently placed for the beach, town centre and St.

Mary's Catholic Church. They later retired to Knott End on Sea, a short ferry ride across the River Wyre.

There was one other family migration at this time, that of my parents John and Win Coyne who in 1951 moved 120 miles south to live in Coventry. It may have been that my mother was keen to return to her home town where Coventry's economy was booming. The city's car factories enjoyed full employment during the 1950s and 60s such that industrial wages in the city were then the highest in the country. Twentieth century Coventry was Britain's fastest growing city until 1975 when the 'Chrysler Crisis' signalled the onset of decline. In the 1950s amid this post-war optimism John transferred to Coventry City Police where he was given the number P.C. 168.

During the 1950s John progressed well in Coventry. Soon after arriving in 1952 he was sent on a Home Office Detective Training Course (*ix*) at Eccleshall in Staffordshire. In his early days he dealt with all the everyday petty crime a constable dealt with (as can be seen from the selection of press cuttings overleaf) along with traffic duty and 'walking the beat'.

His move into the Criminal Investigation Department (CID) meant a step up into the area of more serious crime and a new rank of Detective Constable. In January 1954 he worked on a famous unsolved murder case, when a local woman named Penelope Mogano was murdered at her home in Holland Road. This was not far from where we were then living at 276 Sadler Road in the Radford district, and John was one of fifty officers assigned to the case along with detectives from Scotland Yard. This was a case involving painstaking door-to-door enquiries, a task my father would have excelled at. A year later he received a first commendation from the Chief Constable (x) for *'good police work'* in apprehending a serial offender accused of larceny from clothes lines on a grand scale! John, and another detective spotted a man answering his description while patrolling in a police car. By the end of the decade he had been promoted to Detective Sergeant, when he received a second commendation on the 21st July 1959 for the arrest of three men for armed robbery, and assault while armed, during a raid on FW Woolworth's large city centre store.

Early 1950s Press cuttings, Coventry Evening Telegraph

John had clearly taken to detective work and in 1960 he was sent to the national Police Staff College for a course at Bramshill House in Hampshire which he attended around the 24th July. During the course a football match was arranged. John, by then just 40, and around fifteen stones in weight was required to play in goal. He returned to Coventry with his ankle in plaster and using a walking stick having broken his ankle taking a goal kick! He had one other football memory of 1960. Following Blackburn Rovers unfortunate 0-3 defeat to Wolverhampton Wanderers in the FA Cup Final his desk at Coventry CID office in Little Park Street was draped in black, the colour of mourning.

The 1950s of course also had its share of births, deaths and marriages in the family. In fact the deaths of many of the older Coynes meant something of a generational change took place at this time. Firstly the marriages, both at St. Alban's in Blackburn. On the 12th September 1953 Frank Coyne, aged 24 years, married Florence Riley. They were to live at 5 Ailsa Road in Shadsworth. Secondly, on the 28th May 1955 Sheila Coyne married Terry Hoyle who worked in the newspaper industry with the *Lancashire Evening Telegraph*, based in Blackburn town centre. For the rest of the decade they lived at Mary Ann Coyne's house at 179 Whalley Range. The following children were born during the decade beginning with myself, shortly after the feast of Stephen in 1953 (my mother always held me responsible for her spending Christmas in hospital)

1953	Stephen John Coyne	Meriden, Warwickshire
1956	Michael Hoyle	Blackburn
1957	Janet Anne Coyne	Blackburn

The first death of the 1950s – and one we were only aware of quite recently – was that of James Edward Coyne who died at a place called Ambassador Beach, near to Windsor, Ontario. His address at the time was 576 Dougall Avenue in the city. James had lived on Dougall Avenue for at least 18 years. On the Voter's List for 1935 he lived at number 490 with 'Mrs Margaret Coyne' and an Arthur Fitzgerald, likely James' stepson. James' entry records him working as a 'decorator' and since Arthur was a 'painter' it is possible they worked together. By the time they next appeared in 1949 James –then aged 69 – had retired and with Arthur having left home James and Margaret had moved to number 576 on the same road., A death notice appeared in the *Windsor Daily Star* on the 4th August 1953 when he was described as the *'beloved husband of Margaret Ann'*. James was buried at the Victoria Memorial Gardens in Windsor who kindly provided the image of his gravestone

The final resting place of our mysterious James Edward Coyne, Windsor, Ontario, Canada

So ended the life of one of the most mysterious figures in our family history, one whose presence looms large in our story long after his 'disappearance'. I found also that his second wife Margaret, who died in 1966, was around the same age as James so it seems likely that Arthur Fitzgerald and a daughter, Mary, mentioned in the newspaper death notice (xi) were both Margaret's children from her previous relationship.

The 1950s was also defined by the deaths of the family's older generation – the last of Peter and Mary Ann's nine children who had lived through two World Wars. In February 1957 James' sister Frances Frost died aged 69 years. Frances and Hughie had lived for a long time in London Road, just behind Whalley Range. She spent much of her life in the cotton mills which continued to close amid terminal decline. Just over two years later elder sister Emma McHugh died aged 79 years. Emma was our oldest family member and the oldest person we have a photograph of. She was a strong rather severe figure of Victorian rectitude, and well-remembered within the family! Her marriage in 1921 was all too brief and the children of the 1950s remember her as somewhat scary. She had also worked in the mills in her younger days and latterly ran the fondly remembered baker's shop. In the 1920s she may have funded Frank X. Coyne's pharmacy studies setting him up for life. It seems there was more to Emma than at first apparent. I learnt recently from a cousin, Peter Fielding, that Emma and Nellie (Ellen) enjoyed holidays in Westport, County Mayo, during the same decade *(xii)*. Clearly they put their inheritance funds from 1922 to good use. Emma was our last connection with the Manchester years of the family.

She died of pneumonia, complicating a heart condition, at Queens Park Hospital and while ill had stayed with her niece Josie at 4 Tintern Crescent. Before the funeral she 'lay in state' in an open coffin at the house for several days. Surely a late Irish tradition. By the following year, 1960, two further deaths of Ellen Kennedy and Mary Ann Coyne brought the Coyne's sixty year residency on Whalley Range to an abrupt end resulting in the sale of both Beaumont Terrace houses. Emma had made a will in 1955, appointing nieces Winnie and Josie as joint executrix. Each were to receive £100 with the balance going to her surviving sister Ellen with whom she had lived for all her long life. When probate was granted at Lancaster on the 5th May 1959 her effects were valued at £926.10 shillings.

Ellen by then was not well herself. She also had a heart condition and had become afflicted by dementia. She had to leave her home in Blackburn and spent her last days in Fleetwood cared for by her daughter Winnie. She died at Rossall Hospital on the 16th May 1960, aged 76 years. Administration was granted at Lancaster on the 1st July to both daughters and her effects were valued at £1,484 1s 10d.

The generational change was complete when my grandmother, Mary Ann Coyne, died later the same year on 26th October. She died of a carcinoma, a cancer, at Blackburn Infirmary. A letter survives detailing her funeral arrangement (xiii) recording that she had a *"wax polished coffin with silver handles, engraved plate, wreath holders, end rings and crucifix, upholstered in Swansdown and silk"*. A Requiem Mass took place at St. Alban's on the following Saturday attended by members of the Coyne,

Bentley, Hoyle and Eccles families. The list of mourners included Hughie Frost, Frances' widower, and Harriet Conroy, an old family friend with another good Connacht name *(xiv)*. Mary Ann was buried at Blackburn Cemetery in a grave in which lay her father Fergus Power, and husband Joe. Administration of her effects was granted to son Frank on the 19th December, the sum of £788.9s.

Mary Ann Coyne on the steps of 179 Whalley Range, late 1950s.

My grandmother's house was finally sold to Blackburn Corporation on the 7th March 1961 for £442 1s 6d. This was the last of four houses owned or rented on Whalley Range either side of two world wars. In addition there were other family houses in nearby Cowper Street and London Road.

Visiting the area years later it still resonates as the area of Blackburn with the strongest family connection. The houses were first built in 1870 and have survived numerous demolitions in the locality. Nos. 143, 175 and 179 still survive today, where the area now houses some of Blackburn's Asian community who settled in the town, as elsewhere in Britain, from the 1960s onwards. On a happier note there was also one wedding at the time, when in 1958 Patricia Eccles, eldest daughter of Josie and George, married Noel Jordan in Blackburn.

If we again look at the family finances it may look as though, by today's standards, that the sums left by the three elderly widows were modest indeed. In fact in all three cases it would have been possible to buy a house, at the values of the time, with the proceeds. This was a sign of rising prosperity, where owner occupation of houses enabled wealth to be passed on to the next generation and certainly by 1960 all the economic indicators of rising living standards were by now apparent. Frank X. Coyne in Birkenhead, being in business, enjoyed a more affluent lifestyle once the war was over. By 1950 he was the owner of a Mark 1V Jaguar car, DLV 824, when he also bought an MG sports car for daughter Margaret's seventeenth birthday.

Frank X. Coyne in the ruins of Ancient Rome in 1951.

Ann and Margaret next to the Jaguar at a French hotel, c.1950.

My father also bought his first car in the mid-1950s – I believe it was a grey coloured Standard Ten, a 1930s model built in Coventry before the war. A few years later in June 1958 John and Win bought their first house, 365 Burnaby Road, Coventry, a three bedroomed semi-detached house overlooking a busy junction, for £1,950. It was bought with a mortgage from the Abbey National Building Society. A change in the destinations of family holidays also shows the rising living standards enjoyed by many. As we shall see in Chapter Seventeen it was the late 1960s and in particular the 1970s which saw the arrival of foreign holidays in the family, away from caravan holidays in Devon and Cornwall and numerous trips to Blackpool. Again, Frank and Ann with daughter Margaret led the way having travelled abroad from Birkenhead since about 1950.

As the photographs show Frank drove the car down to the south of France (to Nice and Cannes) in the late 1940s, and in 1951 in another photo 'Queen' (popular name for Ann Coyne), Frank and Margaret are seen at the Colosseum, and among the ruins of Ancient Rome. This was some return journey from the Wirral for the 1950s, although the roads, less expansive than today, were much quieter. As we approach the modern day and our story comes to a close, our focus now moves to Canada to see how the family fared after emigration.

i. *It was once said he would never use two words where one would do.*
ii. *Some 60 coupons were allowed each year for all except baby clothes. One dress required 11 coupons and a man's suit 26 coupons.*
iii. *Recollections of Margaret Mearns, formerly Coyne. She also remembered her cousin Tim at this time when he was at Birkenhead Boys School and Margaret was at Birkenhead High School.*
iv. *The' RMS Aquitania' was built in 1913 and was a 4 funnel sister ship of the famous 'Lusitania'. In 1947 she*

	had just returned to commercial routes after serving as a troopship.
v.	*There is a death reference for an Eveleen Scannell at Withington on 14th December 1966.*
vi.	*Leave was granted from Foretop Division, HMS Raleigh, from Friday 30th May to 08.15 on Monday 2nd June.*
vii.	*'PC Complimented', report Burnley Express 17.1.1951.*
viii.	*Kelly's (Gore's) Directory of Liverpool, including Birkenhead 1946.*
ix.	*29th April – 19th July 1952 as per official photograph.*
x.	*Police Order, 9th March 1955, Coventry City Police.*
xi.	*Margaret Ann Coyne died 9th January 1966, 'Windsor Daily Star' death notice.*
xii.	*Recollections of Peter Fielding. We are unaware of a family connection with Westport although it is possible there may have been one.*
xiii.	*The funeral cost £68 3s 9d (bill of Thomas Talbot and Sons, Funeral Directors).*
xiv.	*The Conroys in Irish History came from the 'MacConroi' or 'Mulconry' families who held territory in the Barony of Moycullen, County Galway.. Close to Coyne territory in fact.*

CHAPTER SIXTEEN

The Canadians

October 1947, Weymouth, England.

On this date, Terry Coyne and family bade farewell and began the great journey to Canada. Just twelve days earlier sister Kathleen had sailed from Liverpool bound for Montreal – she may have just beaten the winter freeze-up of the St. Lawrence Seaway. For Terry's family the journey began with a taxi journey to nearby Southampton where the *RMS Aquitania* was waiting to take them 2,835 miles to Halifax, Nova Scotia.

Passenger List for the Cunard White Star ship RMS Aquitania leaving Southampton on 20 October 1947. The Coyne family are listed from the fifth line down.

A few years ago Jim Coyne wrote a poem for the Coyne newsletter called *Coyne Odyssey to White Rock* in which he vividly recalled the five day journey through the eyes of a seven year old boy.

> "Welcome to Canada, waved the banner at Pier Twenty-One
> As six Coynes disembarked there, our journey half-way done"

The odyssey continued as they next departed from Halifax by CN train at five in the afternoon.

> "We watched the passing vista .. will we be in Vancouver soon?"

Alas not, for there were still 3,834 miles still to travel! The boys enjoyed Montreal which they reached a day later and where they stayed in a hotel with a concierge – very French. They asked their Mum about staying, soon forgotten when it was found they would have to learn French. After two days in the big city it was back on the train, crossing the Canadian Shield for Winnipeg.

> "From 'Peg across The Prairies, those great plains flat and wide.
> To Jasper in the foothills, 'twas such a joyous ride"

Here a second locomotive was added to pull the train up through the Rocky Mountain range and on to Kamloops, down through the Fraser Canyon to reach Vancouver the following day. With the family settled in the Hotel Allen in the city Terry's work then began in earnest. As an ex-serviceman he sought help from the Canadian Legion and was advised to try White Rock. Travelling by a Pacific Stage Lines bus Terry and the boys went to have a look at a little place called White Rock while Bess stayed with Terry junior, then five months old.

A first acquaintance was made at the Ocean Beach Hotel on the sea front, a man named Charlie Brown, while the three boys headed for the beach. On the beach they marvelled that they had travelled from the English Channel to the Pacific Coast in two weeks. The first home they rented was what Jim described as a 'rude dwelling' called *The Rendezvous* where they stayed for the first five weeks.

White Rock, British Columbia

A new life had begun on the other side of the world on the coast of the far-off Pacific Ocean. British Columbia, the most westerly of the Canadian provinces joined the dominion of Canada in 1871. It had the highest winter temperatures in the country, albeit wetter ones. In 1991 the population of the province was still only 2.8 million, about the same as for one of the Coyne family's former homes, Greater Manchester. Canada in 1947 was an exciting country of opportunity, and a longstanding destination for emigrants from both Britain and Ireland. Its vast land area is thirty-five per cent forested and has great mineral wealth.

White Rock is a small coastal community to the south of Vancouver on the Semiahmoo peninsula, hilly and with lots of trees. Its beaches were already popular with tourists when the Coynes arrived. It had a railway station, a pier, and yes, a prominent White Rock on the seafront. For work it was close to one of North America's great cities, Vancouver, and closer still to the border with the USA, from where the towering Mount Baker (10,750 feet) commands the view to the south. In 1912 the population was only 350 when the Great Northern Railway, whose line here clings to the coast, arrived building a prominent wooden station right on the Marine Drive which also served as a Customs post. By 1937 White Rock had a population of 1000, when the Coynes arrived it was still only around 5000, and today is home to a community of 18000. The city of White Rock is joined to the city of South Surrey (population 50,000) on three sides, and it is within these two locations you will find most of our Canadian family today.

A Coyne family gathering at White Rock, British Columbia

Terry had the idea of perhaps farming for a living and the first house secured at 17770 Boundary Road, Surrey, was in fact a farm house close to the US border. This was a bold move since we appear to have no farmers in the family, even back in Roscommon days. Bess, however, preferred to move to White Rock and so the next home was near to the beach, appropriately called *Seaweeds*, and which reminded them of Weymouth. It would seem that Bess, born in the seaport of Liverpool, was never far from the sea all of her life.

With farming no longer an option Terry pursued other openings. From his time in China he could speak both Cantonese and Mandarin, and while in the British Army he had spent time at the Shorncliff Army School of Education where he acquired a teaching certificate. He applied to the Surrey School District but was told he needed two more years of training. With a family of five to support this wasn't possible. Instead he was hired by the Provincial Fire Marshall of British Columbia to investigate a fire at a mental hospital called *Essendale*. He caught the arsonist ... but was also again out of a job.

The family was by now also larger. With one son born in China and three in England, Terry and Bess next had three daughters, the first Canadians in the family. Firstly on the 26th October 1949 they had twin girls who they named Elizabeth (Beth) and Honora (Nora). This was the third instance of twin girls in our branch of the Coyne family. A seventh child was born on 11th December 1956 when their youngest daughter Deborah (Debbie) was born.

One day leaving the bank Terry met the man who found them their first home and was asked *"Would you like to sell real estate?"* Naturally he replied yes, then being a recent arrival from Britain, he had to ask what real estate was. This proved to be a good move when in 1958 Terry opened his own business called *White Rock Realty Ltd* with his own office at 14977 Marine Drive, conveniently placed over the road from the train station and the beach. This was a good location. Travellers arrived by train and his clients would then call at the office. *"He spent the next nineteen years selling farms in the Fraser valley and commercial and residential real estate in White Rock* "said his daughter Debbie. The station closed in 1971 and Terry sold the business in 1977.

By the mid-1950s the family needed a larger house and in 1956 they were able to buy a house for $5,500 in Ocean Park. Many happy years were spent at this house which had steps up to a raised front porch and wooden pillars which held the roof as it extended over the porch. Here the family could sit in the porch in the best North American style.They also remembered skating on the pond in winter, with the beach nearby in summer. There are also memories of rounding the day off with fish 'n' chips before piling into Terry's car at the end of the day. Terry's first car was a *Model A Ford* which he bought from a Native Indian. This was a successor to the famous *Model T Ford* and between 1927 and 1932 some 4.8 million of them were manufactured. He always needed a large car both for the family and for taking clients to view properties.

School and Work

At the time of emigration Tim, the eldest boy was thirteen, Vin was nine, Jim seven, and Terry a baby. In the 1950s the youngest three all attended White Rock Elementary School while Tim entered the world of work joining a Vancouver shipping firm at the age of sixteen. Later the girls began at Ray Shepherd Elementary, and all went to the Semiahmoo Secondary School on 148th Street. Semiahmoo is a local place name given to the area by the indigenous First Nations people. It translates as *'half moon'*.

Vin Coyne next began work, starting a career in the newspaper business. He was first hired by *The Province* newspaper, a British Columbia daily paper since 1898 .He later moved to the *White Rock Sun* where he became Editor at the age of twenty-five, becoming a well- known figure in the city. He went on to serve as a local councillor from 1975 and in 1996 he received the Freedom of the city.

Jim Coyne remembered his first job – as a dishwasher on a freighter bound for Russia in 1958. When he retired from teaching after a 31 year career his school, Frank Hurt, compiled a list of his previous jobs. Alongside the merchant seamanship, he had also worked as a logger, longshoreman, and as a mining prospector in the Yukon before he began teaching at Elementary School in 1970. Later in 1977 he moved on to Frank Hurt. Here he taught a number of subjects, including law, and enjoyed supporting the school's sports teams.

1977 was also a landmark year for Terry senior. Now aged 73 years he sold the real estate business and took a part-time job in the Continuing Education Department of a community college. He impressed the Chief Instructor with his knowledge and experience and was asked to give lectures on Asian affairs which he did for several years. He had realised his dream of becoming a teacher. As we saw back in England the teaching profession employed quite a few members of the family in the second half of the twentieth century and continues so today.

The Coyne twins. Beth (left) and Nora either side of big brother Tim. At the front is Terry.

Other family members found work in a variety of jobs. Young Terry on leaving school in 1963 began at the *White Rock Sun*. He later had his own landscaping business with a client list within ten miles of White Rock. In 1967 Beth and Nora both found work in Vancouver with Beth beginning as a Secretary with a shipping firm and Nora working in insurance. Nora later trained as a Court Reporter and also spent thirty years in insurance before retiring in 2006. Finally youngest daughter Debbie followed her Dad into real estate obtaining a Real Estate License. She later worked in fundraising roles firstly for a hospital foundation and then in Further Education.

The Next Generation

By the late 1950s the family was ready for the next phase. The first Canadian marriage took place when Vin married Jean Walters in 1959. Tim married Mary Stevenson in 1967, followed by Jim's first marriage to Wendy Wittaker in 1968 and Terry's first marriage to Linda Houston the same year. In 1967- which latter-day historians like to call the *'Summer of Love'* – both twin girls married within a few months of each other. Firstly in May Nora married Clayton Collum followed by Beth who married Derwyn Dunbar in August. After Clayton died Nora married again to Teddy Cameron in 1989. Beginning with Bill here is a chart showing the first Canadian generation of the Coyne family.

Year	Name	Parents
1954	Bill Coyne	Vin and Jean
1962	Cathy Coyne	Vin and Jean
1965	David Coyne	Vin and Jean
1968	Brian Coyne	Terry and Linda
1970	Tricia Coyne	Tim and Mary
1970	Michelle Coyne	Terry and Linda
1970	Sara Coyne	Jim and Wendy
1972	Michael Coyne	Tim and Mary
1972	Vincent Coyne	Tim and Mary
1972	Natalie Dunbar	Beth and Derwyn
1979	Lindsay Coyne	Terry and Linda

Michael and Vincent were twins – sadly Michael died as an infant. After the older brothers and sisters moved out of the house in Ocean Park, Terry, Bess and the youngest, Debbie, moved to a smaller house in White Rock at 14093 Magdalene Avenue. In 1985 Debbie married Michael Mellenger. Three years earlier Jim remarried to Marion Kuzenko while in 1991 Terry remarried to Linda Sewchuk.

End of an Era: The Death of Terry Coyne

On August 30th 1983 Terry Coyne died at the age of seventy-nine years. Known to the family as *'Poppa'* Terry had led a remarkable life since his birth in Blackburn back in 1904. He was the oldest child of his generation and saw his father James Edward Coyne leave the family home when he was still a child. He began work at the age of ten while still at school. He lived through two World Wars, and during a lengthy military career saw active service in the second one. He was the first Coyne to set foot again on Irish soil – albeit in the uniform of the British Army (*i*). He first joined the army while underage. He spent ten years of his life living in China while working as a Shanghai policeman. In 1932 he returned on leave and married Bess, his wife for fifty years. During the Second World War he was part of a famous secret organisation, the Special Operations Executive. He was interned in Thailand by his Japanese captors for three years and eight months.

Throughout his life Terry travelled many thousands of miles by sea, not in the least when in his forties he took his family to Canada to begin a new life. Settled now in British Columbia he built his own business and spent many happy years living in White Rock. He was also the father of seven children. His descendants, the Canadian family of Terry and Bess represent the largest part of the Coyne family today. In total the family is comprised of their six surviving children, ten surviving grandchildren, two great grandchildren, and two great great grandchildren.

On September 6th 1983 a Memorial Service for Terry was held at the First United Church in White Rock. Terry was clearly one of our most interesting family members and we should be proud of what a working class boy from Blackburn achieved during his life. Our family has often had different compartments so now perhaps the history is together all in one place. There may even be more to come since the British Army records which cover Terry's time in Ireland are not yet publicly available, a reminder that what we know is only that which the records reveal - never more apparent than the story which unfolded from the wartime documents . Finally, in terms of family history, we should remember it was Terry who in 1971 travelled back to England and began the renewal of contact with his family.

"It wasn't until they spent the summer of 1971 in England that Mum finally felt that Canada was home!" said Debbie Mellenger, touching again on the issue of identity. After Terry's death Bess lived out her years at 15158 Royal Avenue, up on the White Rock hillside enjoying views over Semiahmoo Bay and the Salish Sea. The family attribute her longevity to the "ever-changing ocean scenes from her window". On the next page is one of the last photographs of the couple together.

Where the Wildgeese Roam

Other deaths in the family in Canada are listed in the Postscript section at the rear, including those of the Wecko family whose story is covered next.

Bess and Terry Coyne pictured in 1982

The Wecko Family of Alberta

When Kathleen Coyne emigrated separately, also in 1947, she alighted from the railroad at a small town in Alberta called Medicine Hat, population 26,000. A *'war bride'* it was another year before she married Michael Wecko, who had served in the Canadian Army Anti-Tank Corps during the Second World War. On the 2nd November 1948 they were married at St. Patrick's Catholic Church in Lethbridge, a church dedicated to Ireland's patron saint just the same as in Elphin, County Roscommon, where our journey had begun. The Wecko family were earlier Canadian immigrants having arrived from the Ukraine in 1921 settling in the predominantly agricultural province of Alberta, east of British Columbia, and just east of the Rocky Mountain range with its peaks as high as 14,000 feet.

Michael and Kathleen had one child, Barbara Eileen, born in the early 1950s. From electoral registers it has been possible to follow their movements around the province and it would appear that Kathleen spent her first decade and a half in Alberta moving to where Michael found work, firstly in coal mining. Farming, forestry and mining – three industries long associated with Canada – were to comprise his working life. Kathleen, meanwhile, worked at the *Coleman Journal*, newspaper of the town where they lived. In 1952 they left Coleman for Tilley, followed by a move to Hinton in 1962. Around 1965 Michael was employed as a *'pulp cutter'* in Jasper and in 1968 they became residents again of the town of Coleman in the south-west corner of Alberta. Here between 1968 and 1976 he worked as a miner at Coleman Collieries after the industry began to pick up, before retiring at the age of sixty-eight years.

Barbara married Ken Taje and had two sons, Richard and Kristoffer. In 1992 she was living in Grand Cache, Alberta, but now lives over on Canada's eastern coast. The distances between Alberta and White Rock being in excess of 700 miles there were not too many chances for the two Canadian families to meet up. Nonetheless visits to Uncle Mike and Auntie Kathleen were made. Barbara recalled how excited the three of them had been *"the summer we visited White Rock" (ii)* .Kathleen also stayed in touch with her brothers in England by letter. Both the Weckos died in 1992 and are buried at the Mountain View Cemetery in

Lethbridge. Staff there sent me an image of Kathleen's gravestone which read 'In memory of a *Loving Mum and Grandma. 1913-1992. Gone Home'*

i. *Terry told the family he had served in the British Army during the period known as the War of Independence. Fighting broke out between a newly insurgent IRA and British forces during 1920-21. At this point he was clearly underage, he was still only fifteen in January 1920 and still sixteen in mid-1921. It is not known which regiment he served in since there were many within the Army's deployment of 57,000 men. Army records of this period are not yet publically available.*
ii. *Email 2017. It is thought this visit took place either in 1968 or 1969. It was the first time Terry and Kathleen had met in decades.*

CHAPTER SEVENTEEN

Towards the Modern Day

By 1960 the United Kingdom was at something of a watershed. Behind was the slow recovery from the war, although economic performance was still dependent on a pre-war infrastructure, the same often smokestack industries required to continue in service as manufacturing struggled along in often dilapidated buildings. In the Midlands and the North the soot-blackened townscape was still evident despite the efforts of the Clean Air Act and the fact that towns like Blackburn now had a lot less chimneys than they once had. On the horizon was an era of modernity. If Prime Minister McMillan had spoken of the 'Winds of Change' throughout the Empire, signalling a retreat from the colonies, it was Labour's Harold Wilson who in 1964 advocated the *'White heat of technology'* as an instrument of national renewal. On the railways the Steam Age was soon to disappear under rapid electrification; the first motorways appeared (i) to soak up the increasing car ownership; while air travel began to replace the ocean liner as the transport of choice for the long-distance traveller.

Increased consumerism brought the new televisions – built in the new industrial estates before the effect of Japanese and Far Eastern competition began to bite. With full employment, rising wages, more holidays and an improved quality of life – perhaps with knowledge of what was to emerge in the 1980s and 90s – *"You've never had it so good"*, another McMillan quote, was to prove remarkably prophetic? The public sector continued to grow with a large expansion of Further Education. For the first time it was possible for children of working class background to advance in life, benefiting from free education alongside a free health service.

This birth of the 'modern day', although still pre-computer, was unrecognisable from the war ravaged decade of the 1940s. Next black and white television was replaced by colour, while bright new shopping centres and housing schemes – not yet condemned as 'concrete jungles' – became the architectural showpieces of the 1960s.

The newfound destinations of family holidays began to emerge. Since the advent of the 'package holiday' in the late 1960s and the ease of travel to Europe in particular we saw postcards begin to arrive from farther afield. In 1970 from Austria; 1971 from Italy and Germany; 1972 the Blackburn Coynes posting from the Hotel Magalluf Park, Majorca; 1973 Frank and Ann Coyne visited Lloret de Mar; 1974 John and Win went to Copenhagen in Denmark; the same year the Hoyles were in Austria; while 1979 saw Florence and Frank Coyne in Dubrovnik, in what was then Yugoslavia.

As before rising living standards meant house moves. By 1960 Frank X. Coyne had moved south. The Birkenhead pharmacy on Woodchurch Road was sold and the family moved to Bristol to live. His daughter Margaret saw this as a further sign of the Coyne family's need to be 'on the move'. Apparently Frank looked out at the dismal weather one day in Birkenhead, said *"just look at that weather!"* and made plans to move. The house they moved to, 3 Coombe Lane, in Bristol was the first of many houses Frank and

Ann were to move to throughout the south-west. Frank didn't own a shop again, instead working as a pharmacist for a multiple until he retired at the end of the decade. Margaret had also by now followed him into pharmacy and it was while in Bristol she married Alfred Dyke, in February 1963.

Back in Blackburn the last two births of my generation took place. In 1960 Sheila and Terry Hoyle had bought a house at 1 Ripon Street in Queen's Park *(ii)* when their second son, Ian, was born on the 12th June 1961. Earlier on 24th March Peter Andrew Coyne was born to Florence and Frank, the same name as his great grandfather who had brought the family to Blackburn in 1880.

Over in Yorkshire, Marie Bentley had by now become the School Secretary of Whitcliffe Mount School in Cleckheaton, a position she held for many years delighting in the stories of school life. Her husband Stan, meanwhile, commuted daily from their home in Pyenot Hall Lane, Cleckheaton, to Leeds where he worked as a tailor for the local firm of Joseph May and Son. Situated in Springwell Street in Leeds the firm had a four-storey clothing factory, established in 1927, making woollen suits and overcoats under the *'Maenson'* trademark, which were once exported widely.

It was in the 1960s that John Coyne's career with Coventry City Police advanced. Not long after attending the course at Bramshill House he was promoted to Detective Inspector on the 17th October 1961. On the 1st April 1965 the *Coventry Evening Telegraph* reported (iii) that he had taken charge of the Coventry branch of the newly-formed Midland Regional Crime Squad which began operations on the same date. The branch had offices at Coventry central Police HQ and included a Detective Sergeant and two Constables. Other staff were comprised of officers from the Warwickshire, Leicestershire and Rutland forces. Their job was to work with other branches of the Regional Crime Squads to investigate major crime in the Midlands. The report added that the branch had their own vehicles *"equipped with multi-channel two-way radios"*. This was a time when the police had to reorganise to cope with the new motorway system which gave criminals the opportunity to commit major crimes far from home and return rapidly by motorway. Popular television series such as *Z Cars* and *Softly Softly* reflected these changes.

In April 1967 John was promoted again to Detective Chief Inspector, aged 46 years, and spent his last two years in the police force continuing to head the Crime Squad (*iv*). His promotion was also reported in the *Lancashire Evening Telegraph,* which added that his brother Frank was a Detective Constable in Blackburn, and his brother-in-law Terry, an employee of the Telegraph.

In June the same year the Squad was praised in a news feature (*v*) where John is pictured poring over a map with other Squad members. Throughout the region one hundred detectives from all the major towns and cities could now be summoned at a moment's notice to attend major crimes – recent cases included the murder of a girl in Shrewsbury, a rape at Charlecote, and around Christmas 1966 no less than six murders in Birmingham. DCI Coyne features in the article where he is described as a *"tough, quiet-talking Lancashire man"*. I have no doubt he would have liked this description!

Coventry Evening Telegraph, Wednesday, June 14, 1967

Regional Crime Squad detectives in conference listen to Detective Chief Inspector John Coyne as he pinpoints the spot where the next round of investigations is to take place.

Elsewhere in the family Pauline Eccles was the next to marry when in 1964 she married Barrington Ward in Blackburn. Following the death of Hughie Frost in 1964 it meant that the last survivor of my grandparents' generation was James Edward's estranged wife, Catherine Coyne. She had been living in Southport on the Lancashire coast when she died on the 9th May 1965. She had been on her own since her daughter Kathleen emigrated in 1947 and had, sometime before 1950, moved to be near her son James, who was living at 17 Highfield Road, Croston – a village to the south of Preston. She was eighty-four when she died of a throat cancer at 20 Park Road, Southport.

Still on the Lancashire coast, John Fielding, eldest son of Winnie and Joe, married Theresa Dunderdale (known as 'Terry') in 1967 at St. Mary's Church in Fleetwood. John, a plumber, spent most of his working life at Rossall School, an independent fee-paying school established in 1844, which occupied a 160 acre site to the south of the town. They later had two children, Simon and Emma Fielding, born in 1969 and 1972 respectively.

Before the Second World War Frank X. Coyne was the first, and at the time only, family member to benefit from Further Education. This was to change in the 1960s, a time of widespread expansion of education. In 1967 Susan Coyne went to Sheffield City College of Education, her cousin Paul Bentley went to Lancaster University the following year, while the other Fielding brothers, Peter, Gerard and Paul, at different times all qualified as teachers. At the end of the decade Peter Fielding, who had been working in the insurance business, was elected onto Blackburn Borough Council, as the youngest Labour councillor at the time serving as the councillor for the Ewood Ward for four years. All five were to spend all, or part, of their working lives as teachers.

It was early in 1969 when John Coyne's police service came to an end when he retired on medical grounds. Police Officers at the time were required to complete 25 years' service to qualify for a full pension. John had served 23 years when he became ill with a stress – related condition. He was 'off sick' from work during 1968 when he was assessed by the Police Doctor, a Doctor Navin, who decided he should retire early . Since the stress had been caused by working anti-social hours on often long-extended duties the decision seems harsh today. No attempt was made to find less arduous duties, while the reduction in pension meant a financial penalty and the need to find a new job.

John was retired on 7th January 1969, no doubt encouraged by a letter he received a week later from the Blackburn Branch of the Police Federation expressing sadness at the turn of events and wishing him well for the future. On the 17th March *(vi)* he began a new career in the motor industry taking up a staff job in Parts Supply at the Standard Triumph car factory in Coventry, variously rebranded as British Leyland and later Unipart during his ten years with the firm. After his previous job he found the work much less challenging but busied himself with out-of-work activities with the Royal British Legion and NARPO, the police pensioner's organisation. At this point John and Win bought a caravan and this was to lead to a significant development in our family history.

The Coyne Family Reunion of 1971

The caravan, an eight berth static Pemberton, was bought in 1969 with the proceeds of John's pension pay-off. After consideration of several sites, limited by Coventry's long distance from any coast, my parents decided to buy one on a site at Ashley Heath *(vii)*, a rural location surrounded by pine trees on the edge of the Ringwood Forest, close to the border between Hampshire and Dorset. It was close to the New Forest national park and crucially, a mere ten miles from Bournemouth with its beaches, and nearby Poole Harbour. John was able to relax here and soon recovered from his illness. The caravan was given a Blackburn name, *Roe Lee* – many site visitors unfamiliar with the names of Blackburn parks would for years after enquire when Mr. Lee would next be down! The caravan served many a family holiday over the next sixteen years.

It was in 1970 that Terry Coyne, on holiday from Canada with Bessie and his youngest daughter Deborah, and returning to England for the first time since 1947 paid a visit to his home town of Blackburn. It seems likely he had not been back since his visit in 1932 when he visited his mother, while on leave from China. He didn't have a lot to go on since the Whalley Range houses had both been sold, but he did know of the police connection. He went into Blackburn Police Station, explained who he was and that he was related to two brothers called Coyne who were "both on the police". He was put in touch with Frank Coyne and during the conversation mentioned he had two brothers in England, James and another Frank who was living in Dorset at a place called ......Ashley Heath.

The next time John visited his caravan he called at the house in Ashley Heath, just half a mile away, knocked heavily on the door and asked if it was James Coyne's house? It was not but Francis Xavier Coyne lived there, his elder cousin who he could not recall meeting as a child. Frank had recently retired to the area after living for a while in Exeter. His daughter Margaret, now separated, had also moved from Bristol a few years earlier and also lived nearby. From here on regular family visits took place assisted by the fortuitous location.

James and John met later in Redditch. James had left Lancashire for a second time in the late 1960s when worked declined at the Croston cotton mill. By 1957 two – thirds of Lancashire's cotton mills had already closed and it seems he moved some 100 miles to Redditch in Worcestershire when he got a job at an engineering firm (*viii*). He moved to a house at 22 Millsborough Road, a

1930s redbrick terraced house, on a hill about a quarter of a mile from the town centre. The properties on Millsborough Road were unusual in that they had a third floor. Somewhat large for a single man James may have rented a room from a landlady, although it is known he later had a flat of his own in the town.

The 1970s saw a number of family marriages as the next generation came to the fore. Just one week before Christmas in 1972 Paul Bentley, only son of Marie and Stan, married Janice Bell at Beverley in East Yorkshire. He had just left university and the couple went to live in Harrogate. In 1973 Philip Eccles married Jennifer Chambers in Southgate, London. In 1974 my sister Susan Coyne married Brian Mabbett, an electrical engineer, on 13th April at Coventry Register Office. They went to live in a newly-built house at 9 Kirby Avenue, Woodloes Park, in nearby Warwick and the next year, their eldest son, Jake Andrew, was born on 10th October. Gerard Fielding also married in 1973 followed by his younger brother Joseph Paul who married Michelle Bruchet in Liverpool in 1975. Another marriage took place in 1977 when Margaret Dyke remarried, to Stanislaus Kowalski at Poole on the 12th May.

John and Francis Xavier, Laycock Abbey, Wiltshire, c.1980

Sadly it was not all good news. Back in Yorkshire, 1977 was to be a tragic year for the Bentley family with the sudden and shocking death of Paul Bentley on the 9th August. At the time Paul and wife Jan were on holiday in Germany when he died suddenly overnight. He was just 27 years old and had seemingly had an undiagnosed heart condition. After a cremation his ashes were interred at Harrogate Cemetery on Wetherby Road in the town where he has a headstone (*ix*).

Changing Times

The 1970s drew to a close, now remembered as a time of economic crises with inflation rates at times in excess of 20 per cent, with rising unemployment, and regular balance of payments concerns. The UK, along with Ireland and Denmark, had entered the EEC, the European Economic

Community in 1973, a decision backed by a referendum in 1975, in the hope this would stem some of the economic woes. As the Government of James Callaghan went to the polls in 1979 following what is now called the *'Winter of Discontent'* few foresaw what lay ahead. The return of a right wing Conservative government under Margaret Thatcher was to change the country forever. Out went consensus politics. Our post-war story had seen us benefit from full and stable employment, rising wages, a growing public sector with large numbers of well-paid jobs, and free Further Education. In the decades that followed all this was to change and it is at this point – at another national watershed – that I have decided to draw our story so far to a close.

In 1979 Oliver Paul Mabbett was born to Susan and Brian on the 16th April. In the following year Janet Coyne married Les Murphy, a brewery executive, at St. Alban's in Blackburn on the 20th September. Soon after they moved temporarily to Herefordshire when Les took up a position with Bulmer's Cider, and it was in Hereford that their eldest daughter, Joanne, was born on the 4th December 1983.

Stanley Bentley, meanwhile, had been suffering from a brain tumour, a condition which led to his death on 9th March 1982 at St.Gemma's Hospice in Leeds, the city where he had spent most of his working life. Marie was now a widow, and went on to volunteer at the Hospice for many years after. In the same year on the 10th May, Paul David Eccles was born to Phil and Jenny in Luton, Bedfordshire.

In Canada the death of Terry Coyne in August 1983, aged 79 years, had also signalled the end of an era and it is with the first deaths of this generation that the curtain now comes down on this account of the Coyne Family History. I decided that this story should first and foremost be a history best viewed from afar so I have made no attempt to chronicle events up to the present day. We end our epic tale of almost two hundred years of family history with a conclusion which firstly takes a look at our family's employment position around 1980 to contrast it with the earlier list, a brief catch-up of family reunions, and a page recording what happened to some of the family members who have appeared so far in this book. Finally I will consider our original question of the Irish emigrant journey and how it relates to the Coyne family today.

Reunions

As overseas air travel became more and more popular family members travelled even farther, to places such as the USA, even to Australia. Not surprisingly this trend enabled visits to be made, for the first time, to the family in Canada, and visits by the Canadians to the UK. In 2003 Jim and Marion Coyne visited the UK and in 2009 daughter Shona and I were warmly welcomed by the family at a gathering in White Rock, British Columbia. Two years later in 2011 Debbie Mellenger and her brother Terry Coyne visited family members here and also toured Ireland, where they paid a visit back to the town of Elphin in County Roscommon where our journey began.

At this juncture then is a table of Coyne family employment around 1980 here in the UK which clearly shows the changes from the first half of the twentieth century away from plastering, painting and cotton weaving to a more varied list including manufacturing, the professions, trades and a solid core of public sector jobs.

INDUSTRY	Number	INDUSTRY	Number
Brewing	1	Newspapers	1
Community	1	Pharmacy	2
Engineering	2	Plumbing	2
Factory/production	3	Police	1
Insurance	1	Tailor	1
Local Government	1	Teaching	4

Coyne family employment 1970-1980

Final Commentary: An Irish Journey

Our journey is almost over. Just as the story closes in the 1980s we arrive at a point in 1986 when I first began to take an interest in family history. What appears here is a result of a thirty year interest in the Coyne family history. I have found the journey always interesting, absorbing and fascinating in its detail. It is a story, of course, limited by the information out there, or the lack of it. We began the journey in County Roscommon in the days before the Great Famine, among the famine emigrants themselves, many of whom arrived barefoot in rags. We arrived in England, to this altogether larger, noisier, more unforgiving country with its different ways, politics and religion. The colonial oppressor even. Walking right into the teeth of the Industrial Revolution, our ancestors settled eventually in the choking smoke-blackened inner city of *Cottonopolis* itself. In fact walking everywhere, our menfolk pushing handcarts and ladders up steep northern brows; our womenfolk, with shawls wrapped round to keep out the morning chill, heads down *Lowryesque*, heading towards the unrelenting noise of the cotton mill. In between the poverty and the insecurity stalked illness and infant mortality.

The plastering, the painting and the cotton weaving eventually brought some relief in the form of a larger family income. Some fell by the wayside. In our history we have seen the inside of the prison system at Salford's New Bailey; the Lunatic Asylum at Prestwich; and the workhouse at Withington in Manchester.

Sustaining it all was the Coyne's Catholic faith. All those masses, the baptisms, the first holy communions, the confirmations, holy days, marriages and requiems. So much of our early story is written in Latin and served with the aroma of incense. We provided altar boys and Children of Mary as first St.Wilfrid's in Hulme and then St.Alban's in Blackburn became the churches of family allegiance. At times there was sectarian strife in the wider community. Marriages to non-Catholic spouses, and movement away from close family ties gradually loosened the religious bond, reflecting trends in society as a whole. Perhaps it is Catholicism, once the majority family religion, which remains the last.surviving Irish characteristic? Either that or what was my father's favourite LP, among a tiny collection of music –*'John McCormack Sings Irish Songs'* where the once popular tenor sings Irish ballads all recorded between 1911 and 1927!

Today the Government of Ireland recognises the existence of an Irish-born grandparent as a qualification for an Irish passport. On the Coyne side our ancestry goes back to our great great grandparents. Officially therefore we ceased to be Irish during my grandparents' time which perhaps fits in with how things developed in our history from the First World War onwards. Irish identity perhaps endured a while longer when nearly all the Blackburn Coynes married within the Irish Catholic community. It takes only one generation to lose an accent and alongside this the process of assimilation would have continued. Undoubtedly two world wars and the contributions of family members to the British armed forces encouraged a British identity, although it should be remembered that the Irish were major contributors, in numbers, to the British Army, particularly, right up to 1922. It seems certain it was the absence of family ties back in Ireland which distanced us more than others.

Since 1922 independent, neutral, nationalist Ireland has kept her distance from the UK, at the same time as the Protestant, Unionist community in Northern Ireland remained a part. Among the Irish in Britain today the culture is kept alive mainly by the immigrant communities of the 1950s and 60s supporting music, Irish dancing, clubs and Gaelic sports. Later generations appear less nationalist in cultural identity bringing a rapid assimilation. Taking popular music for example many top British performers have Irish ancestry. We can include Lennon and McCartney in the 1960s; and Morrissey and

Johnny Marr (Maher) in the 1980s for example. All could be considered 'Lancashire Irish.'

In September 2017 the Irish Ambassador to the United Kingdom, Dan Mulhall, in an interview with the *Irish Post*, recognised the issue when he commented on the challenge of *"how to cultivate Irishness in the second, third and fourth generations"*. He felt it was The Troubles which was to blame for the absence of an identification with Ireland in contrast with the United States.

And so unlike our American kinfolk there is no green beer for us on St. Patrick's Day. It seems it was religion rather than politics which defined us. Or as WB Yeats so eloquently put it in his poem *'September 1913'*

> *"Romantic Ireland's dead and gone,*
> *It's with O'Leary in the grave."*

Now in the second decade of the 21st century the world is again changing rapidly. In the 'Global Village' national identities are likely to fade, as once happened in Ireland with the decline of the Gaelic culture. If the Coyne family of Britain and Canada today have other national identities one fact remains. The origins & early history of our family, indeed the family name itself, remains *Forever Irish*.

i.   The first motorway was built in 1958, a section near Preston, followed by the M1 in 1959.
ii. A district of Blackburn, south –east of the town centre, near to Audley Range.
iii. 'Coventry man Heads Crime Squad Branch' (Coventry Evening Telegraph)

iv.   His pay rise on promotion was £210 per annum (Pension letter *1969*)
v.   June 14, *1967 (CET)*
vi.   St. Patrick's Day. A lucky day for Coyne employment? Later in *1986* I began work at Coventry City Council on this date and stayed for *10* years.
vii. Ashley Heath village boasts "the smallest High Street in England". It had its own railway station until *1963*, the remains of which are still visible.
viii. James' niece Margaret thought they were gunmakers.
ix.   Grave reference 4778c, Section 14, Stonefall Cemetery, Harrogate.

POSTSCRIPT

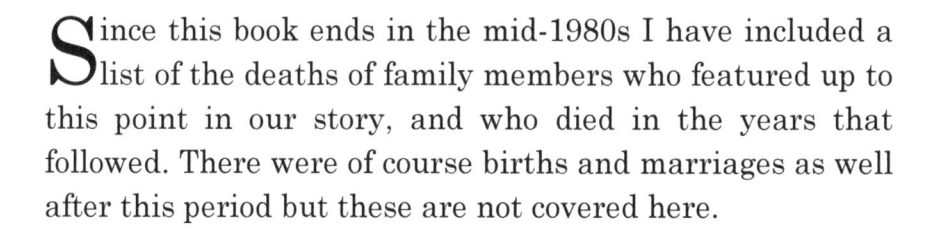

Since this book ends in the mid-1980s I have included a list of the deaths of family members who featured up to this point in our story, and who died in the years that followed. There were of course births and marriages as well after this period but these are not covered here.

Name	Year of Death	Where	Age
John Coyne	1986	Coventry	65
George Eccles	1989	Blackburn	78
Joe Fielding	1989	Garstang	76
Michael Wecko	1992	Alberta Canada	84
Katherine Wecko	1992	Alberta Canada	79
Frank Coyne	1992	Blackburn	64
Win Coyne	1996	Coventry	75
Francis Xavier Coyne	1998	East Dorset	91
Josie Eccles	1999	Stoke on Trent	87
Winnie Fielding	2000	Sefton North	83
Mary Patricia Jordan	2002	Sydney Australia	64
James Anthony Coyne	2003	Redditch, Worcs	88
Bess Coyne	2003	BC, Canada	90
Marie Bentley	2006	Blackburn	84
Timothy Coyne	2007	BC, Canada	72
Sheila Hoyle	2008	Blackburn	75
Terry Hoyle	2012	Blackburn	81

APPENDICES

Appendix 1 - Table of Rent: Coyne houses of Hulme and Chorlton on Medlock, 1864-1899

DATE	ADDRESS	TENANT	RENT	LANDLORD
1864	18 Park Street Hulme	Thomas Coyne	5s per week	Samuel Evans
1873	27 Union Street C on M	Emma Coyne	6s per week	J'mah Roberts
1879	6 Naylor Street Hulme	Francis McCausland	5s9d per week	John Crane
1883	4 Dorrington St Hulme	Thomas Edward Coyne	4s 10d per week	Mr. Hignam
1888	24 Anson St C on M	Annie Coyne	4s per week	W.J.Birtenshaw
1898	28 Boundary St Hulme	Amy Coyne	4s9d per week	Mrs. Mounsey

Extracts from Manchester Rate Books to 1900

Where the Wildgeese Roam

Appendix 2 - Coyne Family Addresses in Hulme and Chorlton on Medlock

	Address	Year(s)	Names
1	18 Park St	1862-1871	Thomas and Emma Coyne
2	6 Naylor St	1876-1877	Emma and sons
	29 Naylor St	1876	John and Hannah Coyne
3	32 Tamworth St	1876	Mary Cowper
4	2 Boundary St	1879	John and Anne (Hannah)
5	5 Russell Square	1881	John and Anne
6	4 Dorrington St	1881	Thomas E. & Mary Coyne
7	33 Clifford St, Stretford	1881-1883	Emma, Francis McCausland and sons
8	29 Upper Tamworth St Barton on Irwell	1889	Emma and Francis McCausland
9	52 Clayton St	1890	Emma McCausland and William Couttes
10	24 Anson Street	1891	Annie Coyne and children
11	9 Prospect Street	1899	Anne Coyne
12	77 Bonsall St	1901-1911	Thomas and Mary Coyne
	89 Bonsall St	1882	John, Anne and family
13	20 Stanley St	1901	Hannah (Anne) Coyne
14	22 Union St	1906	Peter and Harriet Coyne
15	8 Hall St	1907	Hannah Coyne
16	16 Percy St	1929 - 1930	Mary Rideal Coyne

Numbers 1-16 relate to the streets marked on the Map of Hulme, Chapter 8, page 84.

Appendix 3 - Wages in the Building Trades in the U.K. in the 19th Century: pre-1859

pd = per day

	1836	1847	1848	1851	1853	185·
Wage rate Artisan			5/9 pd		6s pd	5/8 p
Wage rate Labourer		3s pd	3/8 pd		3/8 pd	3/8 p
Hours Summer		58.5 – 60				
Hours Winter		47 (12 weeks)				
Estimated Weekly wage Artisan	30s			£1.4/10		
Location				National	London	Lond

Post 1859: After 1859 an hourly payment system was introduced

pd = per day. ph =per hour

	1859	1865	1866	1867	1874	1893
Wage rate Artisan	7d ph	7.5d ph	8d ph		8.5d ph	7d
Wage rate Labourer	4.5d ph	4.25d ph				
Hours Summer	56.5		55.5		52.5	49.5
Hours Winter					48	
Estimated Weekly wage Artisan	£1.13s	£1.15/4	£1.15s to £1.17s	£1.15s	£1.14s to £1.17s2d	£1.13s
Location	London	London		Burnley	National	Burnley

All wages are pre-decimal in £.s.d. Halfpennies are entered as 0.5d and farthings as 0.25d.

Appendix 4 - Plasterer's Wages in the 19th Century

I have tried to gather together figures to work out how much a plasterer would have been paid in the period when Thomas and Patrick Coyne arrived from Ireland in the nineteenth century. Patrick's son, Thomas, was also still employed in the trade in the 1880s and possibly longer.

Before the analysis it is necessary to look at sources and the limitations of the available figures.

1. The figures used are from *'Wages in the UK in the Nineteenth Century'* by Arthur Bowley. Bowley's figures for the building trades are mainly for London with some for Lancashire and Scotland. Regional variations would not be as extreme as today.

2. The figures tend to be for the building trades generally with the major demarcation between artisans and labourers. Within the trades a plasterer was among the highest earners along with bricklayers and carpenter/joiners.

3. For much of the period there is a difference between summer and winter earnings. In 1847 for example the gap was big with a 60 hour week in summer and 47 in winter which extended for 12 weeks. By 1874, however, the working week was down to 52.5 hours with 9 hours worked on Monday; 9.5 hours Tuesday to Friday; and 5.5 hours on Saturdays. By the 1890s the seasonal difference had disappeared.

4. Payment Systems. Before 1859 workers in the building trades were paid a daily rate, e.g. in 1848 when an artisan

was paid 5/9d per day and a labourer 3/8d per day. After a major building workers strike in 1859 a new hourly payment system was introduced. Today we tend to use weekly payments as comparators hence the figure for the estimated weekly wage.

5. Bowley summarised his work by stating that there was a regular tendency from 1836 for a progression in wages and a reduction in hours. From 1830 to 1900 wages increased by 50 per cent and hours fell by 16 per cent.

6. In 1874 we have a figure specifically for a plasterer – that of 8.5d per hour – which works out at an income of £1.17s 2d in the summer for 52.5 hours, and £1.14s per week in the winter for a 48 hour week. This wage compared well with Bowley's London figure which stood at 9d per hour in 1873.

7. A couple of caveats should be added to these figures. Few workers in the building trades could expect to be fully employed for 52 weeks per year. Supply problems and extreme weather would always stop work and reduce earnings. At times of economic downturn employment would be much harder to find. Although plasterers were in demand, as today they were vulnerable to periods of inactivity.

So how well did our plasterers do? Clearly their wages were at the top end for building artisans; they earned significantly more than labourers and were better able to withstand fluctuations in the trade.Looking specifically at Thomas Coyne in Hulme in the 1860s we can compare his wages with his rental costs. Over the period 1859 to 1973 rents on the Hulme properties tenanted by members of the

Coyne family ranged from 5s per week to 6s per week (see Appendix 1.)

Our figure for a plasterer in Burnley in 1867 has a seasonal range from £1.14s to £1.17.2d. Wages in Manchester would be expected to be similar to this so on this basis the rent element of family household costs appears manageable in the 1860s and compares favourably with the percentages for housing costs today! Once again we should emphasise that periods of inactivity would bring the annual income down to something closer to that of a labourer and explains the constant struggle to overcome poverty.

BIBLIOGRAPHY

Baggoley, Martin	'Blackburn', Britain in Old Photographs series
Bowley, Arthur	'Wages in the UK in the Nineteenth Century'
Delve, Ken	'Bomber Command 1936-68: An Operational and Historic Record
Doolan, Brian	' The Pugins and the Hardmans'
Dudgeon, Piers with Cox, Josephine	'A Child of the North'
Fowler, Spencer and Tamblin	'Army Service Records of the First World War, Public Record Office Reader's Guide No.19
Gough, Richard	'SOE Singapore : 1941-42'
Greenhall, R.L.	'The Making of Victorian Salford'
Hayes, Cliff	'The Changing Face of Manchester'
Imperial War Graves Commission	The Silent Cities'
Jackman, Mike	'The Essential History of Blackburn Rovers'
Kinealy, Christine	'The Great Calamity: The Irish Famine 1845-52'
Neal, Frank	'English- Irish Conflict in the North-West', North West Labour, History magazine No.16, 1991-92
Neal, Frank	'Black '47: Britain and the Famine Irish'
Nicholson, Colonel	'History of the East Lancashire Regiment in the Great War'
O'Donovan Rossa, Jeremiah	'Rossa's Recollections 1838-1898'
Phythian, Graham	'Shooting Stars: the Brief and Glorious History of Blackburn Olympic FC 1878-1889'
Postgate, R.	'The Builder's History'
Smith, Cecil Woodham	'The Great Hunger'
Timmins, Geoffrey	'Four Centuries of Lancashire Cotton'
Tressell, Robert	'The Ragged Trousered Philanthropists'
Wakeman, F.	'Policing Shanghai'
Wilson, Kevin	'Men of Air'
Woodruff, William	'The Road to Nab End'